Flowers for Adrian:

The Life and Death of Adrian Adonis

John Ellul

"And remember, you spell wrestling A-D-O-N-I-S."

‐   *Adrian Adonis, after John Tolos*

Editor and formatting: John Ellul (@ellulcoolj)

Cover design: Dorsa Pedari

Cover photo property of Pro Wrestling Illustrated/Kappa Publishing Group, Inc, with permission.

Interior photos property of PWI/Kappa, Fumi Saito, and Paul Neiss, reproduced with permission.

Love and Rockets image courtesy of Gilbert Hernandez and Fantagraphics

For Jay and Aaliyah love from Dad

Contents

Preface

A note on names throughout the text.

Through this book, the subject is referred to variously by his birth name, Keith Franke (pronounced "Frank-ie"), as well as his more famous wrestling persona, Adrian Adonis.

An editorial decision has been made across each chapter to discern which name was most appropriate in the context of the immediate topic under discussion.

In some places this is an obvious decision, such as when Franke's personal life is being examined, or when Adonis' wrestling career is under review. Upon occasion, such decisions are less clear cut, but the most obvious approach has been followed at all times.

Similarly, when referring to the former owners of the World Wide Wrestling Federation (WWWF) and World Wrestling Federation/Entertainment (WWF/WWE), the text refers to Vince McMahon Senior (or 'McMahon Senior') and Vince McMahon Junior (or 'McMahon Junior'), unless the context makes clear that simply 'McMahon' will suffice.

Wrestlers and wrestling personalities discussed are generally referred to by their gimmick names, unless otherwise indicated.

Every effort has been made to ensure a consistent and logical approach.

Introduction: Who kisses the roses?

"Look at the shoulders, look at the beautiful Roman profile, look at this Italian skin, soft and silky daddy, I am just too much."

- Adrian Adonis, 1981

From the moment he first adopted the name 'Adrian Adonis,' to the untimely end of his life a little over ten years later, Keith Franke was many different things to the wrestling audience. A vicious brawler, a sneering talker, a preening provocateur. Most infamously, as the powdered, prancing "Adorable One" during the first boom period of the World Wrestling Federation (WWF), he portrayed an exploitative gay stereotype, a deliberate lightning rod designed to appeal to the worst impulses of fans in mostly male arenas during the height of 1980s homophobic hysteria.

For many wrestling fans, wrestlers, and historians, it is difficult to settle on the true legacy of Franke, and the "Adorable" gimmick for which he is most remembered. There is praise, certainly, from those who remember him. Legendary wrestling announcer and executive Jim Ross was fulsome in his praise during one interview when Adrian Adonis' name was brought up, recalling him as "a guy full of charisma who could actually wrestle, which is always a winning combination." If only it were so simple.

Even today, a simple Twitter search for Franke's famous ring name reveals a broad church of opinions. At one end of the spectrum there is nostalgic reverence from those who saw Franke in his prime. From younger fans discovering him via the magic of modern video-sharing platforms, there is often surprise, at the grace and deftness with which Franke once floated around a wrestling ring. Then, there is the downright hostile. Indeed, in many cases the name retains a second, seedy life as a small-minded insult that a certain set of online trolls use to belittle anyone deemed unmanly.

"Are you going all 'Adrian Adonis' on us?" - Twitter user, December 2019

The 'out and proud' character of "Adorable" Adrian Adonis only existed on WWF television from January 1986 to April 1987, with a brief recurrence in the fading American Wrestling Association (AWA). This represents a tiny fraction of Franke's overall career, giving some measure of the notoriety his performance achieved in a relatively short space of time. It also obscures much of his life and career. A family man; given up for adoption at just a few days old; one of the most

3

technically gifted wrestlers of his day; agile; inventive; a vicious southpaw; a wicked talker, with a brutal sense of humour. Little of this nuance cuts through the eyeliner.

Despite the impact Franke had as Adonis, and the profile which came from working for the biggest wrestling company in the world at the height of its first boom period, Franke appears to largely be forgotten about within modern wrestling circles, except for those references on social media. In the aftermath of his death in 1988 at the age of 34, tributes were brief and fleeting for the man from Buffalo, New York. Thirty-five years later, little has changed.

Perhaps this is simply because even at his most high-profile Franke was, at best, a mid-card attraction – a wrestler who worked hard but never rose to the main event status of wrestling's upper echelons frequented by the likes of close friends Hulk Hogan and "Rowdy" Roddy Piper. This is no insult, and before his weight ballooned in later years, Franke was at one point considered one of the most technically gifted and versatile wrestlers in the world.

If this is the case, there is more to write about this version of wrestling history. Plenty of wrestlers who have achieved far less have been talked about far more. In Adrian Adonis we see a case study of an industry's struggle to adequately reconcile its problematic past. A wrestling character apparently created to elicit the hate of testosterone-fuelled audiences. Is this the real reason why the years pass with barely a mention of the life and work of the man behind the perfumed veil? As a wrestling fan, it is hard to avoid the question; are we too embarrassed to talk about Adrian Adonis?

This seems the case for WWE, for whom Franke took up the controversial character of "Adorable" Adrian Adonis, back when it was the World Wrestling Federation (WWF). Still the premier professional wrestling outfit just as it was in the mid-1980s, WWE today is a multi-billion-dollar company, publicly traded, and beholden to a cornucopia of investors, sponsors, and other stakeholders.

Franke does not feature in the company's Hall of Fame, or any of the similar professional wrestling institutions. As of 2023, the WWE Hall of Fame boasted more than 200 inductees, including some who never worked for the company. You won't find him as a playable 'legacy' character in the company's yearly 2K computer game series. It's not simply a modern conundrum. Back in 1988 his death was not even acknowledged on WWF programming or in its publications. Wrestling was ready to forget Adrian Adonis before he even left.

When a lot of wrestling fans conjure an image of Adrian Adonis, it isn't one they wish to behold for very long. It is unclear where this discussion leaves Franke, who earlier in his career portrayed a New York biker, moving between different regional territories as a tag-team specialist. He floats as a conundrum, deserving of more recognition than he receives, inextricably linked to a name and character that many would prefer to forget.

Franke wrestled for several years before he became 'Adorable,' in numerous territories across the US and Canada, as well as stints in Japan and Australia. Initially he performed under his real name, then as "Gorgeous" Keith Franks and later as "The Golden Boy" Adrian Adonis. Wrestling fans with long memories can look beyond the effeminate character that Franke depicted for a couple of years at the tail-end of a notable career. The industry that he dedicated his adult life to has been unable to do the same.

When legendary tough guy Frank 'Bruiser Brody' Goodish was murdered by a fellow wrestler in a Puerto Rico dressing room in July 1988, he was instantly immortalised as an icon of the pseudo-sport. A violent, volatile grappler, Brody gained a devoted following, especially in Japan, for his brutal style, and built the parameters of much of what is today known as the 'hardcore' wrestling motif. So much so, after winning the category of 'Best Brawler' in the *Wrestling Observer* newsletter seven times in nine years from 1980 to 1988, the award was permanently named after him and remains so to this day.

More than one wrestling company held tribute shows, and published magazines highlighting his achievements. Books and documentaries have followed in the past three decades, many of which rightly delve into the detail around the horrific circumstances of his death, and the questionable legal process that followed and allowed his attacker to walk free and continue a successful wrestling career.

To be in the shadow of a more important, bigger name was always Franke's way, whether that be future Governor Jesse Ventura, or kindred spirit Roddy Piper. Even in death, with Brody's shocking murder taking place just days after Franke's fateful van crash, Adrian Adonis could not have the spotlight for himself.

The commemorative treatment of Andre the Giant, another wrestling star of the 80s who died several decades ago, has likewise been vastly different to that of Franke in the years that have passed. Andre Roussimoff was a special attraction all over the world, including in the WWF during the time of its international expansion between 1984 and 1988. Like Adonis, he died 14 months after his final WWF appearance.

When Roussimoff died in January 1993, the following week's episode of *WWF Monday Night Raw* featured a moving tribute and ten-bell salute. Andre, however, was not simply a professional wrestler; he was a marvel. A movie actor, a frequent guest on mainstream US chat shows, it's not surprising that his death was heralded as the passing of a legend. A much bigger star than Adrian Adonis and deserving of a much bigger send-off accordingly.

Closer parallels to the treatment of Adrian Adonis in memoriam may be seen in the deaths of former WWF performers Dino Bravo and "Texas Tornado" Kerry Von Erich, which occurred within three weeks of each other in February and March 1993. While neither were on the WWF's payroll as active wrestlers at the time of their deaths, their stature and history with the Federation should have been enough to garner at least a mention on the weekly TV shows. They did not.

It is likely that the WWF was disinclined to associate itself with the 'negative' connotations with both deaths. Von Erich died by suicide the day after being indicted for a parole violation; Bravo was shot 17 times in his living room, a speculated 'mob' hit for his involvement in an illicit cigarette-smuggling ring. No such murky circumstances befell Keith Franke. The man simply had the misfortune of being a passenger in the wrong van on the wrong day.

Killed in a car crash on U.S. Independence Day 1988 alongside two fellow wrestlers while travelling in far-flung Newfoundland, Franke unwittingly gave many younger wrestling fans their first opportunity to confront the vulnerability of a TV hero.

Wrestling newsletters and local news reports made mention, but Franke was not remembered as he might have been. He was 'Adorable Adrian,' little more than a punchline by the end. The name is largely forgotten and, where it is remembered, it resides as a byword. A shorthand for bloated laziness, for unmanliness, and for the exploitative tendencies that lie within the world of wrestling.

In April 2021, wrestling legend Hulk Hogan paid a visit to an unassuming storage facility in his native Florida. Documenting the trip to his social media followers, Hogan was there to sort through boxed up mementoes from his wrestling career. Among the grappling-themed bric-a-brac, a picture caught Hogan's eye. Barefooted, Hogan picked it up, and sat his bruised, aging torso down on a box to consider it a little closer. Briefly, he was transported back in time, nearly forty years, as two athletic young men growl into the camera. Making sure to post it online, so fans could see his tenderness, he gave a brief remembrance of a former friend.

> *"Adrian Adonis and I were attached at the hip, from [the] AWA until he passed, we always had a blast and always tore it down, brother."*

It was not the first time. Shortly before the thirtieth anniversary of Franke's death in 2018, Hogan posted a picture of his late friend on Twitter. Beaming into the camera directly from December 1983, a hopeful young couple were pictured outside a church in the middle of Sunset Boulevard, the man grinning with a mischievous glint in his eye to match the unseasonably sunny day, ready to enter the cathedral for Terry Bollea's wedding.

6

Within five years of posing for that photo with his wife Bea alongside the great and good of the early 1980s wrestling fraternity, Franke was dead. Hogan reflected wistfully on the passing of the years to his millions of followers, many of whom had likely never heard the name. The Hulkster opined simply: "Miss my boy 'AD,' Adrian Adonis," before adding that Franke was indeed a "crazy brother."

It should not be a surprise. The pair worked together in numerous wrestling territories throughout the 1980s, from the American Wrestling Association (AWA) to the WWF and Japan, enjoying a bond that would endure through numerous incarnations, at least until one backstage incident in 1986.

It speaks volumes of Franke's influence to have made such an impression on Hogan, a man who has glad-handed everyone in both the professional wrestling business and the wider entertainment industry in his forty-plus-year career as a wrestler, B-movie actor, and reality TV star. Of the hundreds of people Hogan has known over the years, Keith Franke remains one thought about in the quieter moments.

At his early 1980s peak, respect for Franke was not just forthcoming from fellow wrestlers. In November 1983, a month before Franke attended Hogan's wedding to Linda Claridge, the *Wrestling Observer* newsletter ranked three men jointly as the best wrestler of the prior year. One was, of course, perennial great Ric Flair, the golden-haired "Nature Boy" who that month toppled Harley Race to win his second NWA World Heavyweight title at the inaugural *Starrcade* extravaganza. The second, Bruiser Brody, was similarly busy in November 1983, winning the prestigious Tag League in All Japan Pro Wrestling with partner Stan Hansen. The third was Adrian Adonis.

A rapid weight gain culminated in Franke adopting the "Adorable" Adrian Adonis character. The persona was a pastiche of the renowned 1950s TV wrestling showman Gorgeous George, and borrowed from flamboyant, androgynous Welsh wrestler 'Exotic' Adrian Street. Immediately beforehand though he was regarded as one of the most technically proficient and convincing professional wrestlers of his day. There was also a time early in his career when the 'Adonis' moniker seemed perfectly natural for one with rugged good looks, and less the cruel irony that it would later become once his figure bloated so horrendously.

The 'Adonis' tag replaced the earlier nickname of 'Gorgeous.' The moniker 'Apollo' was also ascribed to Franke by one local newspaper profile in 1977. It was not meant as a joke when it was first adopted. A handsome man with striking features, the Adonis handle was meant with sneering sincerity in the early days. Perhaps he lacked the physique of musclebound buffoons like Tony Atlas or Ivan Putski, body-types that the lay-person might more quickly recognise as 'built like a Greek God.' But labelling Keith Franke an Adonis in 1978 was not some sarcastic jibe.

As his career progressed, and Franke took less and less care of his body, the name would become a sad joke at his own expense. The Adrian of 1986 or 1987, an Adonis? Nothing could seem more ludicrous.

The final factor in the puzzle of Keith Franke, and the key component missing in so many professional wrestlers who fail to make it past the mediocre, was his ability to capture the crowd's imagination with his work on the microphone. Bragging, boasting, and belligerence is a must for any wrestler looking to 'talk the people into the building' and put butts in seats. As with his in-ring work and his appearance in those early days, Adrian Adonis was one of the best at the art of the stream-of-consciousness 'promo,' –

> *"It's hard to explain how you get this great. It's not from eating your Wheaties, it's not from going to bed at 9 o'clock and getting up at 5. It's from being a man. I refuse to be a puppet for those so-called big shots. I refuse to be dancing on strings, I am my own man, my own person, and I make a lot of people believe it. And right here, in this area, I have just started to terrorise. Violence, it's a banquet on which I feed."*
>
> *- Adrian Adonis, Southwest Championship Wrestling, 1983*

With an improvised delivery packed with cultural references of the time, Franke's interviews painted visceral pictures which wouldn't fly today for all manner of reasons. One such example would be his tendency to interpolate a particular passage from *The Godfather* movie, referencing Adolf Hitler.

Adrian Adonis knew how to make people care outside of the ring just as much as inside it. For the majority of his career, he was always the heel, always hated, always laughed at, always despised. Maybe this impacted how he viewed the fans in return; or maybe he was just too good at playing bad. Either way, an anger permeated his on-screen interviews, often meandering, with vague references to a damaged childhood, sometimes veering on the prophetic. No more so was this the case than when he warned the Brisco Brothers ahead of an imminent tag-team showdown:

> *"But I'll tell you something, Jack and Jerry Brisco, I'd rather burn out than fade away."*
>
> *- Adrian Adonis, World Wrestling Federation, 1985*

Picking up a line from a 1979 Neil Young song, Franke unknowingly pointed to his own demise with words later immortalised when they appeared in Kurt Cobain's suicide letter.

The looks, the ability, and the voice; who could ask for more from a professional wrestler? For some wrestling fans of the mid-1980s, that 'something extra' that

Adrian Adonis provided was not to their taste and they were not shy about letting Franke know it. As the WWF hoped they would, crowds revelled in chanting homophobic slurs at Adonis as the company mined archaic prejudices to foment hostile feelings against this supposed 'villain.' Franke did his job and created a bad guy that fans loved to hate. This came at a cost to his own legacy and helped set wrestling back years.

Wrestling began in 1986 for Adorable Adrian, which was rather late for Keith Franke, a man who had worked since adolescence to be a major wrestling star. Some might say Adrian Adonis died in 1985. Of course, Keith Franke died three years later – but the character died the minute he dyed his hair platinum blond and wished everybody a "gay new year" for 1986. Nowadays, with all information at our fingertips, memorialising all the young dead wrestlers of the 1980s, 1990s and 2000s has become a cottage industry. Many are canonised, some rightly so, some less so.

So, one last question – when did we all forget about Adrian Adonis?

Chapter 1: Adrian's Adonis

"He had the kind of body that would shame Adonis,

"And a face that would make any man proud."

- *Sister Sledge (1979)*

While the memory of Adrian Adonis fades from view a little more with each passing year, Keith Franke's influence remains, whether wrestling fans realise it or not. His bruising, bouncing style saw him bump across the ring to emphasise the force of opponents' attacks. While far from the only wrestler to embody this style he was a direct influence on many, including future WWF champion Shawn Michaels, with whom Franke briefly crossed paths in the AWA.

You do not have to look far to see the imprint of Adonis throughout WWF's history in particular. Adrian Adonis used the DDT as a finishing move in Federation rings well before Jake "The Snake" Roberts. He was renowned for his sleeper hold – *'Good Night Irene'* – well before "Million Dollar Man" Ted DiBiase ever subjected anyone to a 'Million Dollar Dream.' He hooked on a sharpshooter years before Bret Hart, and he sprayed perfume well before Rick Martel displayed any kind of arrogance.

Thanks to Adonis, Brutus Beefcake became "The Barber" and added a whole new dimension to his character. To this day, Adonis is one of only two male performers to have their heads shaved upon losing a match as part of the annual *WrestleMania* attraction – twenty years before company chairman Vince McMahon did so as part of his showdown with future United States President Donald Trump in 2007.

Adonis is the only wrestler to have received, at different intervals, the on-screen tutelage of legendary managers "Classy" Freddie Blassie, "Captain" Lou Albano, Bobby "The Brain" Heenan, Jimmy Hart and Paul Heyman. A member of the Hart Foundation back when it was a manager's stable rather than a tag-team, he is also credited by Jim Neidhart of convincing the team to switch to its iconic pink and black motif.

As a tag-team specialist he featured in the first televised WWF match immediately following the infamous 'Black Saturday' takeover of the Georgia television slot and faced Bruno Sammartino in the Italian American superman's final ever Madison Square Garden main event. His cultural impact also came in the form of a *People Magazine* feature, and as the subject of pioneering new wave 80s comic book, *Love and Rockets.*

In short, it is easier than you might imagine to list Franke's lasting influence. Franke earned his pro wrestling acumen the way most wrestlers did in the 1970s. Travelling through different regions he learned contrasting styles and how to use them to complement each other. In front of often hostile crowds, he developed a sense of how to enrage and entertain; when to hold back, and when to bring forth. On the circuit he learned from legends and peers, and absorbed their influence, from big stars like Ray Stevens and Harley Race, to journeymen pros like Dennis Stamp.

Franke had all the components needed to be a successful, multi-dimensional pro wrestling character. Working the first year of his career under his real name he made an unremarkable impact. In the years that followed he made progress, raising his profile in several territories as "Gorgeous" Keith Franks. But something was missing. Aside from the wrestling, the talking, the charisma, he needed something extra. He needed a name.

By the early 1980s Franke could count himself among the better talkers of the pro wrestling fraternity. This was during a time when the brash, aggressive interview style that wrestlers would become known for was less common than it would become.

Alongside his tag-team partner and future Governor of Minnesota, Jesse "The Body" Ventura, Franke adopted and adapted the jive-talking patter of musclebound heavyweight "Superstar" Billy Graham and beloved everyman "The American Dream" Dusty Rhodes. Both were premier stars of the 1970s remembered more for their verbal dexterity than in-ring capabilities, which they themselves borrowed from Muhammad Ali. Ali, of course, cited a different inspiration.

Ali observed from fabled 1950s wrestling star Gorgeous George that it paid to be hated. He noted: "I saw fifteen thousand people coming to see this man get beat, and his talking did it. I said, this is a good idea!" Where Ali went, others followed, including generations of professional wrestlers, many perhaps not even realising they were following a path carved by one of their own.

When it comes to working the microphone for the purposes of putting yourself over in front of an often-cynical crowd, the best pro wrestling talkers all have their calling cards. Whether it be Ric Flair's grandiose insistence that "to be the man, you gotta beat the man;" or 'Stone Cold' Steve Austin's hostile warning of "that's the bottom line because Stone Cold said so;" the best wrestling catchphrases capture the public's imagination, embed a Pavlovian response in front of a live crowd, and help build the identity of the man behind the mic.

Franke had a rolodex of phrases he could trust to build the crowd's antipathy towards himself. The one he often used as his finale was by far the most pretentious and infuriating, perfect in its simplicity, for a wrestling bad guy:

"And remember, you spell wrestling...A-D-O-N-I-S."

- Adrian Adonis, Southwest Championship Wrestling, 1983

Wrestling historians would instantly recognise the slogan, which was adopted from the verbal calling card of Canadian grappler John Tolos. A multiple-time tag-team champion in numerous promotions with brother Chris including in the old WWWF, Tolos would amuse and enrage fans throughout the 1960s and 70s with his familiar refrain: "There's only one way to spell wrestling, T-O-L-O-S." Adonis, a wrestling fan from an early age, would have been keenly aware that he was following Tolos' example.

Like a lot of things about Adrian Adonis, the origins of the name he loved to spell out to the marks in the crowd are just as elusive. Where the name 'Adrian Adonis' came from, and why it stuck, are not completely clear, beyond some reasonable deductions that can be made.

George Wagner inspired the look of dozens of wrestlers who would follow, chief among them "Nature Boy" Buddy Rogers. Prior to adopting his more famous sobriquet, Rogers employed a different nickname – "The Blond Adonis." Even earlier in his career, while working under his real name, newspaper columns occasionally referred to the Camden, New Jersey native as the "Camden Adonis." Years earlier, wrestling trailblazer Jim Londos was occasionally dubbed the "Greek Adonis," a variation on his more famous "Golden Greek" tag.

The alliterative nature of the name helps it roll off the tongue and was among the earliest examples of the wrestling monikers repeating identical initial sounds in successive words. This helped ensure a name stuck in the memories of fans, many of whom were adolescents that might otherwise forget a more complicated name. This simple, playful structure has established another of the inarguable principles of any good wrestling character: the importance of a catchy name. Consider Hulk Hogan, Roman Reigns, British Bulldog, Macho Man, Kofi Kingston, or [Bret] 'Hitman' Hart, to name a few.

The curiosity of a man with a feminine first name like 'Adrienne' (borne from the northern Italian city of Adria, neighbouring the Adriatic Sea), would have certainly raised a few laughs among the male wrestling crowd.

Famously, John Wayne, the manliest man of them all, was actually Marion. Likewise, 1970s British wrestling star Big Daddy was really Shirley to his friends and family. Not to mention Johnny Cash's *'A Boy Name Sue.'* The hit record, performed live in concert at wrestling mecca Madison Square Garden in 1969, recounted the tale of a young man who set out for revenge on his deadbeat dad, responsible for saddling him with "that awful name".

Who was this man who paraded around with blonde locks, answering to what sounded suspiciously like a girl's name? Had he no shame? For Franke, generally a heel throughout his career, this was precisely the reaction he was looking for.

Franke first wrestled as Adrian Adonis on 30 January 1978, under the Georgia Championship Wrestling arm of the National Wrestling Alliance (NWA) umbrella, on a card in Augusta which also featured Ric Flair, Dusty Rhodes, Ole Anderson, and Stan Hansen. Five days prior he wrestled for the final time as "Golden Boy" Keith Franks as a late substitute in the opening match of the NWA's 'Superbowl of Wrestling' super-show.

No obvious explanation is given for the sudden change, but wrestling pioneer Terry Funk staked a claim in his 2005 memoir, *More Than Just Hardcore*:

> *"Another guy who did that was someone I got to know much better in San Antonio years later, named Keith Franke. Keith gained more fame using a name I gave him, Adrian Adonis."*

The legendary former NWA Heavyweight Champion welcomed Franke into his family's Western States promotion in Amarillo, Texas, in 1978 and has taken credit for coining the name that stuck with Franke for the rest of his career. Whether a poor memory, good old-fashioned wrestling hyperbole, or incomplete archiving of wrestling records, we are met with a conundrum.

Namely, Adonis did not start wrestling for the late Dory Funk Sr's NWA offshoot until August 1978 – by which point he had apparently been wrestling under his new pseudonym in Georgia for at least six months, a period when the younger Funk was touring St Louis, Houston, and Florida. It is quite conceivable that their paths crossed on the road and Funk, world champion in 1975, passed on some wisdom to the rookie Franke, still only four years into his professional career at that point.

As was the duty of the NWA champions of the era, Funk appeared on cards for the association's regional members when he held the big belt and did pass through Toronto during Franke's year there. Indeed, on the single occasion they appeared on the card together, 19 July 1976, Franke appeared in newspaper ads referenced as the 'New York Adonis,' a nickname the local paper ascribed to him at least once before, the previous October. Is this when Funk took him aside and laid the seeds for what was to come?

There are other possible sources. Franke was proud of his New York Italian heritage and was referred to as both the "New York Adonis" and the "Italian Stallion" in promotional material before his name change.

14

Some have speculated that it was a risqué reference to Italian American mobster Joe Adonis, who operated in New York in the 1940s and 50s, before dying in his native Italy in 1971. Maybe a coy reference to Talia Shire's 'Adrian,' foil to Sylvester Stallone's boxing hero in *Rocky*, the highest-grossing film of 1976. Both names appear, separately but tantalising close, in 19th century Oscar Wilde novel *The Picture of Dorian Gray*. Perhaps Funk and Franke were in the same book club:

> *"He has stood as Paris in dainty armour, and as Adonis with huntsman's cloak and polished boar-spear. Crowned with heavy lotus-blossoms, he has sat on the prow of Adrian's barge, looking into the green, turbid Nile."*

Whatever the case, it was not a short leap from Franke's previous nickname of 'Gorgeous,' and the newspaper tag of 'Apollo,' to settle on the equally resplendent 'Adonis.' It retained the infuriating arrogance to make fans seethe and sneer, amplifying it further by having the temerity to recall the Greek god of beauty.

It is tempting then, when analysing the name 'Adrian Adonis,' to focus on that mythical second name. The feminine tones it imbued upon its carrier over the years, subtly at first, and then flagrantly, as well as the cruel joke it eventually played on Keith Franke's once handsome visage. But what about the 'Adrian'? Simply a suitably androgynous name that fitted well in an alliterative coupling – or something more?

The city of Adrian, located in southeast Michigan, sits at the heart of Lenawee County, not far from the state border with Ohio. Home to around 20,000 people, denizens enjoy a busy cultural scene, from the Croswell Opera House, the county museum, numerous parks, and a vintage downtown district. As you might expect, official city material describes Adrian as 'great,' 'thriving;' and 'a city of culture and innovation.'

Originally named Logan, the area was renamed 'Adrian' in reference to the Roman emperor Hadrian, from a suggestion by the city founder's wife in the 1828, maybe keen to imbue the fledgling settlement's local identity with a little Mediterranean culture.

Adrian is the birthplace of Norman Bel Geddes, universally recognised as the originator of twentieth century American industrial design, famed for pioneering an aerodynamic, streamlined style while working on everything from theatre and film set design, world fairs and cars to houses and packaging. It was also the manufacturer of the short-lived but immensely popular Lion motorcar.

All great accolades. But does Adrian also have an unlikely claim to another, altogether more flamboyant character? A man so striking, some might even call him, dare we say, an 'Adonis'?

15

Born in 1881, Paul Stoner Smith from Mount Zion, Illinois, was that man.

Smith had a baseball career which spanned more than a decade in the early part of the twentieth century, the majority of which was spent in the minor leagues, before it was cut short by the First World War.

The high point of his career was a brief spell in 1916 for the Cincinnati Reds of Major League Baseball's National League, where they remain today. His brief sojourn in the majors took in a modest total of ten games, 44 turns at bat, and five runs recorded to his name. His obituary points to a two-week spell for the more famous Boston Red Sox, home of the mighty Babe Ruth, in October 1916, mere days before the team secured that season's World Series, although this does not match up with official MLB data.

Prior to arriving in Cincinnati and taking the step up to the big leagues, Smith plied his trade for two years with the now-defunct Montreal Royals in Minor League Baseball's International League. It was a far more fruitful stay for Smith, who made 83 appearances in 1914, and 88 the following year. While statistics aren't recorded for his debut year with the Royals, Smith notched 51 runs, including four home runs, for 1915.

It is conceivable, however, that none of this would have been possible for Smith had his prodigious talent not first been spotted at a training camp while he was still at his previous club, the Adrian Champs of the Southern Michigan League. The Champs were the third of four incarnations of the short-lived amateur baseball team serving the city of Adrian, which started life as the Adrian Yeggs (1909-11), then Adrian Lions (1912).

The Lions name came from local sponsor the Lion Motor Car Company and stuck until the company's factory burned down in 1912 and put the firm out of business. In need of a new name, and still basking from securing the league's pennant for 1912, the reigning champions called themselves just that: the Adrian Champs.

As the pennant went elsewhere the following year, so did the name, and the team was again reborn as the Adrian Fencevilles (1914). Both the Fencevilles and the Southern Michigan League itself folded in 1915. The team's solitary year as champions coincided with the single season their line-up could boast future Major League player Smith, who played 78 games for the Adrian Champs in the 1913 season, registering 302 appearances at bat, and 100 hits.

Something of a renaissance man for his time, Smith's obituary details the many pursuits he packed into his colourful life. Part of a machine gun battalion on the Western Front; a lengthy career as a wildlife agent when he returned home; an unsuccessful candidate for Macon County Sheriff; and, briefly, a triallist for the Chicago Bears NFL team. Records of Smith's life are hard to find and may indeed be tinged with a hint of the type of embellishment normally reserved for professional wrestling. One other improbable accolade minor league ball player Paul Smith may be able to lay claim to is that of being the original Adrian Adonis.

As unlikely as it may seem, a pair of articles from the sports pages of the *Washington Herald* in the spring of 1914 present the first known occurrence of the phrase which would go on to be forever associated with a prancing, preening professional wrestler.

Sportswriter William Peet reported from a local training camp held to scour prospects for the local Washington Senators. Of the attendees, many of them minor league ball players present by invitation only, Peet was struck by the potential of Paul Smith, and was effusive in his praise. Taken aback by his arresting appearance as much as his ability on the mound, the writer recognised Smith as "the blonde giant from Michigan," his height and hair colour clearly more than enough to catch the eye for the team's next scouting report.

The March 15, 1914, edition of the *Washington Herald* carried training camp notes from the University of Virginia, overseen by Clark Griffith, former major league pitcher and then manager of the nearby Senators. Somewhat preoccupied with what the trialists were eating in their break periods, he noted:

> *"Not only does Paul Smith, the Adrian Adonis, bat right and left-handed, but he can throw with either mitt. Like most of the other recruits, he is also a good two-handed eater."*

Ironically, over-eating would certainly be an accusation that could be levelled at Smith's wrestling namesake towards the end of his wrestling career. A second article five days later provided a more detailed update, with Peet repeating his alliterative praise. *"Paul Smith,"* is, we are told again, *"the Adrian Adonis."*

> *"Paul Smith, the blonde giant from Michigan, has made a favourable impression upon manager Griffith and Smith stands an excellent chance to stick with the club as utility outfielder."*

With a final flourish, foreshadowing that punditry cliché that would hound British soccer players tall enough to be playing basketball, we are told that Smith is *"remarkably fast on his feet for a big man."* The final comments would again reasonably describe wrestling's Adrian Adonis at his agile, nimble best.

The Adonis from Adrian? The handsome hunk of south Michigan? It sounds plausible enough, at least. The man who made the difference, how they marvelled at this statuesque figure, bound to homely Michigan from the Heavens. How they revered him, this local Apollo. This Michigan-bred, Adrian Adonis.

Drawing inspiration from baseball for a ring name would not be without precedent in the squared circle. One of the most popular wrestlers of all time did just that.

Virgil Runnels, another former NWA heavyweight champion, first used the 'Dusty Rhodes' name in 1968, a year into his career.

It was at the apparent suggestion of a colleague who initially proposed he call himself 'Lonesome Rhodes,' the name of the lead character in a 1957 Elia Kazan movie. In truth, both Runnels and the movie likely took inspiration from James "Dusty" Rhodes, star outfielder for the New York Giants in their World Series triumph of 1954.

Paul Smith resumed his minor league career after the war, playing for Milwaukee in 1920, before brief spells with Syracuse and Rochester, followed by retirement in 1921. There's no indication that Smith was a particular star to young children in the cities he represented, from Michigan, to Montreal, to Cincinnati. Nor that he was significant enough to be remembered by those same baseball fans as they grew to adulthood. But perhaps that nickname, if it appeared in more than just those two single paper columns, caught the imagination of some.

Maybe it lived on in the mind of a young boy who grew up some 200 miles away from the city of Adrian in Hammond, Indiana. Such a boy would be Dory Funk Senior, born two years before Smith's retirement, and well after his brief sojourn for the Adrian Lions was over. Did his father tell him tales of the great 'Adrian Adonis,' who once plied his trade on the pitcher's mound a few cities over? Did Funk senior bear the name in mind when he pursued a life in the ring, and later set up his own Western States regional promotion, eventually passing the playful phrase of 'Adrian Adonis' onto his own sons? Maybe Terry Funk did christen Keith Franke after all.

It is a possible origin story for the Adonis name, and one which has gone unnoticed, like so many things associated with the life of Keith Franke. The Adrian Adonis name would go on to define and, to some extent, eclipse Franke's birth name. Like a method actor who has taken his role too seriously for too long, in later years Franke would struggle to delineate between the two.

Chapter 2: Nobody's my people

"Nobody's my people."

- *Adrian Adonis, July 1984*

Adrian Adonis was born in January 1978 for a run in Georgia Championship Wrestling; or was it the August of that year, at the behest of the Funks down in Amarillo? We know for certain that *"Adorable"* Adrian first debuted in the spring of 1986, at the direction of WWF honcho Vince McMahon. Or was the dye truly cast when fans at 1981 Allentown TV tapings screamed a gay slur repeatedly at street brawler Adonis, clad in biker leathers, while McMahon silently observed from the commentator's desk? For Franke himself, even something so simple as his earliest beginnings were hard to decipher.

Keith Franke was born in Buffalo, New York, on 15 September 1953. To whom is less clear. Franke gave numerous in-character wrestling promos throughout his career, particularly in his earlier 'New York City street-tough' persona, in which he would allude unfavourably to his upbringing. In one, he recounted being abandoned as a baby and put up for adoption. As with anything in the murky world of professional wrestling, this could have been simply an example of a wrestler giving a colourful backstory, but it was in fact the case.

> *"I've had bad partners; I've had people try to take advantage of me ever since I've been six years old. But I've always got revenge."*

- Adrian Adonis, WWF Championship Wrestling, July 1985

Modern wrestling promos are closely scripted affairs, engineered to ensure finely-honed 'superstars,' many reared in a purpose-built WWF performance centre, hit all relevant talking points and avoid going off-script. This was not the case in the 1970s and early 80s. Wrestling in those days was an all-around less coordinated affair, with wrestlers and their on-screen proclamations under far less scrutiny, even from the organisations for which they worked. If a wrestler could 'get the match over,' and talk fans into buying a ticket to the arena, he could say what he wanted – within reason.

As "The Golden Boy" Adrian Adonis, Franke entered the World Wrestling Federation for the first time in October 1981, jumping ship from the Minnesota-based American Wrestling Association with tag partner Jesse "The Body" Ventura. In one of his earliest appearances, he was provided a valuable chance to showcase his verbal skills to this new group of fans in the form of a pre-match ringside interview, hosted by WWF commentator Pat Patterson. Patterson, transitioning at this time to a backstage role which would soon see him established as Vince McMahon's right-hand man, questioned the newcomer about his legitimate amateur wrestling pedigree.

> *"Let's just talk about the beginning of time, the beginning of a style, about a man that was moulded. I'm talking about a kid from birth that was left on a doorstep in Manhattan, that worked his way out of the gutter, Jack. Worked at the docks at 17 years old, and I'm talking about taking on people and I'm talking about knocking them down one-by-one.*

> *"And then I'm talking about going into big-time football and then I'm talking about the Junior Olympics. I'm talking about scholarships to ten major colleges, turned them down, you know why? Because the teachers were prejudiced, they didn't like my attitude."*

At this point Adonis removed his sunglasses and flicked his wavy blond hair. He turned to Patterson with a rhetorical question that reverberated tellingly when it came to dissecting Adonis and his relationship with the wider world:

> *"Can you imagine somebody not liking Adrian Adonis' attitude?"*

It picked up a theme initiated by Patterson who mentioned on commentary on one of Adonis' earliest WWF appearances that the new arrival to the north-eastern wrestling scene had *"been on the streets since the age of 14, he's been in trouble ever since."* The motif continued beyond his first WWF tenure, with Adonis warning one opponent ahead of a 1983 match in Southwest Championship Wrestling:

> *"I don't care. Fourteen years I lived with life, death on the streets, what do I care man, I'm out for reputation."*

Off-screen, Keith Franke's real-life background received some focus early on thanks to a local newspaper feature. Nearly three years into his fledging career Franke had gained experience in several local wrestling circuits acquiring knowledge and know-how in each one, fleshing out his style and feeling his way into the role of a true professional wrestler. People were starting to take notice.

On March 9, 1977, the *Bakersfield Californian* published a profile on Keith "Apollo" Franks as a promotional item ahead of a local grudge match the following evening at the now-defunct Strongbow Stadium. Franke's opponent was to be Roddy Piper. The two real-life friends would meet again almost ten years to the day as part of the WWF's record-breaking *WrestleMania III* extravaganza, in front of a supposed 93,000 fans.

While the Bakersfield venue might not have expected quite that capacity a decade prior, people had evidently been excited enough by Franke's performances in the area to merit this brief media spotlight. In the article, readers learned that Franke, an avid fan of pro wrestling as a child growing up in New York City (in truth, New York state), resolved to become a wrestler himself at just nine years old. From going to matches to catching every show he could on television, Franke dedicated himself to achieving his dream of a life in the ring.

The article jumped to Franke's high school amateur wrestling excursions, and his formal wrestling tutelage under the auspices of fearsome trainer and former professional Fred Atkins but did not shed any further light on Franke's childhood. The paper cut a year off Franke's age (he was 23 at the time of the piece), but left one charming artefact:

> *"All that hard work is paying off for the 22-year-old handsome Italian Adonis."*

The 'Italian Stallion' would also be a nickname Franke would briefly toy with before settling on the less ethnic 'Golden Boy.' Amusingly, in the article's penultimate paragraph, Franke was keen to point out that he is *"not a physical fitness fanatic or 'musclehead'"* – something which he would never need to stress in later life.

Five years later the media would once again come calling to speak to Adrian Adonis. This time the coverage was national. Six months into their first foray with the World Wrestling Federation, tag-team partners "The Golden Boy" Adrian Adonis and Jesse "The Body" Ventura – collectively 'The East-West Connection' – were the subject of a spread in the pages of *People* magazine. In the May 24, 1982, issue, graced by Jane Fonda on the cover, the pair featured in an article titled, *"Wrestlers Jesse Ventura and Adrian Adonis Discover the Good Life as Bad Guys."*

Mainstream coverage of wrestlers was rare in this period immediately prior to the Hulk Hogan-infused wrestling boom of the mid-1980s, especially for those who were not main event stars. For media appearances to breach 'kayfabe,' and share behind the scenes details from the fiercely secretive world of professional wrestling, such as a performer's real name, was rarer still.

A pattern emerges. Adonis was once again tagged as a year younger than his actual age, with the writer describing him as 27 rather than 28. Perhaps Franke encouraged it, or perhaps the interview took place prior to the previous September. Details of Keith Franke's true start in life emerged in the article:

> *"Adonis' battles began early in life. Born on Manhattan's Lower East Side, he was raised in the Buffalo area by his adoptive parents, Kenneth and Kay Franke. The Golden Boy, then known as Keith Franke, hated schoolwork, had the grades to prove it, and engaged in gang fights every day after school,"*

Years later, Roddy Piper, who had his own chequered start in life after leaving home under a cloud at 14, confirmed Franke's adoption and further described him as an orphan. He told a Twitter follower in July 2012: *"Adrian Adonis was an orphan, that's why he viewed me as his brother."*

Piper's claim was expanded on in the 2016 book on Piper's life written by his children after his death the year prior. He and Franke, he felt, developed a kinship borne out of similar tough circumstances, and a bond that endured throughout their careers:

> *"He thought I was his brother," said Roddy. Adonis was an orphan and Roddy used to speak of himself in similar terms...They'd bonded over much more than their common age and early starts in the business."*

So, Keith Allen Franke, son of Kenneth and Kay Franke. Not, as Wikipedia once claimed, *'the second son of wrestling manager Keith A Franke senior and Dolores Elizabeth Franke.'* Both are entirely fictitious individuals, when matched against official records. Don't believe everything you read online.

The same page has in the past listed multiple errors. A rogue 1954 birthdate has cropped up persistently. Whether a well-meaning contributor simply had access to faulty information, or someone was seeking to cause mischief is not clear. What is clear is a lack of clarity has persisted pertaining to the man who portrayed Adrian Adonis, even on items which should be the most basic building blocks of his identity.

People Magazine, it turns out, was half correct. Keith Allen Franke was the adopted son of Kenneth and *Hortense* Franke, Horty to her friends. He was taken in by the couple from the small town of Kenmore, New York, just north of Buffalo, having been put up for adoption at a few days old in Manhattan's Lower East Side.

The New York City neighbourhood of the early 1950s that Franke was born into was quite different from the gentrified reality that visitors enjoy today. A working-class district densely populated by, at various points, Spanish, Italian, Jewish, and Irish settlers. It is clear from his promos and newspaper clippings that Franke was aware that his biological parentage was European and Italian, often referencing his 'Roman' features in interviews.

Adopted yes but not an orphan. Kenmore provided a settled upbringing for the young Franke. He certainly did not find himself out on the streets at the age of fourteen, but his childhood was not without upheaval.

Kenneth Franke was two weeks past turning twenty-three when he married Hortense Ada Rockelman on August 24, 1940, the day before her nineteenth birthday. The couple first lived in the picturesque Taunton Place in north Buffalo, before eventually settling on a quiet, suburban street at 5 Hobmoor Avenue, Keith Franke's first home. With its tree-lined streets and lush surroundings, the sedate neighbourhood is far removed from the notorious New York City district of Hell's Kitchen which Franke would years later claim to emanate from during his leather jacket-clad biker phase.

Blonde haired and blue-eyed with a light complexion, Franke senior was a Buffalo native like his wife, and attended the city's Burgard Vocational High School. His cherubic appearance matched an angelic voice and during his senior year he and 14 classmates took up the important role of bass in the glee club, the Craftsmen, performing during the school's silver jubilee in 1935.

It was not long before the glow of marital bliss was interrupted for the Frankes, when Kenneth was drafted into the US Army as part of the United States' growing war effort in the latter part of 1940. Franke was assigned to the airplane division of the Curtiss-Wright Corporation, splitting his time between a manufacturing complex on Elmwood Avenue, and a second factory built in 1941 at a site which now houses the Buffalo-Niagara International Airport.

The slightly built Franke, registered as 150 pounds and two inches shy of six foot when conscripted, spent the remainder of the war helping to produce Curtiss-Wright's famous P-40 fighter planes, known variously as the Warhawk, Kittyhawk and Tomahawk. The Buffalo plant was even responsible for producing the P-40s which defended Pearl Harbour during the Japanese attacks in December 1941.

Horty Rockelman grew up in the heart of the city with her parents, self-employed mechanic father Victor, mother Ruth, and brother Earl, three years her senior. The family lived first in Hoyt Street before purchasing their own home in Tioga Street, a short distance from the city's Delaware Park.

Victor – Adrian Adonis' adopted maternal grandfather – passed away in April 1980 at the age of 85, after a lifetime residing in Buffalo. He made his living in the town as the owner of Rockelman Appliance Service, founded in 1947, shortly after the end of the Second World War. Still operating today, the outlet sits on a typical retail park on one of the main roads through Buffalo.

Despite Kenneth Franke being called upon for national service, the newlyweds were not separated as many families were during the conflict, with Franke able to support the war effort working in construction plants based in the city. This would prove fruitful for the young family as they welcomed their first child, Karen Ruth Franke, in August 1942.

Karen, who inherited her middle name from her maternal grandmother, attended Riverside High School until she was sixteen, a mere stone's throw from the Niagara River, as the name would imply. Sadly, the Franke's eldest child would also pass away at a young age much like her adopted younger brother. Karen

23

Campbell, married and living in East Amherst, died aged 52 in July 1995, two days before the seventh anniversary of her brother's death.

Kenneth Franke himself died a few days before Christmas 1993, aged 76, while Keith's adopted mother Hortense passed away from cancer in November 2016. Still residing in Kenmore at the time of her death, Hortense's obituary in the *Buffalo News* noted her thusly:

> *"Dear wife of the late Kenneth Franke; beloved mother of Susan C. Franke and the late Karen Campbell and Keith Franke; adored grandmother of two grandchildren and five great-grandchildren."*

With the war safely behind them, the 1950s brought stability for upwardly mobile families like the Frankes who settled into life as young parents in upstate New York. Kenneth returned to civilian life, putting his wartime skills to good use by working as a serviceman and repairman, and the couple adopted Keith shortly after he was born in 1953. In December 1955, the family welcomed younger sister Susan.

As Keith Franke's daughter Angela Perides learned at an early age, her father enjoyed a strong relationship with his maternal grandparents in his formative years, spending time at their family home much like Angela herself did when she was young. She noted:

> *"They were really close with my grandmother Franke's family, who owned a furniture store in town, like an appliance store, Rockelman's. I'm not very familiar with New York but it was Amherst, Buffalo area.*

> *"I remember going there when I was younger...downstairs was the whole house and then upstairs there was [another] whole house. So, my grandmother and grandfather lived on the upstairs and then her dad and mum lived downstairs."*

Never one to refuse food, as many could attest years later, the young Keith Franke quickly learned that some shrewd manipulation of his grandparents' living situation could work to his benefit. Perides explained:

> *"My dad would in the morning go downstairs and have breakfast with his grandpa, Grandma Franke's dad [Victor], he'd have breakfast with him, and then come upstairs and have breakfast with the family and then come back downstairs at 11 o'clock and have breakfast with his grandma. So, he would have three breakfasts, almost like he was just into everything, he had so much energy."*

Keith was adopted by the Frankes when he was just a few days old, shortly after his birth on September 15, 1953. According to Perides, the Frankes had been trying to conceive a second child for several years without success following the

24

birth of daughter Karen. As she was told, the couple were approached by their obstetrician about an opportunity to adopt, at very short notice.

When the couple confirmed their interest, the physician advised that he was aware of a young lady who lived in the area with an unexpected pregnancy which she wished to give up for adoption. The mother's only requirements, he told the couple, was that the baby was not placed with an Italian or Catholic family since that was the father's background. When the Frankes confirmed they were neither, they received the new-born at seven days old and brought him home as their own.

Keith's younger daughter Gena Banta recounted a very similar story, although recalled being told that the adoption was arranged by the local Catholic church and took place at five days old. Either way, the Frankes were delighted to add a second child to their family. She said:

> "Basically, a young couple out of wedlock got pregnant and my grandmother was told she couldn't have anymore children, she'd had my aunt Karen and they wanted another child and I guess back then it was a lot easier to adopt, got him when he was five days old; they never wanted to be contacted."

The Frankes were honest with young Keith from the outset about his background and informed him early in life that he was adopted. Keith showed little interest in knowing more about his biological background according to his daughters, which Gena has interpreted as a reflection on how comfortable he was with his adoptive parents. She added:

> "I asked [my mother] if he ever wanted to reach out? [She said] no, he was perfectly happy with the life that he had. That was interesting, how secure he was with his relationship with his family."

Perides holds a similar view, adding the detail that her father's birth certificate retained his birth mother's maiden name of O'Grady. She also recounted being told by her grandmother that her grandfather believed he saw a woman in the local neighbourhood watching Keith from a distance when he was playing outside at around four years old and was convinced it was her. Despite this, Keith's real mother never made contact and he never showed any interest in contacting her.

Keith's adoptive parents made sure he felt loved and appreciated despite the circumstances, and clearly the upbringing he received from the Frankes helped him prosper. Rather than feeling isolated or different because of his adoption, Franke would brag to schoolfriends about his unique status, prompting the disbelieving pals to seek out his mother for confirmation. Perides said:

> "He always knew, he would tell everybody, and my grandma said that [friends] would ask him – and this little boy would say, 'Oh Mrs Franke,

Mrs Franke, is it true? Is Keith adopted?' And she would go 'Well, yes, he's adopted.' 'Well, he told me he was and we thought he was lying,' and she goes 'No, no, he is.'"

Keith was aware of his Italian heritage, which he would pay tribute to in later life via an Italian flag tattoo on his right forearm. Early in his career he briefly used the nickname "The Italian Stallion." Years later Keith befriended comedian and actor Joey Gaynor. A chance encounter with Gaynor's mother led the pro wrestler to inform the pair that she shared a maiden name, Caputo, with one of his biological parents, presumably the Italian American father he never met. The discovery led Franke and Gaynor to speculate that they may be cousins.

The Frankes lived at 60 Lorelee Drive throughout Keith's childhood, during which time he attended Alexander Hamilton Elementary School, often creating quite the challenge for sixth grade teacher Miss Krickledorf with his rambunctious nature. As they got older, Keith and neighbourhood friends rode to bus to Herbert Hoover Junior High School. Junior High was the first place that Franke took up wrestling, the endeavour that came to define him.

Despite the relatively tranquil surroundings, the adolescent Franke was at times an angry young man. Stories abound of the teenage Keith frequently getting into arguments with teachers during the school day, and fistfights with classmates once school was out. He developed a reputation across neighbouring schools of someone not to be messed with, as referenced in the *People* article.

Paul Neiss befriended Keith around this time when the pair were both eight years old. Franke senior brought his son along to join Neiss's football team, the West Side Tigers, a junior side sponsored by Neiss's father's employer, the Ellwood Fire District. Neiss remembered:

> *"My dad was our coach. My dad told his father to bring him out the following year. We played a few times and he was a little bit bigger than most kids but he had this drive to always win. When he came out the next year he was bigger but right on the edge of the weight limit to play at our age.*
>
> *"According to my dad, Keith was the measuring stick to see if boys could play football for him. Any time someone came to join the team, you had to go against Keith in just about every drill and even when we scrimmaged. I was no exception. I got my fair share of bumps from Keith and it seemed like no one could ever move him or block him. He was the toughest kid I ever played against including college football.*
>
> *"My uncle brought his son out to play football for my dad and he had to go against Keith the whole practice. After, my uncle asked my dad if he was trying to get his son killed!"*

26

People started to notice this talented youngster, and after a while the coach of a team from the west of Buffalo enquired about Keith and Paul lining up for his squad on a different day of the week. Despite a two-year age gap between the boys – now 10 and 11 – and their new teammates, Neiss' father took them to play. He recalled:

> *"Keith being a very aggressive player was always the first one to go offsides. We were to go together but Keith always beat everyone off the ball. The thing I remember most about him during this time was that whenever you tried to block him or tackle him, he would just laugh. It was impossible to take him off his feet or hurt him. We played together for another year before he had to move to a heavier weight division, but the stories were basically the same, he loved contact and he loved the competition."*

It was not all fun and games for Franke as a young man. According to Banta, family legend has it that her father was *"super mischievous and always into something."* Perides said that he often had to be separated from other children to avoid conflicts in the classroom and theorised that if he was growing up today, he might be diagnosed with a condition such as attention deficit hyperactivity disorder (ADHD). Describing a particular clash relayed to her by her father's mother, she said:

> *"He did get in a lot of fights, my grandmother would say. He would get in fights and neighbourhood mothers would come to her and tell them, 'Your son should be punished he beat up my son, my son is however old,' and my grandmother would say 'Well no, Keith is only ten and your son's thirteen, well he's bigger,' well, he would get in fights usually he was sticking up for a smaller kid that somebody was picking on or he was sticking up for somebody else, like a bully he would go to fight for the underdog. And my grandmother always said that he would always help the smaller person."*

As a teenager, Keith attended Kenmore East High School. Many of the anecdotes around Franke's high school days revolve around his sporting prowess. While he was not overly academic, he did for a time enjoy an auto mechanics class. As with junior high, this too required a bus ride, this time to the local adult education centre where the lessons took place.

By eleven, Franke was developing into a budding multi-sport athlete, competing in wrestling, football, baseball and hockey. As a member of the Bills Bombers he twice won junior baseball trophies within the Buffalo Kiwanis youth league. It was around this time he also played as a defensive lineman for the Ken-Ton (Kenmore-Tonawanda) Panthers junior football team, briefly under the tutelage of future NFL coaching great Jim McNally.

A couple of years later Franke tasted further sporting success as a defender for the Tonawanda Bantam All-Star ice hockey team. The squad won the state's championship before successfully raising $2,000 from appealing to local businesses, to enable them to compete in national finals in Minneapolis.

Unlike older sister Karen who went to school in Buffalo, Keith attended one of the two public secondary schools in the family's tiny hometown. Just north of the city of Buffalo, the small town of Kenmore is in many ways a typical twentieth century American suburban village, with its tree-lined streets stretching out from the town centre. Atypical of most of suburbia but ever-present in Kenmore is the area's collection of waterfalls, situated less than a half hour drive from Niagara Falls and its neighbouring State Park.

While academia may not have appealed to the young Franke's tastes as much as his family may have liked, Kenmore East did present the boy with a path to the goal he had since he was nine years old. As soon as he was old enough, Franke joined the high school wrestling team. Wrestling served a dual purpose, allowing Franke a constructive outlet for his adolescent frustrations, and placing him on the path towards a future career.

At Kenmore East, Franke was a member of the junior varsity wrestling team while still a sophomore in 1968, and the varsity team the following year. Both years he wrestled under the guidance of Coach Kerwin "Skip" Pine. Coach Pine had a storied career as a high school wrestling coach, retiring in 1994 after more than three decades. He would subsequently be inducted into the Upstate New York arm of the National Wrestling Hall of Fame in 2013.

During this period, Pine led several teams to championships and coached numerous tournament winners. Among his accolades were 52 'section 6' place finishers in the New York Public High School Athletic Association (NYPHSSAA), and 15 champions, as well as two New York State champions. One of those, Bob Rust, went on to finish second in the NCAA University division wrestling championships in 1970.

Joining the Kenmore East Bulldogs was a fine decision for Franke as he quickly excelled in the amateur ranks. Pictured in the school yearbook of 1969, Franke is listed in a team photo with the unmistakeable glare at the camera which would chasten many a pro wrestling fan and opponent in later life.

Elsewhere in the same yearbook he can be spotted on the side-lines of the 'Ken-East' bench studiously watching a match in progress. The year marked a fourth consecutive sectional title for the team, with 12 victories from 14 matches against local rival schools including Kenmore West and Niagara Falls. Franke played his part as the team retained its Section VI Class AAA Championship.

By the following year, now a senior, Franke was a leading member of the team and represented the Bulldogs well at a pair of tournaments in the spring. On February 21, 1970, Section VI Class AAAA Wrestling Championships, with matches taking place on the home turf of the Kenmore East gymnasium, the Bulldogs entered the eight-team, one-day tournament as favourites, and emerged victorious with 120 points. Franke secured victory in the 250-pound heavyweight division, with a pinfall over Steve Pachla in a little over two minutes.

The team and Franke would be less successful two weeks later when they progressed to the state qualifiers at the Erie Tech Sports Arena in Williamsville on March 7, 1970. Despite a 7-0 decision victory in the championship quarterfinals, and a one-minute pin-fall triumph in the semi-final, Franke could not quite match his first-place showing of the previous month. Despite a valiant showing, he was pinned in the first period of overtime in a match lasting nearly seven minutes and had to settle for second place overall in the single's heavyweight competition.

Channelling teenage angst into a constructive outlet had proven a winning decision for Franke, who benefited from the structure and dedication he gained from joining his high school wrestling team.

Despite his success Franke did not graduate high school, instead opting to drop out during his senior year. According to his eldest daughter his intention was to pursue a career as a professional athlete. A self-taught ice skater, Franke initially pursued ice hockey before making the short trip to Canada where he briefly played amateur football.

A try-out for a Canadian Football League team proved unsuccessful. It was this sojourn which stirred Franke's true passion, prompting him to call home and inform his parents of his latest plan. Perides said:

> "He kept calling my grandma, he called, and he told my grandma he wanted to wrestle, and she goes 'You better get in shape.' Because he would just go and drink the whole [carton] of orange juice, she goes, 'no you are just being gluttonous, you need to lose weight and get self-discipline,' she told him all of it."

Back in Buffalo during this time Franke started working out at owner Nick Mortilaro's Western New York Athletic Center on Englewood Avenue, befriending other regulars. A gym-goer more than his physique suggested, Franke struggled to keep weight off his whole life.

The adolescent Keith's lack of self-control of his eating habits was not his only problem. In the period immediately following high school, Franke bounced around a number of low-level jobs and hung around with a tough crowd. There was none tougher at the time in Buffalo than the Kingsmen Motorcyle Club, North Tonawanda Chapter. Simply put, a biker gang.

The Kingsmen still exist in the area today and is classified as a criminal organisation. Back in the early 1970s, the notorious motorcycle gang members tended to be younger in age, and mainly attracted the attention of authorities for fighting with rival gangs. Franke did not associate long with the Kingsmen but long enough to have his own bike and logo-emblazoned jacket, which he wore around the group's Oliver Street headquarters in North Tonawanda.

There were legitimate jobs alongside the not so legitimate activities too. At one such place, a gas station, Perides described how he technically worked there but in reality *"basically had all of his friends doing all the work and he would smoke weed, sitting out drinking beer with all the friends."* He also put his imposing stature and physical nature to good work elsewhere as a bouncer at local bars, including one on Elmwood Avenue, and another further afield, McAvans of Syracuse.

Affable and talkative by nature, Franke was a social animal and had no problem building friendships to sustain him while he figured out how to take the first step on his next adventure. Buffalo hangout Chooch's Bar was a regular haunt, as Franke befriended many of the local patrons, including owner John "Chooch" Miceli. Companionship came in many forms, such as the bull terrier that Franke rescued from a fighting ring and took in as his own, christened Taurus.

A couple of other associations marked this formative period in Franke's youth and perhaps fermented an appreciation of the camaraderie he would later enjoy within professional wrestling. Around 1971 Franke found the perfect outlet for his love of rough-housing and partying as a member of Kappa Beta, a local fraternity with about eighty members which rented a house on Normal Avenue, on the western side of Buffalo.

By now eighteen, Franke attended meetings, partied, and held his own in mass fights with rival groups, on one occasion scaling a flagpole mid-fight, or so legend has it.

One fraternity brother has since described the harrowing moment that showed Keith's true character during one Saturday night house party. When he was told of a young woman being sexually assaulted by fellow chapter members in an upstairs bedroom, Franke stormed the room and attacked the offenders, helping the victim escape. At the next fraternity meeting, Franke attended, explained his actions, and quit the fraternity shortly after, appalled by what he had seen.

From dropping out of school to his dalliances with rowdy biker gangs and frat boys, Franke started to grow frustrated with the rut he found himself in. He knew where he wanted to go, but not how to get there. He would find the answer without even leaving Buffalo.

Franke's hometown and the friendships he made there left an indelible impression, with many friends telling stories of bonds that lasted beyond fame and fortune, and ups and downs. One of those was his junior football teammate Paul Neiss. Reflecting on what it was like to reunite with 'Adrian Adonis' in the mid-1980s at the Meadowlands Arena, Neiss remembered:

> *"I got to see [him] after many years in his dressing room at the then called Brendan Byrne Arena in New Jersey. I scammed my way in to see him and he thought it was great."*

Chapter 3: Fred Atkins and Crystal Beach

"There's no question if this man could behave, or could have when he was a kid, he would've went a long way in amateur wrestling. But he got thrown out of school, everything he tried to accomplish, he never made it, he was always in trouble."

– Pat Patterson, 1981

As referenced in *People*, Franke's first forays into life as a sportsman upon leaving school did not involve wrestling, but ice hockey and football. He quit high school during his senior year (class of 1971) without graduating and attempted to break into semi-professional football in Canada. The *Bakersfield Californian* expanded on this claim with the detail that Franke played two seasons for the Hamilton (Ontario) Tigers, while continuing his wrestling training.

With the Hamilton Tigers an ice hockey team, it is possible the newspaper is referring to his endeavours on the ice, or rather to the Hamilton Tiger-Cats, of the Canadian Football League (CFL), albeit this is a professional outfit rather than the semi-pro level Franke reached. A member of this team becoming a professional wrestler would have been far from unusual, however.

Angelo Mosca, voted into the Canadian Football Hall of Fame in 2012, was an all-star twice in his near decade-long career with the Tiger-Cats. Mosca started wrestling in the off-season in 1969 and took to the squared circle full-time following his football retirement. Another Tiger-Cat of the early 1970s was George Wells, who completed a similar if less successful football-to-pro wrestler transition. A stalwart of many territories from the 70s to the early 90s, Wells is mostly remembered by modern fans as the opponent of Jake "The Snake" Roberts at *WrestleMania II,* a card which also featured Adrian Adonis.

Franke does not feature on the extensive player rosters of the Hamilton Tiger-Cats for the late 1960s or early 1970s. It is most likely that Franke featured for the practice or development roster of one of these teams but did not turn professional. Another possibility is that he played for one of the country's semi-professional football leagues, such as the Northern Football Conference which formed in Ontario in the mid-50s. However, while this league did once boast a team of 'Hamilton Wildcats,' this was not until 1978.

Franke initially wrestled in the amateur ranks, building upon his high school success. As he would boast accurately on WWF programming almost a decade later, Franke was selected to participate in the Junior Olympics. The *Bakersfield*

Californian article of 1978 claimed he won the gold medal in the heavyweight class of the wrestling competition at the 1972 AAU Junior Olympic Games.

An annual competition hosted by the US Amateur Athletic Union, the Junior Olympics first took place in 1949 and by the early 70s was regarded as the uppermost competition in the US for junior athletics. Results don't exist to verify the claim of Franke's success at the 1972 meet, held in Spokane, Washington, but according to claims made by the organisers at the time, more than a million junior entrants participated in the Chevrolet-sponsored event. Franke did well to place in his division at all, let alone win, if he indeed did so.

In the closed shop that was professional wrestling, an introduction to a trusted trainer usually came via a personal recommendation from someone with connections. How Franke made this jump is not clear. One possibility is that he received advice from Buffalo-based bodybuilding champion and coach, Dr Joe Lazzaro, whom Franke met in his early years.

Back home from his initial excursions, Franke found there was no better place to start asking about opportunities than with his local wrestling promotion. The Buffalo territory at the time was run by local entrepreneur and former wrestler Ignacio "Pedro" Martinez. Martinez launched the National Wrestling Federation (NWF) in Buffalo and Illinois in 1970 outside of the umbrella of the National Wrestling Alliance.

Though it only lasted for four years, the NWF held the distinction of hosting wrestling's first 'Superbowl of Wrestling' card, which attracted several thousand spectators to Cleveland, Ohio's Municipal Stadium in August 1972. As a hopeful teenager, Franke approached the group with his enquiries about how to break in.

It was the Buffalo-based regional promotion which helped Franke plan his next move. One young wrestler ion particular proved vital, someone with whom Franke would become colleagues in the World Wrestling Federation, and one of his first opponents as a professional.

Two years' Franke's senior, Jon Wisniski preceded the future Adrian Adonis in the business by four years. Wisniski, who would eventually find fame as Greg "The Hammer" Valentine, had the notable advantage of being the son of famed pro wrestler Johnny Valentine.

Prior to taking his father's storyline surname, Valentine initially made in-roads as Johnny Fargo, the kayfabe brother and tag-team partner of Don Fargo. The Fargo 'brothers' first competed as a team for the NWF in Cleveland and Buffalo, winning the promotion's tag titles on one occasion.

It was at one of these shows in the early 1970s, according to Valentine, that he first met Buffalo-based wrestling fanatic Keith Franke. Back then, Franke was an eager outsider and had yet to start his training with Fred Atkins. Valentine recalled Franke's early days in a 2021 interview:

> *"I met him up in Buffalo when I was a young kid, when I was Johnny Fargo, and he'd follow me round, he wanted to get into wrestling and there was this old timer [Fred Atkins] who lived right across from Buffalo over on Fort [Eerie], right across the river on the Canadian side and he would have Adrian pulling logs, he had Adrian in shape, had him out on the beach, and Adrian could actually shoot wrestle, he knew some amateur wrestling and he was pretty good at it."*

With his background in amateur wrestling and having already made his way to Canada to try his hand at a football career, it is no surprise that Franke gravitated towards Fred Atkins, a notoriously tough trainer and former professional wrestler based in Toronto, for his early professional wrestling training. Originally from Westport, New Zealand, Atkins took the young Buffalo native under his wing between late 1973 and early 1974.

During a career that spanned more than 35 years, Fred Atkins, born Robert Fred Atkinson, won regional titles in Australia, America, and Canada, before settling into a second career as a referee, announcer, and trainer. Emigrating to Toronto, he started a lengthy association with promoter Frank Tunney, and worked extensively for his Maple Leaf Wrestling promotion for much of his career, capturing the organisation's British Empire Heavyweight Title in the process.

Atkins loved the territory so much he stayed permanently and eventually became a naturalised Canadian citizen. Old school in every sense, Atkins developed a reputation for his disciplined and intense training style, imparting wisdom as a coach to several up-and-coming wrestlers during the 1960s and 1970s.

Living a modest life with wife Edna Mae, known as "Teddy," and daughter Robyn, Atkins was well-known in the local community and respected by wrestling matchmakers across the world, who would send him their up-and-coming prospects to be whipped into shape. Promoters making these arrangements would act as sponsors, paying their charges to train with Atkins, in the hopes that they would return as promising mat technicians.

Atkins began training other wrestlers in the early 1960s, with one of his earliest apprentices being Luke Brown, who would compete in Maple Leaf as Man Mountain Campbell, and elsewhere as the Masked Mauler. Brown achieved his most notable achievements in wrestling as one-half of the Kentuckians tag-team with Grizzly Smith, father of Jake Roberts.

Around the same period, Atkins also took under his wing Arthur "Art" Thomas. A former US Merchant Marine, Thomas was spotted in Chicago by the original "Nature Boy" Buddy Rogers, who told WWWF promoter Vincent J. McMahon about his find. McMahon sent him to Atkins for a year of schooling, which preceded a successful career as "Sailor" Art Thomas.

One of Atkins' most famous trainees was Shohei "Giant" Baba, a former baseball player from Japan after a career change. He was dispatched to train and live in the States after a series of meetings with Rikidōzan, the father of Japanese wrestling. Atkins' connection came through Kazuo Okamura, better known as The Great Togo, who played Rikidozan's manager during tours of the Pacific Coast area in the 1950s and 60s.

Okamura and Atkins struck up a friendship, and when Rikidozan needed a US-based trainer for his new prospect, his right-hand man knew whom to recommend. In return, Atkins had two Japan tours in April-May 1963 as a wrestler and January 1968 as a referee, both of which were booked by Togo. Atkins also acted as Baba's storyline manager when Baba wrestled as a heel in the early 60s US territories.

Another of Atkins' notable proteges came about through an international connection. Young Indian wrestler Jagjeet Singh Hans was introduced to Atkins by another wrestler who faced the Kiwi in India. Atkins agreed to take both on as trainees and in 1963 they emigrated from their hometown in Punjab to Toronto, submitting themselves to a year of constant workouts and four-mile daily runs. Hans would establish himself as Tiger Jeet Singh, a name coined by Atkins. He portrayed a despicable heel for most of his career, initially gaining success as part of a tag-team on the Maple Leaf circuit with his trainer.

There could have been more. One wrestling tale has it that 1960s and 70s legend Johnny Valentine considered sending his son Greg to train with Atkins prior to starting out. Instead, he opted to send his offspring to the infamous Calgary 'dungeon' of Stu Hart, deemed by Valentine senior as the *easier* option.

Hawaii native Don Muraco got into the business and quickly became aware of Atkins' feared reputation. Muraco, who would later become one of Franke's closest friends in wrestling, said:

> *"[Keith] was broke in by a guy named Fred Atkins, I never knew him. He was a tough [guy], up in Buffalo, Hamilton, Ontario, that whole segment of wrestlers who came in from that part of Canada. There was Stu Hart's area, Hamilton, there was the Montreal, like three different schools across Canada, and Fred who I never knew, I never met, was the one who broke in [Franke], and he was a hard guy, legendary, you know this is all hearsay, but he was a legendary tough guy."*

Though a wrestler through and through, Atkins is also remembered these days for his long tenure as a referee for the Tunney promotion. This notably included officiating the NWA heavyweight title change of early 1977 when Harley Race defeated Terry Funk in the Maple Leaf Gardens to win the title for a second time.

Atkins specialised in physical fitness and conditioning rather than wrestling holds and manoeuvres, as was typical of the time. Basic training included cable weights and running on the sands near his Crystal Beach home in Ontario to get in shape, his own favourite pastime even when he had no proteges accompanying him. Toronto-based sports journalist Greg Oliver co-founded the *Slam! Wrestling* website and covered the death of Franke in his 1988 newsletter. He has also profiled Atkins more than once on his website. Oliver explained:

> *"The thing with Fred Atkins is he was a firm believer in, not the repetition in the ring that has become the norm, he was more about the total-body workouts, and he was really big on conditioning, so they'd be going for runs along the beach, they did a lot of stuff in his garage. The guy later worked with the Buffalo Sabres hockey team, so he was a well-respected trainer of athletes, and not just of pro wrestlers. I suspect it must've been really old-school training and I'm pretty sure [trainees] wouldn't have been smartened up [to the wrestling business] until quite a ways along the way."*

Patrick McMahon (no relation to Vince) performed for Maple Leaf Wrestling in the early 1970s, shortly before Keith Franke arrived for his training with Atkins. Emphasising his Irish roots with the in-ring persona of Shillelagh O'Sullivan, he later told *Slam! Wrestling:*

> *"He had a mat in his basement, a horsehair mat and that was it, a mat on the concrete floor. Amateurish stuff, it was real wrestling that we learned from Fred, you know what I mean? It wasn't the acrobatic stuff, it was the real stuff. It cost us when we started to wrestle because we were doing the real shoot wrestling. We were doing that and the other guys were surprised, and they didn't want to work with us because we were too rough with them."*

When not training wrestlers in the gym basement of the modest bungalow of the Lake Erie tourist town he called home, Atkins also acted as a pre-season conditioning coach for National Hockey League (NHL) clubs the Toronto Maple Leafs and the Buffalo Sabres.

According to the Toronto Sun, Sabres player Pat Hannigan had heard Atkins' reputation as a fierce fitness trainer and suggested the club take the then-unusual step of hiring the displaced Kiwi to its staff. In what is a now common occurrence but was virtually unheard of in the early 1970s, Atkins in the 1971-72 season was the only full-time conditioning coach employed in the NHL at the time, even joining the players on away trips to make sure they were sticking to his strict training regime. Talking to the *Vancouver Province* shortly after joining the Sabres' staff in December 1972, Atkins explained his methods:

> *"Endurance is the key to everything...and there is no substitute to give you endurance. Plain, old-fashioned hard running is what gives these kids' body toughness."*

The arrangement was far from seamless. The Sabres' players did not react too favourably when Atkins started applying his methods, such as two-mile runs five times a week, as well as endless push-ups. Rationalising the grumbles in January 1973, Atkins told the *Philadelphia Inquirer*:

> *"Nobody accepted me and what I was doing. And it's what I expected. They thought all they had to do was play hockey. Well, their record showed that wasn't true."*

He was correct that the move was not met with universal acclaim from the players, but Atkins was more than ready to deal with the frosty reception in his own imitable style. A *Toronto Sun* article recounts a tale of an unnamed Sabres player and frequent goal scorer refusing to take part in exercise drills off the ice. Bravely, or stupidly, he even proceeded to mock Atkins' cauliflower ears and antipodean accent. Teammate Peter McNab recalled:

> *"You do not push Fred, he will not take it. Fred said, 'Oh, that's enough of that,' gave him a good quick cuff, and the guy, who I'm not about to name, found himself on the floor. You could just feel everybody's respect perk up."*

While Atkins' methods may not have been popular, they worked, with the Sabres boasting a vastly improved win-loss record, including going unbeaten in 23 home games at one point. Atkins' side hustle as a conditioning coach for professional hockey players did not last, despite the success it brought the team. In October 1973, a dispute about pay saw Atkins removed as physical training instructor for the Sabres, despite his methods being credited for helping the team get off to a fine start in the previous season. While Atkins claimed to have been the victim of cost-cutting measures, team general manager Punch Imlach told the *Vancouver Sun* that Atkins "priced himself out of business."

It's little wonder that Franke made his way to Ontario, first for semi-professional football, and then for wrestling training. Despite being in different countries, Atkins' home on the northeast shore of Lake Eerie is a stone's throw from Buffalo. The Frankes, like many of their friends and neighbours, likely spent their summers taking the short ferry ride from Buffalo to visit Crystal Beach's amusement park that served generations of tourists. Oliver noted:

"Crystal Beach is a tiny little hamlet just near Niagara Falls and it's basically best known because there's an amusement park there, but it was right across the border from the US, so very easy for wrestlers to work on both sides of the border. Keith would just be going across the border, it would probably take twenty minutes depending on the border to get there, based on where he lived."

Franke's record as an amateur gained him an audience with Atkins. While no stranger to hard work and physical dedication himself, Franke obtaining Atkins' training is an achievement in itself, given how closed the wrestling business was to outsiders. He was not the beneficiary of sponsorship from a top wrestling star or promoter, many of whom invested time and money sending burgeoning talents to Atkins for fine-tuning. Rather, Keith Franke backed himself and made his own way to Atkins' doorstep, determined to do things on his own terms. Oliver added:

"I'm not even sure how he would've found Fred in the sense that it was such a closed business, so unless Keith got to know someone like Pedro Martinez, that was running the Buffalo promotion, or one of the wrestlers, who would've said 'Go see this guy,' other than that I don't really know how they would've hooked up."

To begin with, the irascible old physical fitness tyrant with the spartan regime was not convinced by Franke's prospects. According to Franke's late mother, retold to Angela Perides, Atkins declined to train the young man at first on account of his unimpressive physique. She said:

"He went off, met with Fred Atkins, and Fred had told him 'I'm not going to train you, you have no discipline, you're not in shape, you need to lose weight.' So he came home, he was all grumpy about it and my grandma goes, 'I told you'. He dropped all the weight, and Fred took him on, and Fred would call my grandma periodically, and he told him if you are not being respectful, or this and this, I will drop you. So, he would call and ask my grandma if he was being respectful or not, but yes, he did drop out of high school and then he went off and started wrestling."

Eventually, Atkins agreed to take on the young Buffalo native, who relocated to Crystal Beach for a year of intensive coaching. During that year Atkins developed a paternal bond with the young man and would discuss his new trainee's progress and attitude with Franke's parents during regular phone calls.

The months which followed were gruelling but worthwhile, and the experience left a lasting impression on Franke about the benefit of discipline, a dedication which would slip noticeably from view in later years. He told the *Californian* in 1978:

"Atkins had his own idea on nutrition. I never once saw a slice of bread. One day Fred caught me coming home from the store with a bottle of milk

39

and he threw it in the street. Sure, it was rough, but it was such an honour to have him for a trainer. I will always be indebted to him. He's a remarkable man."

Fred Atkins passed away on May 13, 1988, at the age of 77 at the Welland Country General Hospital from complications related to a short illness, less than two months before the death of his young Buffalo trainee. It is possible that news got through to Franke of the passing of his trainer, though it is unlikely he had time to attend the funeral of the man who got him started in the wrestling business. Later that same week, he flew out for what would be the final tour of his sporadic career with New Japan Pro Wrestling.

Chapter 4: The early years

"I called him 'The Kid.'"

-   Dennis Stamp, 2007

While wrestling was not yet the massive money-making operation it would become ten years later when Vince McMahon Junior set upon a national expansion, pro grappling in the United States in 1974 was still very much a busy and bustling landscape. Member territories of the National Wrestling Alliance (NWA) catered for fans across the country, with hotbeds in Atlanta, Vancouver, the Carolinas, St Louis, and Toronto, to name a few.

The territories were well-defined with borders generally well respected between promoters, while the NWA itself wielded great influence throughout the professional wrestling industry. The NWA heavyweight champion of this period was Jack Brisco, a technically brilliant wrestler with an accomplished amateur background. Brisco toured the territories as a special attraction for regional promoters to entice fans in their region, the NWA business model.

Other major players in the mid-70s American wrestling scene were the northeast's World Wide Wrestling Federation (WWWF), run by Vince McMahon Senior, and the American Wrestling Association (AWA), overseen by Verne Gagne in Minneapolis. The WWWF would later withdraw from the NWA as a precursor to striking out on its own in 1983, while the AWA had been independent of the NWA since 1960.

Freedom from the NWA brought its benefits, as 1974 began with the release of *The Wrestler* movie, starring Gagne and a clutch of AWA stars alongside Ed Asner in a low-budget cinematic effort, thinly based on Gagne's life. Inside the ring, business was booming. In September the AWA drew 22,000 spectators to the Comiskey Park baseball stadium in Chicago as fans flocked to see Gagne successfully defend his AWA world title against Billy Robinson.

In the New York territory, Bruno Sammartino was six months into his second lengthy reign as WWWF heavyweight champion. A sold-out Madison Square Garden crowd watched the Italian superhero wrestle his way to victory in a tag-team main event in the first week of July 1974, yet another in a string of unparalleled sell-outs Sammartino had to his name by the end of his career. His final ever Madison Square Garden main event would also be as part of a tag-team match, opposite Adrian Adonis of all people.

For Keith Franke, both the AWA and WWF would come later. In 1974, Eddie Graham's Championship Wrestling from Florida (CWF) was renowned for its mixture of scientific wrestling, from the likes of Jack and Jerry Brisco, and colourful characters such as 'The American Dream' Dusty Rhodes and 'Cowboy' Bill Watts. The territory was popular with wrestlers and fans alike due to the action-packed style and the climate. Graham was well-respected as a promoter, running his own territory and also serving a term as NWA president between 1976 and 1978.

In the Sunshine State, Franke worked a month of matches at the bottom of the card for Florida, one of the major regional promotions of the National Wrestling Alliance. Franke wrestled around a dozen bouts between 28 July and 27 August 1974, completing a single four-week tour for the promotion, as early-card filler underneath the likes of Rhodes, Florida heavyweight champion Watts, promoter's son Mike Graham, and tag champs the Hollywood Blonds, Buddy Roberts and Jerry Brown.

With his name mis-spelled to its phonetic format, the *Tampa Tribune* of July 28, 1974, noted the pending debut due to take place that evening: "newcomer Keith Frankie will face The Samoan in the opening match at 8.30pm." The match with The Samoan (local pro Reno Tuufuli) was booked for the Fort Hesterly Armory, a stronghold of the Florida promotion, although no record of the outcome has survived. Results from the *Palm Beach Post* two days later show that Franke was victorious in his match of July 29, however, beating Frank Martinez in six minutes. Two months shy of his 21st birthday, Franke was on his way – even if his surname was being variously spelled as 'Frank,' 'Franke,' 'Frankie,' and 'Franki.'

The Florida scene would later introduce perhaps the most important rookie ever to enter to the wrestling business, when Hulk Hogan first stepped between the ropes on a Florida card in August 1977; as luck would have it, during Franke's second run in the promotion. For now, however, this was not about being a big name; it was about getting match practice. Victories were hard to come by for Franke in the first month of his career, putting over the likes of old acquaintance Greg Valentine, Les Thornton, and even fellow newbie (and 1975 NWA co-rookie of the year) Jay Clayton. Clayton *"took only five minutes to beat Frankie with dropkicks and a crossbody press,"* one newspaper reported.

For Franke, like so many other rookies before and since, the experience of being in the locker room around the pros was far more valuable than any predetermined win in the ring, even if only for a month. Surrounded by the likes of Watts, Rhodes, the Grahams, ex-WWWF tag champ Toru Tanaka and Don Muraco, who would go on to become one of Franke's best friends in the business, Franke soaked in the experience, as he would in every territory he frequented.

Bookings were patchy for the young hopeful in his rookie year and more than two months passed before he secured his next assignment. It was worth the wait however, and in late autumn of 1974 Franke made the first of a few appearances on home turf.

The Buffalo territory had experienced a change by the time Franke made his debut. Due to a combination of bad business deals and waning interest, Martinez closed the NWF in Buffalo in April 1974. Super Pro Wrestling, the key brand of Upstate Wrestling Inc, began promoting shows in the area, where its television programme replaced the long-running Studio Wrestling show. Talent from Rochester and Pittsburgh would criss-cross the region, while the World Wide Wrestling Federation (WWWF) began running shows in the area more frequently too.

Franke wrestled a single match under his real name for the WWWF, the only time he did so, taking on Terry Yorkston on November 12, 1974, at the Onondaga War Memorial in Syracuse, New York. Toronto native Yorkston was a short way into his own in-ring career but would become more well-known after transitioning to the role of referee for the Tunney's Maple Leaf Wrestling in his hometown. Yorkston also refereed WWF matches when the Federation came to Toronto, including Adrian Adonis' count-out loss to Junkyard Dog in front of 74,000 fans for the WWF's 'Big Event' card in 1986, as well as a rare appearance by the East-West Connection in January 1982.

In the spring of 1975 Franke made his first appearances north of the border as he returned to where his training took place. He took part in two shows in Vancouver and Toronto, places which would also feature more prominently in his later career. On February 15, 1985, he lost to Yasuyuki Fuji for Vancouver's All-Star Wrestling. The following month he did the honours for the famed Pampero Firpo on the March 23 card in his first appearance at Toronto's famous Maple Leaf Gardens.

More bookings for the WWWF followed. Friends and family were able to watch the young man who left town to pursue his dream at the Buffalo War Memorial on June 7, with 'Keith Franks' in the opening match against the masked 'Executioner.' Sammartino headlined the card, a short drive from Franke's childhood home, as the young man marvelled at sharing a dressing room with one of the icons he had admired through adolescence.

At the Rochester War Memorial Franke took on fellow opening match attractions Jack Evans and Jack Varsky on June 17 and July 8, respectively. Despite the unremarkable opposition and lowly position on the card, Franke marked his first year in the business with undeniable, albeit slow, progress.

As the summer ended, Franke's time as an earnest journeyman trying to shoehorn his way into a notoriously closed-off business changed for good. He was invited to join the NWA's Vancouver territory, All-Star Wrestling, as an opening match attraction. He started on September 1, 1975, and spent the next twelve months in the territory, developing in-ring fundamentals and mat psychology under the auspices of promoter Gene Kiniski, another former NWA heavyweight champion.

In a 2017 interview with *Slam! Wrestling*, Kiniski's son Kelly, who followed in his famous father's footsteps, explained how new wrestlers including Franke came into the territory in the 1970s and spar with the younger Kiniski who was still in high school at the time:

> *"As soon as football season was over, wrestling season would come about, and that's when he used to bring pro wrestlers down, like Keith Franks, [who] was Adrian Adonis; Dennis Stamp; Khosrow Vaziri, [who] was the [Iron] Sheik. They used to wrestle me, and if I got too salty they'd drive me into the wall. I felt like the pro wrestlers were the toughest guys walking. They didn't only have to work out for three hours with me on the mat. Then they had to go drive to wherever they were wrestling and go wrestle a professional match."*

Vancouver became a serious presence in the wrestling world in the late 1960s, when Kiniski joined Sandor Kovacs and Don Owens to promote the territory, under the parent company Northwest Wrestling Promotions (NWP). The area shared talent with nearby NWA affiliate Pacific Northwest Wrestling (PNW) in Portland, and its *All-Star Wrestling* television programme was shown in syndication in many parts of Canada, emanating from arenas in Vancouver, Victoria, and smaller towns in the region.

Headliners in the territory included the mighty Don Leo Jonathan, a huge star for Canada for years and a frequent opponent of Andre the Giant, as well as the ageing Gene Kiniski. Future star Jimmy Snuka made frequent visits from Portland as he developed into a major attraction and often stayed at the home shared by Franke and Dennis Stamp. A few years Franke's senior, Stamp started in Vancouver in the spring of 1975 and took Franke under his wing, acting as a mentor to the young man he called 'The kid.' Discussing his time in Vancouver in a 2007 interview, Stamp recalled:

> *"He [Jimmy Snuka] was in Portland and I was in Vancouver, and Adrian Adonis had come in and he was wrestling under his own name then, Keith Franke, and he didn't know anything and I ended up kind of taking him in and teaching him and we became very, very, very, very close friends, and so we had a two-bedroom apartment, furnished two bedroom apartment all bills paid, $140 a month, it wasn't very nice but we couldn't believe we could get it."*

Despite the larger paydays and paid-for hotel accommodation offered to a star like Snuka, Stamp recalled the man from Fiji preferring to be around 'the boys' at every opportunity:

> *"And so, Jimmy Snuka they'd bring him in to Vancouver sometimes, they'd fly him in from Portland which is about 300 miles, but they'd fly him in, and he says, "Ah man, you guys, you got an apartment, right," and I said yeah, and man, he says 'do you mind if we stay with you,' and I go 'Jimmy, they're gonna pay for you a big hotel downtown, they'll pay everything.' He goes, 'I don't wanna stay downtown I wanna stay with you guys.'*

> *"I said 'man you're more than welcome to stay with us anytime you want, I just thought you'd rather just have a nice big hotel room,' he goes 'no, no, by myself? No, I'd rather be with you guys, it's more fun.' So, when he would come, when he would fly in from Portland he would stay, he would stay with us in our $140 a month apartment, but we did have fun."*

As with Stamp and Snuka, Vancouver bore many connections that would endure for Franke throughout his career. In a ten-man battle royal a month into his stay, Franke shared the ring with future tag team partner Jesse Ventura, who made his own debut the previous year. Also in the ring was local tag-team the Kelly Twins, Mike and Pat, who the following month would win their first and only NWA Canadian tag-team title.

More pertinently, the pair would be in the same van as Franke and Dave McKigney on that fateful journey in Newfoundland thirteen years later. This period in Franke's nascent pro wrestling career would have profound ramifications for the rookie in many ways; not least of all the familiarity with the Kelly Twins and other local talent that brought him back to the area when looking for work more than a decade later as his career stalled.

In *Professional Wrestling in the Pacific Northwest* (2017), Steven Verrier described Franke's first year in a positive light, noting his run as a "fairly popular mid-card babyface," with appearances during the year in Oregon and Washington, among other areas. The area gave Franke his first TV exposure, performing several times at television tapings for *All-Star Wrestling* at the BCTV studios in Burnaby, British Columbia.

Franke tangled with most of the roster during his year-long stay, a colourful cast of characters including the fearsome Masa Saito; recent WWWF tag champ Dean Higuchi; former Canadian Football League players – a favourite of Kiniski – George Wells and Bruce Smith; fellow Atkins trainee Tiger Jeet Singh; and the legendary Jerry Graham. Flatmate Dennis Stamp recalled the era vividly in 2007:

"One time, the four midgets were there, these were old days when, ok, at that time I was making about $300 a week, and the kid was – I call him the kid – Adrian was making maybe $200 – so it took every dollar we had just to get around, I mean we couldn't afford any higher rent, so when the midgets came to town they all stayed with us, so Adrian had been in, I was in a closer town, so I got in earlier, and he was in a different town, and he comes in wasted, it's three o'clock in the morning, and he says, 'Dennis,' 'What?' he said, 'there's a black midget in our kitchen walking around on our counters looking at our cabinets!' I said, 'Leave me alone and go to bed!'"

Working alongside Jerry Graham, however briefly, would have been a massive thrill for the newcomer. The flamboyant and flashy Graham was a marquee performer for the popular New York territory throughout the 1950s and 60s, a time when he captured the imagination of many young fans. Graham was the on-screen leader of the kayfabe Golden Grahams wrestling family, a multiple time tag-team champion, and someone who embodied the charisma and showmanship upon which many wrestlers would base their own characters – including the future Adrian Adonis.

Graham struggled throughout his career with alcoholism, weight problems and erratic behaviour, some of which bear resonance towards the man Franke would become. By 1975, Graham, in his early 50s, was largely retired and occasionally training other wrestlers, and picking up low-level bookings when his financial position demanded it of him. The six-week tour of Vancouver was one such booking, as Graham had once again burned his bridges with the WWWF after walking out of television tapings in July 1975.

No matter how brief, Franke idolised Graham and would have loved the time working alongside him, travelling together and absorbing Graham's immense knowledge of the business. They worked one match opposite each other, with Graham putting over his young admirer in a quick undercard showing. Though fleeting, Franke was captivated by the golden-haired, ample-framed, smart-talking New York favourite and it is not hard to see his attempts to embody much of this later in his career.

Franke worked several shows for the Portland territory as part of the talent-trading agreement, and also popped up again for the WWWF and Toronto's Maple Leaf Wrestling. He got off to a good start in Portland, described by Oregon's *Statesman Journal* as a "well-regarded newcomer" prior to his September 18, 1975, bout against 'Bruiser' Bob Remus (the future Sgt Slaughter) in Salem, Oregon for Elton Owens.

Wrestling in Portland accounted for almost half of Franke's year in Vancouver. Based in Portland, Oregon under promoter Don Owen, the Pacific Northwest was long considered one of wrestling's main territories from the 1960s to 1980s. During this period, many top names in the business regularly came through, with the group's syndicated television show airing from Portland Sports Arena, a converted bowling alley. Franke's name was generally standardised as 'Franks,' with the occasional 'Frankes' creeping into some newspaper reporting.

The territory in 1975 was rich with developing talent that would go on to greater things, such as the future Adrian Adonis and Slaughter, Ventura and Snuka, alongside local mainstays Dutch Savage, Bull Ramos, and Johnny Eagles. The area played host to the only recorded singles match between Ventura and Keith Franks, won by Ventura on March 6, 1976.

A typical opening match enhancement talent, or jobber, Franke's first stay in Portland was relatively unremarkable and not many fans would have noticed when he left the area in the summer of 1976. The same would not be the case when he returned less than three years later.

Over in New York, Franke worked a pair of dates on October 22 and 23, 1975. On the first card, headlined by WWWF tag champs The Blackjacks, Franke put over Mexican star Francisco Flores at Rochester's Henrietta Dome Arena. The next night, he took on Manuel Soto, although no result is recorded for the match at Binghampton's Broome County Arena.

Across the Christmas and New Year period Franke twice faced the fearsome Mongols tag team, twice former WWWF international tag champions, in further appearances at Toronto's Maple Leaf Gardens. On December 28, he teamed with Dominic Denucci, and a week later partnered with Sweet Daddy Siki. Franke was on the losing team on both occasions, the latter in front of a purported crowd of 12,000. He would return in July to face faux German terror Waldo von Erich before leaving the territory.

Though his stay in Vancouver may not have grabbed many headlines, Franke didn't need it to. As with Franke's time in Florida, and his sojourns in many of the other wrestling hotbeds he would pass through over the next three years, this stay was about learning on the job and getting as much ring-time as possible. That is not to say he didn't merit any media coverage at all. In fact, from early in his stay in the region, local newspapers were already coining evocative phrases to describe the young hopeful.

For the *Alberni Valley Times* of December 4, 1975, Keith Franks was a "Handsome New Yorker" set to take on "Colorado Giant" Sky Hi Morse. Two months earlier the same paper, on October 23, even promoted him as the "New York Adonis," a name which would crop up elsewhere a few months later.

By March 1976, *The Province* of Vancouver bemoaned a particularly drab in-ring effort, as Franke and Eric Froelich "*wrestled to the inevitable, weekly, stately draw,"* a wider complaint about predictable, plodding fare served up by the promotion on an increasing basis around this time. The very same paper changed its tune markedly by July 12, 1976, as it outlined the card for an upcoming event, with its hyperbolic reference to *"Young Keith Frankes, dubbed the most improved wrestler of the decade."*

A week later *The Province* gave a final brief spotlight to Franke as it listed the results for the previous night's action. Keith Frankes, *"the New York Adonis,"* battled Buddy Rogers Jr (another draw, naturally).

Just as intriguing as the reappearance of the 'Adonis' nickname in its putative form is the man who headlined this particular show at Vancouver's Pacific Coliseum. Reigning NWA heavyweight champion Terry Funk put away 'Big' John Quinn handily, winning both falls in a best of three falls match. Perhaps backstage at this show was the 'sliding doors' moment when the veteran encouraged the novice Franke to employ the newspaper nickname on a more serious basis – more than three years before their paths would cross again in Amarillo.

Chapter 5: Around the territories

"First impressions, she did not like him at all.

"Obnoxious cocky New York attitude, know it all, oh my gosh, get away from me!"

- *Angela Perides, 2021*

Keith Franke's fruitful stay in Vancouver transformed him into a proper wrestling journeyman, and he moved through territories at an impressive pace over the next three years, picking up something new from each one. The twelve months spent in Canada remained his longest tenure in any one area until late in 1979, when he entered his second year with the AWA.

Taking in spells in the Carolinas, California, a return to Florida, Georgia, Amarillo, and a short but notable stay in Portland, Franke studied at the feet of veterans, legends, and old hands, learning different styles and honing his craft. The multitude of wrestling territories across the United States of the mid to late 1970s provided rookies a fertile training ground for those willing to learn and improve, as Franke's development demonstrates.

For Franke, this period saw him gain temporary nicknames and a long-lasting pseudonym. He took part in his first on-screen angles and long running feuds and established lifelong friendships with fellow performers, none more significant than "Rowdy" Roddy Piper. Working in California was particularly productive, where Franke met the woman he would later marry one night after the show. In the ring things were on the up too, as the man from Buffalo pinned the NWA heavyweight champion of the world less than three years into his career.

Wrestling in the summer of 1976 reached a crescendo with the *Showdown at Shea*, an ambitious card held on June 25 in front of 32,000 fans from the imposing home stadium of the New York Mets. The show included the miraculous return of WWWF Champion Bruno Sammartino to face off with Stan Hansen, the man who accidentally but legitimately broke his neck two months prior. Also featured was the ill-advised boxer versus wrestler contest pitting Muhammad Ali against Antonio Inoki, as well as another wrestler/boxer bout, as Andre the Giant faced Chuck Wepner.

In the same month, AWA Champion Nick Bockwinkel turned back the challenge of promoter and perpetual babyface Verne Gagne at a major show in Comiskey Park. Bockwinkel was a few months into an epic five-year reign, with Bobby Heenan installed at his side perfecting his role as the prototypical heel manager.

Terry Funk reigned as NWA heavyweight champion throughout 1976 and was named Wrestler of the Year by *Sports Review Wrestling* magazine. Funk would be dethroned by Harley Race in February of the following year as Race embarked on his own two-and-a-half-year reign, defeating opponents in all corners of the NWA – including a young Keith Franks.

Meanwhile, in December 1976, the landscape of the wrestling business shifted for good when media mogul Ted Turner gambled on turning his Atlanta TV station WTCG into a national programming service. The station, which was later rebranded as WTBS and TBS, carried NWA member organisation Georgia Championship Wrestling's weekly show, instantly making GCW the first US wrestling promotion to be broadcast nationally.

In October 1976, days after finishing up in Vancouver, Keith Franke arrived in Mid-Atlantic Championship Wrestling (MACW), another major member of the National Wrestling Alliance. Previewing the following day's action, the *Rocky Mount Telegram* noted on October 5: *"In another singles match Sgt Jacques Goulet, a villainous veteran, takes on newcomer Keith Franks".*

According to Lanny Poffo who was already working Mid-Atlantic at the time, Franke's entry to the area came on the back of a recommendation from Vancouver booker Gene Kiniski.

Mid-Atlantic was based in Charlotte, North Carolina under the ownership of Jim Crockett Promotions (JCP). In many ways the spiritual predecessor to World Championship Wrestling (WCW), the WWF's closest competitor of the 1990s, Mid-Atlantic was wrestling's stronghold in the Carolinas. Keith Franks wrestled in opening matches and throwaway tag bouts for Mid Atlantic, a long way from the likes of Ric Flair, Greg Valentine, and Wahoo McDaniel at the top of the card.

His stay in the Carolinas was not completely void of benefit, as Franke, still performing as Keith Franks, got to tussle with the Poffo family, father Angelo and sons Randy and Lanny, as well as stars such as Tony Atlas, Boris Malenko, and Crusher Blackwell.

The Poffo brothers would work alongside Franke again years later. He as Adrian Adonis, and they as "Leaping" Lanny Poffo and "Macho Man" Randy Savage. The younger Poffo remembered his time in the Carolinas fondly, including working with Franke. He recalled:

> *"That was Jimmy Crockett and family, the Crockett organisation. They were in North Carolina, South Carolina, Virginia, and expanding all the time. They were an excellent promotion and the biggest star there was Ric Flair, and Wahoo McDaniel, and Ricky Steamboat.*

> *"I worked with [Keith] in 1976 or 77, he came in and there was a tag-team match, Randy and I against Adrian Adonis and sometimes Vic Rosettani, that was his friend from Buffalo, New York and Toronto, that's the area he was from.*
>
> *"Gene Kiniski was a very good friend of his and helped him to get booked a lot. He was a great talent, and a very good person before he got into the drugs."*

An old hand several years his elder, Vic Rosettani was a native of Hamilton, Ontario, who was in the Florida territory when Franke made his first appearances. A veteran of the AWA and elsewhere, the pair crossed paths again in Mid Atlantic. Contrasting the Keith Franks of 1977 to the Adrian Adonis of a few years later, Poffo noted a stark difference. He said:

> *"He was very serious about having a good match, and he usually had a great match, and he was good to work with. And then, all of a sudden, he wasn't anymore. You know, when he gained a lot of weight and sometimes he would go in the ring under the influence, but he didn't do that before, so it was like two different things."*

In addition to everything he learned in the ring and on the road in the Carolinas, Franke picked up some other attributes that would hang around a while. According to a listing of delinquent taxpayers published in the May 11, 1978, edition of *The Charlotte News*, Franke moved on from the North Carolina city without paying the princely sum of $66.99. More pertinent was a lasting friendship with at least one of his fellow wrestlers, as Franke again found himself gravitating towards another veteran of the territories.

Rolland "Red" Bastien was in the Carolinas after a period as booker and wrestler in Fritz Von Erich's Big Time Wrestling in Texas, the group later renamed World Class Championship Wrestling. Bastien was the man responsible for giving a young Roddy Piper his first shots in Dallas and San Antonio, and the pair formed a tight bond, with Bastien acting as best man at Piper's 1982 wedding. He had a similar influence on Franke and acted as something of a mentor to the pair of young upstarts.

For the first time in his fledging career Franke also participated in two longstanding wrestling traditions by wrestling on Thanksgiving, and on Christmas evening.

Some of the biggest names in the industry made their way to the Greensboro Coliseum on November 25, 1976, as well as 11,000 fans for Mid Atlantic's big Thanksgiving night card. Headlined by a two-ring battle royal, with a supposed $20,000 prize money, special guests including Andre the Giant, Dusty Rhodes, Superstar Billy Graham, and more gave a special holiday treat to fans not used to seeing so many big names on their local shows. Newspaper adverts for the night show Franks was double-booked and also on the poster for a concurrent MACW card at the Norfolk Arena, although he competed in the battle royal.

On Christmas night, Franke was back in action for the holidays, tagging with Bastien in Hampton, Virginia, against Lanny and Randy Poffo. Bastien spoke to the *Charlotte News* to promote the bout in an interview printed on Christmas morning and described a typical festive period for a wrestler with a family in 1976.

> *"I'll be wrestling in Florida, the Carolinas, Baltimore and Virginia,"* he told the paper. *"We'll have Christmas dinner and open the presents the day before."*

The pair teamed again the following month, losing to NWA Mid-Atlantic tag champs the Hollywood Blondes (one of whom, Buddy Roberts, Franke would team with himself down the line). After teaming with another future tag partner, Ron Starr, in January 1977, Franke brought an end to his busy three-month spell in the Carolinas.

Within days of finishing up with Mid Atlantic, Keith Franks' arrival in a new territory was once again touted by the local paper in advance of his debut. In the start of extensive coverage of Franks in the Bakersfield Californian over the next six months, readers were told on February 3, 1977, that Keith Franks was to debut that evening at the Strongbow Stadium with a "tough assessment" against Professor Toru Tanaka – formerly a WWWF tag champion, among other accolades. Franks was impressive in his debut and won the match, an immediate sign of progress for the young man.

Franke's latest assignment was all thanks to Bastien who had helped arrange Piper's debut in California a year earlier by way of his relationship with the local booker, Leo Garibaldi. According to Piper's autobiography, Bastien suggested the switch when the pair were together in Texas, as he was aware Garibaldi was looking for younger talent. Piper wrote:

> *"The first thing I did when I got to L.A. was head over to the arena to find Garibaldi. He looked me up and down and said, "Who the hell are you?" I told him that I was Roddy Piper. "Who?" Roddy Piper, Red Bastien sent me. And he said, "Oh yeah. The locker room is down there."*

Garibaldi was the booker for the territory, which has based around Los Angeles, and Mike LeBell was the promoter. Mike's half-brother "Judo" Gene LeBell was a huge star for the group and would become a renowned martial artist and stuntman with a feared reputation as one of the most legitimately tough guys in the world.

NWA Hollywood, sometimes referred to as NWA Los Angeles, was a transformative experience for Franke as he chanced upon two of the defining relationships of his life, and absorbed the unique wrestling culture like never before. Headquartered in LA, based primarily out of the Los Angeles Olympic Auditorium, NWA Hollywood promoted cards throughout southern California including Oxnard, San Diego, and Bakersfield. The proximity to the Mexican border brought a heavy Hispanic influence to the circuit, both in terms of crowds and in-ring personnel.

The territory was overseen by the LeBells, whose mother Aileen Eaton was one of the few female wrestling promoters of the territories era. The brothers took over running the towns in 1966 and reapplied for membership of the NWA two years later following an earlier split. In 1971, the promotion set a national gate record for an event headlined by a brutal battle between Freddie Blassie and John Tolos that sold $142,158 worth of tickets.

By the late 1970s the company, while still a significant piece of the US wrestling network, was struggling to return to the heights it hit in the early part of the decade. Business peaked years earlier when the Blassie and Tolos feud set the box office alight, followed by frequent returns from Blassie, and a strong heel run from Tolos.

As other regions forged ahead, California relied more heavily than ever on its Latino stars, such as the Guerrero sons, Black Gordman, and others. In towns like Oxnard with its large Mexican American population, fans continued to cheer for their countrymen, and took an interest in the younger talent like Franks and Piper.

One such group of fans were Oxnard natives and future comics auteurs Los Bros Hernandez who fell in love with the territory and interpolated wrestling themes throughout their critically acclaimed comics. Middle brother Gilbert would later immortalise Franke years later after his transformation in the pages of his *Love & Rockets* comic and document his shock at realising that Adonis and Franks were in fact the same person.

The Grand Olympic Auditorium, situated in downtown Los Angeles, was a centrepiece of the Los Angeles promotion and the venue for the group's weekly television show, aired on Wednesday nights. The Olympic plays an important, often overlooked, part in the sporting history of the United States and hosted some of the biggest boxing and wrestling events for several decades from its opening in 1925.

The building also acted as the backdrop for scenes in many historic movies, including the first three *Rocky* films and *Raging Bull*. Interviewed for director Stephen DeBro's *18th & Grand: The Olympic Auditorium Story* documentary shortly before his death, Piper described the atmosphere and legacy of the building:

"I know what a gladiator in Rome must've felt like, just a little bit. Unbelievable down there, the dressing room, the pipes with dirt, water, a cement hallway, and all of a sudden there'd be a hole knocked out [for a dressing room]. "You come out of your hole. That aisleway where you used to come down to the ring, you'd come up these stairs and you're behind them, which was good.

"The people that sat there they had boxes of popcorn, and they'd stick the knife up in the popcorn. It was the first time I got sliced, you know. When I'd go by, they'd go [slice] and they'd be gone...The crowd would close."

Piper recounted how Garibaldi complained on behalf of the wrestlers to Mike LeBell about fans with knives getting too close to the performers, only for the promoter to respond, "Well that's what they pay for."

Defined in large part by the Blassie-Tolos feud, Los Angeles was regarded as a violent yet absorbing territory, bloody and action-packed. As the decade drew to a close and business stumbled. While tye-died, tough-talking Superstar Graham was dethroning Bruno Sammartino for the WWWF title and turning the New York territory onto glorious technicolour, LeBell increasingly resorted to crazy angles and wacky gimmick matches. One such stunt took place after Franke's departure, in 1981, when the promotion debuted a new character called simply 'The Monster,' with the straight-faced claim that he was built in a laboratory. The ill-fitting attempt to catch the wave of the changing face of wrestling became notorious among wrestling fans, and snared the unwanted honour of Most Disgusting Promotional Tactic of the year from the *Wrestling Observer* newsletter.

John Tolos, in particular, clearly had an impact on Franke in more ways than one. The "Golden Greek" spent years tussling with Blassie as one of the biggest stars of wrestling in the heyday of the Southern California territory. Tolos trash talked the crowd at the Olympic on a regular basis. His most memorable refrain was later adopted by Franke as a tribute to one of his favourites, first in Southwest Championship Wrestling in 1983, and then as a call-and-response with manager Jimmy Hart in the WWF three years later.

During Franke's own stay in California, fans were still on board with the waning group, for now at least. Keen to see legendary ring announcer Jimmy Lennon open proceedings, fans tuned in to watch as wrestlers grappled in the oversized ring of the Olympic, backed by the enthusiastic commentary style of Luis Magana – or "Mr Olympia" as he was affectionately known. They were keen to see Franke too, evidently, with the "electrifying newcomer" setting upon an unbeaten streak in his first weeks, including a surprise victory in a tag-team elimination match.

Coming in with a sustained push for the first time in his career must have been a pleasant surprise for Franke. Indeed, California represented an era of firsts in

Franke's career, as fans and promoters alike were clearly impressed by his smooth good looks and decent physique, not far from muscular. He participated in the first proper angles and feuds in his careers, cut promos, gained a nickname, challenged for major titles for the first time, and won championships, the first place where his career as a performer truly followed a narrative arc. He also made a lasting friendship which would endure for the rest of his life, as the careers of both men twisted and intertwined over the next decade.

Behind the curtain, Keith Franke and Roddy Piper hit it off immediately by all accounts, drawn to each other as a result of their shared level of experience in the business, their similar ages, like-minded personalities, and their tough starts in life. In the ring, they participated in a lively feud with one particularly notable angle.

Piper was already in California when Franke arrived, being used as a manager as well as a wrestler due to his slight frame, a role he was originally brought into the WWF to play in 1984. Franke, six months' Piper's senior, arrived on the scene as a babyface. That would all change when Piper exposed Keith Franks to his supposed penchant for hypnotism. Another desperation gimmick during the desperate times of the LA circuit, Piper was billed as a master of hypnosis and demonstrated his 'talents' on his new friend to help him "quit smoking." Piper wrote years later:

> *"Mike [LeBell] came up with a routine where I would hypnotize people. So, one night I get to the arena and LeBell hands me this plastic gold chain and I'm on TV hypnotizing Keith Franke. I'm telling him 'You're going to lose the match, you're going to lose the match.'"*

Piper found the gimmick both humiliating and troubling. Veterans in the dressing room, from Andre the Giant to Harley Race, laughed at the ridiculous charade taking place years before the entertainment aspect of pro wrestling was such an embedded part of the enterprise. More worryingly, LeBell and Garibaldi became inundated with calls from impressionable fans who had seen the in-ring escapade at a show and demanded the help of Piper's pretend hypnotism talents.

Under Piper's spell, Franks stomped around the ring like Frankenstein's Monster, devoid of his own free will, following Piper's orders. Piper's 'skills' eventually saw Franks become his henchman, positioned to take out Piper's archenemy Chavo Guerrero. The hypnosis spot was used the following year on a more high-profile basis. Released in February 1978, *The One and Only*, starred Henry Winkler as a Gorgeous George analogue during the golden age of 1950s TV wrestling, a movie which also featured a cameo by Piper.

Franks and Piper formed a tag team, known as (if not officially promoted) as 'The 22's', derived from their shared age. Eventually Piper turned on Franks, leaving him a 'good guy' once more. Any time spent on opposing sides in the ring was far from reality however, as Piper and Adonis maintained an incredibly tight bond from their time in California to the latter's untimely death.

Franke had a fleeting run with the area's top belt, the NWA Americas heavyweight title, dethroning the Hangman on May 13, 1977, before dropping the belt to Mando Guerrero a week later. He also picked up significant experience as a tag-team wrestler in California, winning the territory's NWA Americas Tag Titles on two brief occasions; once with Piper, and once with Mexican veteran Black Gordman, who would end his career with around 30 reigns of the same title with various partners.

Gordman is well known for his long-running partnership with the Great Goliath. He is also regarded by many as the true inventor of the DDT (as the Diamond Twist), the once devastating finishing manoeuvre brought to national and international prominence in the late 1980s by Jake "The Snake" Roberts in the WWF. Franke, as Adonis, would later use the DDT in tribute to Gordman on WWF TV and was asked to stop using it when Roberts joined the Federation to avoid diluting its impact.

Coverage in the *Californian* referred to Franke as both "Apollo" Keith Franks, a nickname which didn't stick, and "Gorgeous" Keith Franks, one which did, and adverts and articles for the first time emphasised his "New York City" origins, quietly erasing his childhood in Buffalo. The 'Gorgeous' tag stuck around after Franks' initial heel turn and he retained it in other territories. One unverifiable source relates at least one occasion Franke was promoted locally as 'Gorgeous Keith Franke, The Human Orchid' at least once towards the end of his run in LA, although no confirmation is possible.

The 'Human Orchid' name if employed would be an undoubted reference to Gorgeous George, someone Franke took more direct inspiration from years later. More pertinent here was the tough New Yorker gimmick which became an integral part of Franke's character in the AWA and WWF but was first established in Los Angeles. While the papers worked hard to promote Franke, LeBell was working just as hard to establish his young new hopeful.

On February 18, 1977, Franks defeated Ken Mantell in a match which saw his hair on the line, with Mantell having to leave the territory as a result of the loss. Franks secured the victory by submission despite the interference of Mantell's tag partner Piper. The real-life friends faced off the following week in a blood-soaked affair which ended without a winner:

> *"The bloody Franks then bit Piper on the ear and before the match got further out of hand, it was stopped on a double disqualification."*

The pair met the following month on March 3 in a no-holds-barred rematch, termed a 'Roman Gladiator Death Match.' Rules for the match allowed for no pins, no dq's, no count-outs, no time-limit, and no referee present, with victory only by dragging your opponent to all four corners of the ring, similar to a strap match. Franks won with the help of Terry Sawyer, who appeared to counteract the interference of recently debuted Piper henchman Tank Patton.

The feud climaxed with a cage match; specifically, a 'Freddie Blassie cage match.' 'La Jaula de Freddie Blassie' to Mexican fans, the gimmick closely linked to the man who pioneered it in the region, with a steel cage tightly encompassing the ringposts and ropes, often with a smaller cage suspended high above the ring and containing another wrestler or manager to prevent interference. A bloody affair ended in victory for Franks, with the added bonus that the match also ensured a shot at visiting NWA Champion Harley Race the following month.

In the interim, Franks faced Piper's bodyguard Patton, securing a victory by referee's decision thanks to the call of Johnny "Red Shoes" Duggan on March 19. A week later he defended his title shot against Mexican veteran the Great Goliath in a 35-minute epic to keep his winning streak alive. The pair clashed again days later in a Texas Death Match, with the same result. Franks retained his title opportunity one final time against Patton, this time in an 'I Quit' match on April 4. After two months of build, he was ready for the champion.

On April 10, NWA Heavyweight champion Harley Race came to town to face the young upstart. At Bakersfield's Strongbow Stadium, named for the original Jules Strongbow, he faced a close call, as reported by the Californian, taking the first fall before Franks levelled with a submission. Race then reversed a pinning combination to gain the third fall, despite Franks' protests as having his trunks pulled. The NWA of course had no intention of putting its premier title on this man still little more than a rookie, but the progress for Franke was undeniable. At the age of 23, less than three years on from his first wrestling match, he had shared a ring and gone the distance with the great Harley Race.

What was more, he had taken the champ to the limit, and, for one fall at least, submitted the current reigning NWA Champion. With credibility even in defeat, Franke's career was surely on an upward trajectory. Eddy Mansfield, who worked the territory at the tail-end of Franke's stay, noted in a 2013 interview:

> "I knew Keith Franks in Los Angeles. Keith was a hoot, when I was with him, he wasn't Adrian Adonis then."

His quick ascent may have annoyed some older wrestlers, but Franke was as popular with his fellow workers as he was with the office and fans. Old hand Victor Rivera was one regular performer who worked hard to make Franks look good. The younger man was being set up for a main event with headliner Chavo Guerrero in May, and Rivera worked hard jobbing for Franke, as he was convincingly reduced to a bloody pulp prior to a count-out loss.

The remainder of Franke's stay in California was just as busy as his first two months. He formed a short-lived tag-team with Black Gordman as the pair tussled with the Guerrero brothers, winning the tag belts for a matter of days in April. Three days later he put over Mexican icon and movie star Mil Mascaras in a 28-minute 'no disqualification' slugfest in San Diego.

He embarked upon feuds with Chavo Guerrero and The Hangman, losing to the latter on 30 April and a return match a week later, by count-out when he fled from ringside. Franks finally went over in a third meeting, a Lumberjack match, refereed by Bob Bockwinkel, brother of Nick, while the blow-off to the feud saw Hangman victorious in a cage match. Some reports suggest a fifth match took place between the tour, with Hangman defeating Franks in a mask versus hair match, a lucha libre staple. If so, the match took place on 13 March, almost ten years to the day he would go on to lose his hair after succumbing to Piper at *WrestleMania III*.

Franks and Piper next began teaming regularly in June and July, including a main event against Mando Guerrero and visiting attraction Andre the Giant, and a one-week run with the tag belts of their own. A week after dropping the belts to Mando Guerrero and Tom Jones in a cage match, Franks and Piper were at loggerheads again, and on opposing teams, as Franks and Victor Rivera lost a 'loser leaves town' match to Piper and Big Bad John. Just like that, the whirlwind tour through the LA territory was over.

Comedian Joey Gaynor befriended Franke after a chance encounter at a WWF match years later. As a wrestling fan from Whittier, not far from Los Angeles, Gaynor attended matches at the Olympic, as well as at the Latin American Press Club of Greater Los Angeles on Washington Boulevard in Pico Rivera. He remembered watching his friend years before they met. He said:

> "I remember Keith said he was making $2,000 a night for WWF when it was really exploding. He said 'I'm so glad no more of that $500 a week bullshit and having to rent a place in LA and send money home.' The shit they went through in LA, the shows they put on were amazing.
>
> "Blassie and Tolos made money there but Keith was an up and coming guy. He had to wrestle a Loser Leaves Town Match with Piper. There was a red lightbulb for boxing and he unscrewed the bulb and starts jabbing it, I said 'Did you guys plan that?' He looked at me and said, 'I did.'"

Away from the ring, California proved just as significant a turning point in Franke's personal life. As described by his daughter Angela Perides in a 2020 interview, Franke was frequenting a bar one night after the matches at the Strongbow and met a young lady who would change his life. It was March 1977 and Keith Franks had just battled Roddy Piper in a fearsome 'Freddie Blassie cage' match.

Franke charmed the young woman he would later learn was called Bea Marie Bertrand with his rugged good looks and cheeky sense of humour, and the pair were soon an item – despite the notable obstacle of Bea having a boyfriend waiting outside. Within a year, she had eloped to Georgia with the wrestler, and they were married. Perides described:

> "My mom's family is Basque and there's a Basque restaurant in Bakersfield, it's since closed down, it [was] called Chateau Basque and they knew the old [Basque] bartender and he used to serve them when they were underage and she had a boyfriend who was asleep and she's like, 'Ah it wasn't a serious thing,' so she would sneak into the bar without him seeing her.

> "[My father] was in there and she said she didn't like him at first because she said he was too cocky. And he just kept I guess pursuing her and then she just, kind of, gave in and then next thing you know my aunt was driving her to the airport and she flew to Georgia because he had a show and they eloped in Georgia."

Bertrand was the sixth of seven children, born to parents who raised cattle in Caliente, fifty miles outside of Bakersfield. The men in Bea's family, especially her father Fred, were big wrestling fans who often went to the matches when the wrestling was in town. The Chateau Basque was a favourite haunt of the wrestlers, as well as being a hangout of the Bertrands and their friends. Younger daughter Gena Banta added:

> "[Bea] was born and raised in the Mojave Desert on the ranch that grandma and grandpa bought, an old family place they bought after they were married, no power or plumbing, one of seven kids, by then they had a house in town; during summer when not in school they were on the ranch. They lived there until they got married and then moved back with her dad when they had her sister [and she] was about two.

> "She didn't go to [the match that night] but that's why he was in town. He came in and they started talking and apparently Andre the Giant and some other wrestlers were there. First impressions, she did not like him at all, obnoxious, cocky, New York attitude, know it all, 'Oh my gosh get away from me,' but so confident wouldn't take no for an answer. She actually took my cousin with her on the first date!"

The added detail of Andre the Giant may put the evening in question slightly earlier or later in 1977. Whatever the case, on this particular night Bea was at the bar with her sisters, hoping to be served by Mauricio the bartender. Another of the

Los Angeles crew, Chavo Guerrero Sr, was on hand, and has taken credit for introducing the pair. He told an interviewer in 2011:

> *"For his size, [Keith Franks] was one of the best. He was awesome. He was crazy, but a good crazy. Actually, I introduced him and his wife. Same with [Tatsumi] Fujinami. I introduced "Dr Death" Steve Williams to his wife. I am like cupid; I don't know what's going on."*

Before leaving Los Angeles, Keith Franks even found time to make his motion picture debut, in the 1977 television movie *Mad Bull*, a low-budget vehicle for former NFL player Alex Karras. Franke is seen fleetingly with Piper, Bull Ramos and a few others who happened to be on hand at the Auditorium on the day of filming this tale of a pro wrestler on a quest to avenge his murdered brother.

Franke also spent time in NWA Big Time Wrestling in San Francisco during this period, as did Piper. The pair split time between north and south California with appearances at major Cow Palace shows in Roy Shire's territory, once a hotbed but by now also in sad decline. NWA Hollywood itself continued to operate until folding on Boxing Day 1982.

Three months later the expanding WWF started promoting in the territory. Franke would return to California briefly in August 1982 for a one-off, likely a favour to aid LeBell's ailing territory. Familiarity surely played a role in this brief return. Returning to old stomping grounds was a trademark throughout Franke's career, returning at various points to Florida, Portland, the WWF, and AWA, after time away.

A week after finishing up in California, Franke returned to the Florida territory. He started back on August 15, 1977, a little over three years since making his professional wrestling debut in the same area, going to a draw with future WWF colleague Brian Blair. Eddie Graham was still in charge, and the main eventers had not changed much, with the likes of Dusty Rhodes, Rocky Johnson and Lars Anderson still thrilling the crowds at the Fort Homer Hesterly Armory in west Tampa.

Florida was a far hotter territory in 1977 than most, and Franke had to be content with sliding down the pecking order from what he had recently become accustomed to. The second sojourn in the Sunshine State was less eventful than his stay in California, yet not without its highpoints. Working for the final time as Keith Franks, Franke worked a few matches with Jerry Brisco, generally putting over the man whom he would later feud with over the WWF tag team titles.

While they may have been rivals in the ring, Franke had Brisco to thank for his accommodation in the area. Unlike many wrestlers who journeyed in and out of Florida, Jerry and Jack Brisco were locals. In 1974 they opened the Brisco Brothers Body Shop, a car maintenance depot on North Hubert Avenue in Tampa, at the corner of Buffalo and Hubert. They also owned the neighbouring duplex apartment which they rented out to wrestlers visiting the territory. During his stay, Franke paid for one side while Don Muraco rented the other. The appeal of working in Florida was obvious for many, as Jerry Brisco said in a 2021 interview:

> *"We had all the amenities, the beach, the climate, and all that stuff, but most of all this area was run by a guy [Eddie Graham] who really appreciated talent who could wrestle, who could take care of themselves, and he filled the territory up with those types of guys, so there were a lot of guys that could go down there and that was kind of a requirement and you kind of took pride in it.*

> *"Keith came in and it was that reputation you know, and he was a pretty good size, and you'd tell just by body language, and stuff like that that he could go, I mean he had no problem with anybody working, he was a complete professional also, but he was a good guy, he was an athlete you could tell that.*

> *"He was a good athlete. He showed that early on down in Florida as Keith Franks. He was slim, he was in shape, he liked going to the beach, getting his tan. He was a regular guy, he was a young guy in his 20s, so there in Florida, he enjoyed himself."*

He also continued his informal learning curve in the art of tag-team wrestling, forming short-lived teams with Dutch Mantell and Buddy Roberts. Roberts had already teamed for years as one half of the Hollywood Blondes with Jerry Brown, creating a blueprint for cocky heel tag-teams that he would later perfect as a third of the trailblazing Fabulous Freebirds.

The Freebirds formed in December of the following year in the NWA's Mid-Atlantic loop, while Franke's own arrogant, sneering double act with Jesse Ventura debuted in the AWA less than a year later. Franke absorbed Roberts' influence during their time together in Florida, with the veteran regarded as one of the most underappreciated performers on his time, a label many similarly attach to Franke.

Both would make their name as the technically proficient in-ring workers within flamboyant heel teams of the early 1980s, committing much of the grunt work to cover for more glamorous counterparts (Michael Hayes in Roberts' case), and it is not hard to see a familial link between the two teams.

One notable appearance for the short-lived team of Franks and Roberts came when they were entered a one-night tournament for the Florida tag titles on December 6, 1977. Franks and Roberts were soundly beaten by eventual winners Masa Saito and Ivan Koloff, getting in little offence but doing a superb job of building up their opponents with their selling, enhancing the winners for their later tournament matches in the process.

In Florida Franke also faced Wim Ruska, the only athlete to win two gold medals in Judo in one Olympics, at the 1972 Munich Games, as well as local regulars Rocky Johnson, Mike Graham, Pedro Morales and Steve Keirn, usually on the losing end. He also crossed paths with a young upstart taking his first nervous steps in the squared circle, a hulking young man put under a mask as the Super Destroyer.

While Franks never faced the Destroyer in the ring, the two did compete on the same card on a handful of occasions before the rookie moved on, including on a Jacksonville Coliseum show on August 25, 1977. Under the mask was Terry Bollea, the future Hulk Hogan and firm friend, following in Franke's footsteps by debuting under Eddie Graham.

Franke worked Florida up until mid-December going home for a month for the Christmas and New Year period. Before he did so, he took part on a December 18 card for Milo Steinborn, one of Graham's local promoters, in a line-up billed as the "last matches of 1977," against Dutch Mantel. For all intents and purposes this was Franke's final appearance in Florida. One newspaper advertised Franke for a January 22, 1978, match against Jerry Brisco, although it is unclear if the match took place.

As was common with wrestlers travelling from town to town, friendships were accrued in different areas. Paused when one would move on, then restarted when finding each other reunited in another promotion years later. Florida forged one of these transient relationships in the form of Don Muraco. After meeting briefly in Los Angeles, the pair built a lasting friendship. Muraco recalled:

> *"We became good friends in Florida when he was Keith Franks. He was kind of a preliminary heel and I was almost a top babyface or one of the top babyfaces and in that position we were able to hang out a lot. The office wasn't real wild about it, but we never crossed paths so to speak in the ring or in business-wise, it was a little kayfabe time. But he and I were good friends.*

> *"In Florida, we travelled, and we hung around, and he wasn't crazy, he wasn't the totally crazy guy that he became. You know, he had a substance abuse problem, as many did in that era."*

On January 25, 1978, Franke competed on one final Florida-booked card. The NWA's *Superbowl of Wrestling* took place in front of 12,000 fans on a rainy night at the Miami Orange Bowl, a co-promotion between Alliance and the WWWF, and the brainchild of Eddie Graham.

Franke, in his final ever appearance as Keith Franks, was drafted in at short notice as a substitute for the absent Black Angus, going over John Ruffin on the undercard of an epic sixty-minute draw between warring heavyweight champions Harley Race and Superstar Graham. The late call is another sign that Franke was done with the territory and was moving on. Three days later, Adrian Adonis arrived in Georgia Championship Wrestling.

Entering 1978, Georgia was riding a wave as one of wrestling's premier territories. Stan Hansen was Georgia champion and traded the belt with Mr Wrestling II during the first half of the year. Major stars from across the US made appearances in the Atlanta-based circuit, including Ric Flair from the Mid-Atlantic, Rocky Johnson from Florida, and Bobo Brazil from Detroit. AWA heavyweight champion Nick Bockwinkel started making cross-promotional appearances with his manager Heenan, much to the chagrin of fans, the cocky champion defended his crown against Dusty Rhodes, Bob Armstrong, and others.

It was activity outside the ring which was arguably more ground-breaking for followers of Georgia Championship Wrestling, and the industry as a whole. Since 1972, GCW had aired its weekly television show on Atlanta's terrestrial station, WTCG, which had been purchased and renamed by media mogul Ted Turner three years prior. When WTBS moved onto satellite in 1976, making the station available to cable systems across the country, promoter Jim Barnett negotiated GCW onto the superstation, making it the first NWA promotion to be broadcast nationally. The resulting exposure made Georgia the centre of the wrestling world in many aspects, a magnet for the top talent, and caused friction with other NWA promoters nervous about this apparent move towards national expansion by a group member.

Keith Franke couldn't claim to be a top-tier talent yet but moving into Georgia was a smart move for any wrestler in the late 1970s, given the connections and experience the territory could bring. Though little footage survives, Franke appeared regularly as a mid-and lower-card talent on the group's weekly TV show filmed at the WTCG Studios in Atlanta. Having spent the new year planning the perfect entrance, Adrian Adonis appeared for the first time on the Georgia group's Saturday TV show on January 28, 1978.

Once again, Franke's stay was low on drama, and he was used mainly to put over stars, and fill out tag team matches. He contested the AWA title with Bockwinkel, whom he would later cross paths with briefly during his two-year stay in Minnesota. Bockwinkel defeated Adonis on March 10, 1978, at the Municipal Auditorium in Atlanta, and again six days later, potentially forming the connection which would see Adonis invited into the AWA eighteen months later. One bright spot was a spring 1978 wrestling magazine feature tagging Adonis alongside Tommy Rich and Raymond Rougeau as three of the territory's 'young lions.'

In Georgia, Adrian Adonis tussled with the feared Minnesota Wrecking Crew, Ole and Lars Anderson, as well as facing (and almost always losing) to major stars including John Studd, Abdullah the Butcher, Ivan Koloff, Angelo Mosca, and Stan Hansen. On June 9, 1978, his final night in, he also made up the numbers in a one-night, seven-man tournament for the Georgia title, eventually won by Mosca.

If things in the ring had slowed down more than he may have liked, life outside the ring could not be more different. Franke's relationship with Bea from Bakersfield had blossomed. In the spring of 1978, while Franke was in Georgia, Bea surprised her friends and family by skipping town and flying to be with Franke, and the two were married shortly after. Perides explained:

> "My aunt Sharon drove my mom to the airport and they got married at the courthouse [in Georgia]. She called crying and told her mom and dad after the ceremony."

With his personal life on a roll, it was time for Franke to address his stalling career and get back some of the cache he had when he first met Bea in California. Growing tired of putting over bigger stars, Keith Franke hit the road once more in search of his own spotlight, and Adrian Adonis was truly born.

Chapter 6: Amarillo

"I didn't beat him, but he didn't beat me either,

so that instant I became a superstar."

- *Terry Daniels, 2020*

Less than a week after his final appearance for Georgia Championship Wrestling, Adrian Adonis arrived in Amarillo. Finally, a chance for Franke to flex his creative muscles presented itself. After taking something of a back seat in Florida and Georgia, Franke was ready to take centre stage and truly unleash his new persona.

While the name change may not have happened quite the way Terry Funk remembered it, Amarillo was certainly where the name 'Adrian Adonis' caught attention from the wrestling world. A decade earlier, Johnny Cash scored one of his biggest hits with '*A Boy Named Sue*,' an ode to a rough loner with a humorous slant, and Franke certainly saw the joke in portraying a tough guy with a feminine name. While he had been billed from New York City before, mainly in newspaper listings, Franke over time became more overt in claiming the Big Apple as the hometown of Adrian Adonis, gradually developing a rough-and-ready, leather jacket-wearing biker persona, no doubt drawing on his legitimate past with the motorcycle gang in his native Buffalo.

Franke's mat work was sound. Not just the fundamentals, but the histrionics that are a must in professional wrestling came naturally, as California showed. But after spending the last four years devoid of any real character, Franke was confident the combination of new name and the aggressive edge, wrapped in a package that whispered something slightly effeminate, would be a winner with the crowd. He was right.

The late 1970s represented, in many ways, the calm before the storm of the following decade, and 1978 was positively pedestrian compared to what came later. The flamboyant "Superstar" Billy Graham was dethroned as WWWF heavyweight champion by the bland Bob Backlund who held the belt for most of the next six years before the rise of Hulk Hogan.

The NWA continued to yield the ascent of Rhodes and Flair as its key face and heel for years to come, while Harley Race carried the group's world title throughout the year. Across the territories, groups peaked and troughed, with big shows such as the *Superbowl of Wrestling* attempted on occasion, alongside regional television exposure. While the Georgia territory was heating up thanks to its unmatched TV deal, the same could not be said for Amarillo.

Franke joined Amarillo at a tumultuous point in the area's history, as the group struggled to pull itself out of a downturn. Formally known as NWA Western States, the area had traditionally been run by retired wrestler Dory Funk Senior. When he passed away in 1973, sons Dory Junior and Terry took up the reins. Outside of its base the group frequented Abilene, Lubbock, and other nearby towns, and also enjoyed the occasional visit of big stars of the era such as Harley Race, Andre the Giant and the Von Erich clan of nearby Dallas.

The Funk brothers were still active professional wrestlers across the US and Japan in their own right and did not have the time to be the full-time owners a regional wrestling territory required. More pertinently, as Funk described in his autobiography, he could sense the tectonic plates of the industry shifting and the dying days of the territories ahead. Funk said:

> "In 1979, I noticed something new – cable TV, in particular a wrestling show coming out of Atlanta. I knew there was a change coming in the professional wrestling business.

> "And once that change with national television hit, I knew that we would have fragmentation of this once-mighty alliance as everyone fought to be the national power. Sure enough, that's what ended up happening, first with the WWF and then with Crockett, who ended up in 1985 on TBS, where I first saw Georgia Championship Wrestling.

> "Even in '79, I knew the day of the national wrestling promotion was coming. I also knew how much work it would be for Junior and me to keep Amarillo running. I didn't want a repeat of what happened after my dad died, when I became obsessed with the business to the exclusion of all else, including my family. I knew that had been a mistake, and I would be damned if it was a mistake I was going to make again. Junior and I talked and decided to sell the Amarillo territory to Bob Windham (Blackjack Mulligan) and Dick Murdoch. Before the deal was done, though, I told them both that I didn't think the future was too bright."

The slight air of desperation was to the advantage to at least one person. The Funks were glad to have Adrian Adonis on board, and the 'man from New York City' arrived at the start of the summer with a big heel push. As well as their backing, Franke picked up an important accruement to his act in the form of a new nickname which endured when he joined bigger promotions, as "Golden Boy" Adrian Adonis; once again, with its boastful quality and preening undertone.

The placement of Adrian Adonis near the top of the card in Amarillo happened immediately. On June 15, 1978, Adonis took to the ring at the Amarillo Sports Arena, the group's home base, and pitched the first iteration of his $5,000 'Golden Challenge', a part-work, part-shoot open invitational which neatly matched the 'Golden Boy' moniker.

The challenge was a stunt nearly as old as wrestling itself, which saw an established star – ideally one with significant amateur wrestling prowess – challenge members of the audience to last a certain amount of time in the ring with them, in return for a cash prize. Funk recalled legendary Winnipeg grappler Gord Nelson offering people out for such a challenge during his time in Amarillo:

> *"As Mr. Wrestling, Gordon would take on all comers with the deal being a cash prize for anyone who could last 10 minutes with him. I always admired anybody who did those open challenges, because you don't just get marks out of the crowd you get some tough guys. You never know who you're in there with."*

It was in this tradition that "Golden Boy" Adrian Adonis launched the "Golden Boy Challenge," a version of a wrestling mainstay that was later aped in WWE by Kurt Angle. Angle, who ironically also had the distinction of being shaved bald on WWF television, initiated the 'Kurt Angle Invitational' in the same spirit in 2005. While these too were staged fights with enhancement talent, Angle almost fell foul of Funk's warning from years prior.

The fan challenge dated back years and was fraught with risk. In 1968, "Mr Wrestling" Tim Woods had part of his finger bitten off by an audience member who had been clinched into a hold. Practitioners of the practice understandably dropped off after this, with Masa Saito in Georgia on occasional proponent.

Needing a big opponent to start off strong, Adonis' version of the challenge was taken up by local hero and former NWA champion Dory Funk Junior. Per the storyline rules, challengers had ten minutes to pin Adonis, or he would be victorious, as was the case in this encounter.

The challenge was a simple but effective way of building up Adonis as a major heel threat to the territory babyfaces and followed a tradition dating back to wrestling's oldest incarnations of performers welcoming marks from the crowd to 'try their luck' for a prize. Adonis had a solid enough background as a high school amateur wrestler that he was capable of taking care of the vast majority of untrained (and likely inebriated) members of the audience in a shoot scenario, as well as other pro wrestlers io the need arise. As the *Hereford Brand* described on July 7, 1978:

> *"The Golden Boy is a product of Buffalo, New York, has an extensive amateur background, and was a notorious street fighter. At 6 feet 1 inches, he is a formidable opponent."*

The Funks clearly had the confidence in their new find to pull off the slightly risky stunt. Writing on his website in the late 1990s, Dory Funk Junior explained the logic behind the fan challenge gimmick in wrestling, and their confidence in Adrian Adonis to pull it off:

> *"Adrian was a tough kid when he was in the Amarillo territory. He came in with the hardest gimmick in wrestling, 'Beat the Champ.' It was a straight offer to anyone in the house, a thousand dollars to anyone who could beat Adrian in ten minutes, not cash, silver dollars, in a bank sack.*
>
> *"The challenge was up every night. In effect, every night Adrian was beating up one of the fans. His heat was building and we were doing capacity business. Adrian was a good wrestler and a tough street fighter, a hard combination to beat. Each night, the challenger selected was asked to sign a release, then stepped in the ring with Adrian.*
>
> *"His standard match consisted of some good wrestling by Adrian until the challenger had a sense that this wasn't going to be too tough, then from out of the blue Adrian would cut loose with a hay maker, a straight fist or elbow smash to the face and from that point the fight was over.*
>
> *"With the challenger in a daze, Adrian would win with a leg drop, elbow drop, or drop-kick, not normally devastating moves, but the challenger usually wanted out of the ring by this time. I watched as Adrian went through at least fifteen challenges for the thousand dollars. Taking on anyone in the house is a tough thing to do. Adrian gained respect among the wrestlers and added to his heat and drawing power."*

The gimmick was two-pronged, for pros and amateurs. Adonis would establish his credibility with 'Golden Challenge' matches with his fellow workers. These generally ended in draws against bigger names such as Dory Junior and Kevin von Erich, who faced Adonis on June 22, when they were unable to pin him within the time limit; or victories against lesser names such as Noah Jones and the Super Destroyer (not Hulk Hogan under the mask here). These were just as predetermined as the other matches on the card.

The same could not be said when the challenge was posed to the crowd, and eager fans would be selected to take on Adonis for real. By all accounts these were legitimate shoot fights, with Adonis using his prowess to pin contenders in short order, without hurting them. The same *Hereford Brand* article asserted:

> *"Adonis has stipulated that all challengers must sign a legal release absolving him of all responsibility."*

Whether or not fans such as Byron Citrest, Charles Hudgens, Bob Burgett or Johnny Sierra who valiantly took on the 'Golden Challenge,' signed such documentation has not been recorded. As Dave Meltzer noted in the *Wrestling Observer* shortly after Adonis' death:

> *"Renowned as a tough guy, Adonis used to take challenges from fans while in Texas, offering $100 to anyone in the audience who could last 10*

minutes in the ring with him. I heard Adonis used to wrestle against several fans in real situations, and none lasted more than around two minutes as Adonis had a good amateur background in wrestling."

Oliver Humperdink worked Amarillo at the same time as Adonis, in his role as heel manager for the villainous Mr Pogo, who years later reinvented himself as a 'death match' specialist. Adonis, Humperdink and Pogo tagged together on at least one occasion losing a handicap match against Dory Junior and Ted DiBiase in Odessa on September 26, 1978, and Humperdink seconded Adonis a handful of times, including for a tag match main event alongside Pogo against the Funks in August 1978. In a 2005 interview with RF Video, Humperdink recounted that Adonis's reputation for unpredictability was growing even in these early days:

> *"Adrian Adonis...well, the first time I had seen him was in Florida about in 1977 or 78, somewhere along in there and we were together in Amarillo with the Funks. He was in there doing the 'challenge anybody out in the crowd' thing. So, I've seen him beat the piss out of some guys, shoot. Crazy guy."*

Fans returned regularly to see who would finally put an end to the winning streak of this cocky newcomer and speculated at what big name might arrive to get the job done. On July 13, their wish was almost granted when fearsome wild-man Bruiser Brody stomped to the ring for a rare appearance at the Amarillo Sports Arena and proceeded to wipe the floor with Adonis.

The weaselly "Golden Boy" managed to survive the onslaught from the man with whom he would later share a tragic legacy, being attacked with a chair and thrown around the ring and held out for ten minutes, technically granting Adonis a victory in their only solo meeting.

The wins continued to rack up for Adonis, often in wild and woolly brawls which were a trademark of the territory, and introduced a new, rougher style to his game. Retelling a recent match between Adonis and Noah Jones, the *Castro Country News* of July 13 reported:

> *"Recently these two mat men ended up in an Amarillo hospital for treatment after a free-for-all,"* which may or may not have been legitimate.

The victories carried on for Adonis for several months, including more than one over top area babyface Ricky Romero. Life was good. The same could not be said in every part of the wrestling world in the summer of 1978.

Lonnie "Moondog" Mayne succumbed to one of the tragic hazards of the job when he died in a car accident on August 14, 1978, a sad reality of life on the road for a journeying wrestler of the twentieth century. Though their paths never crossed, there are grim parallels between the lives and careers of Keith Franke and Mayne. Mayne was a huge star in the territories he frequented, particularly Portland, and also made waves during his short career in New York and California despite only competing for a little over a decade, mainly thanks to his outlandish look and wild styling.

Mayne was as wild outside the ring as inside, and it has been speculated that he fell asleep at the wheel when he took to the road after finishing his match in San Bernardino on that fateful evening. Little remembered today by modern wrestling fan, he was just 33 years old.

Moondog Mayne was not the first or last to fall foul of the risks for professional wrestlers travelling up and down the road. To this day the vast majority of wrestlers, even those making big money at major companies, are responsible for their own travel plans. Combined with hectic performance schedules and often late finishes, performers have for decades been left to drive themselves from town to town to make their living, often in hazardous conditions.

Some, inevitably, have done so under the influence as they strive to lessen the pressure of performing and loneliness of life on the road. As with the case of Hercules Cortez in Minnesota in July 1971, or Sam Bass, Pepe Lopez and Frank Hester on their way to Nashville five years later, wrestling has been a hazardous experience for wrestlers even before they step in the ring; It was the same sad state of affairs for many others for years to come. As Dave Meltzer noted in 2003:

> *"There were more full-time wrestlers, and far more wrestling shows, and far fewer deaths of active performers [in the 1970s]. Older fans can name Alberto Torres, Luis Hernandez, Ray Gunkel, Luther Lindsay, and Mike DiBiase (the latter three of whom were older than 45) dying inside the ring. But the biggest killer of that era was the highway. Moondog Mayne, Whitey Caldwell, Hercules Cortez, Bobby Shane, Sam Bass and a few others died in auto, or in the case of Shane, plane accidents."*

Amarillo quickly proved to be a key developmental period in Franke's life as a performer. It was the most gruelling territory of his career up to that point as he worked multiple times a week, often on consecutive nights, racking up over sixty matches in less than six months. From the Funks and others, he quickly absorbed the region's tough, uncompromising brawling style, building on what he had picked up in Vancouver and California.

One thing that did not change during this period in Franke's life was who was by his side. Newlyweds Keith and Bea were still in the honeymoon stage when Franke entered the Amarillo territory, and Bea travelled on the road with him in Texas as she had in Georgia. A wrestler's lifestyle can be tough on any relationship, especially one in its formative stages. Despite the obvious challenges to moving across the country every few months, Bea was ever-present on the road across numerous territories for the first several years of their marriage, returning to Bakersfield around 1982 when eldest daughter Angela was a toddler. She recounted to daughter Gena Banta in 2021:

> *"[Their] communication was always super open and in the beginning of the relationship she did travel with him. They were in Amarillo, where Terry Funk was from and everything, they were there, and they were in Minnesota and Georgia and things were going good and then she got pregnant with my sister and then had hard, and then it was kind of hard because he was travelling a lot more, he wasn't always at home, she was being lonely, not really knowing anyone.*

> *"They decided together that it would be best if she moved back to Bakersfield to be with her family, especially with a two-year-old, so that's when she moved back, in 1982-83 around that time, she moved back to Bakersfield, to be with her family to be with people that could support her while he was off working."*

Adonis also began to perfect one of wrestling's oldest tricks which would go on to serve him well for the rest of his career; the old wrestling maxim to not be afraid to sell your opponent's offence. One of the most remarked about things in all reviews of Adonis' work, even when he gained an unsightly amount of weight, was his selling, an uncanny ability he shared with greats like Terry Funk, Ray Stevens, Race, and Shawn Michaels.

A wrestler too afraid to make himself look weak by 'giving' too much to his opponent can look stiff and uncompromising. A wrestler who sells too much, looks pathetic. A wrestler who gets this delicate balance right, as each of these men have in their respective eras, can work wonders with any opponent.

Amarillo's penchant for gimmick matches, another key sign of a struggling territory in need of a crutch to lean on, gave Adonis plenty of opportunities to fling himself around in any awkward combination required, including copying the fan favourite 'turnbuckle flip' created by Ray Stevens in 1965. The risky and acrobatic move was a crowd-pleaser for Stevens, with the wrestler whipped into the corner, going into a half-somersault and landing with his back on the top turnbuckle, as a way to underline the force and power of his opponent's throw. The move has become more associated with Ric Flair and Shawn Michaels in modern times, with Adrian Adonis a key proponent of the manoeuvre throughout the 1980s.

On Thursday, August 31, at the weekly card at the Amarillo Sports Arena, Adonis hit a snag. Adonis made his usual challenge to the crowd, a familiar routine by this point and a precursor to his billed match for the evening, a Texas Death Match against hometown hero Terry Funk.

Adonis would go on to win the main event by count-out, but that was not what anyone was talking about at the end of the show. As Meltzer reminded fans in the May 20, 2013, edition of the *Wrestling Observer*, the mood in Amarillo changed when a young former Marine agreed to step into the ring. He noted years after the incident:

> *"A lot of wrestlers who were shooters like Karl Gotch, Gene LeBell, Bob Roop and many others used to challenge fans. Adonis in the Amarillo territory was one of the last to do it. He ran up against [Terry] Daniels, who was a Marine, I think, who gave Adonis everything he could."*

Terry Daniels, a young man in his early twenties fresh out of Marine Corps bootcamp who would later go on to play semi-professional football, took up the challenge and caught Adonis by surprise. With his short, squat stature and his real-life military training, Daniels gave Adrian Adonis a far tougher time than he was expecting and the two engaged in a brief but furious real-life scuffle, with Adonis visibly struggling to control the novice.

To his credit, Adonis did not panic, and instead relied on his experience. Positioning himself and Daniels towards the ropes, he leveraged them both over the top rope and they toppled to the ringside. They continued to fight, with Adonis aware that keeping Daniels out of the ring would lead to a double count-out, which was declared in just under two minutes.

Recalling the star-making moment years later, Daniels described the sequence of events that led him to the ring that night:

> *"Well, the way I got started, because wrestling was really big here in Amarillo, and they, Adrian came to town and eventually they did a deal where if you could pin his shoulders in ten minutes, you'd win five grand.*
>
> *"I watched him wrestle a few guys, you know like myself who wasn't wrestlers or in the business, and he just basically demolished them. And I thought, I'd just graduated high school, I'm just out of Marine Corps bootcamp, and I thought man, let me give this a try. So, I went and talked to the promoters and they was like, 'are you sure?' I'm like, 'yeah, absolutely.'*
>
> *"So what I started doing to get ready – Alex Perez was one of the wrestlers back then, I talked to him about it and he basically called me a freakin' idiot because – he didn't use that word – and I'm like yeah, I know, he lent me some trunks and some boots and I did a little bit of training on my own, and the day finally came, and I never talked to him.*
>
> *"The day finally came and I got in the ring, and we ended up brawling, and sometimes when I get in something like that, I really don't remember*

72

what happened until after it's over and people have got to tell me what happened and stuff.

"But I do know that I stood my own and there was one time we ended up outside the ring and the people – I guess Adrian had pushed me down into the crowd – and he grabbed some kind of a copper bracelet or something, he was fixing to hit me with that and one of the fans stopped him from doing that, and [that's in the ring] and it was over with. And it was pretty cool because, I didn't beat him, but he didn't beat me either, so that instant I became a superstar, that instant, and didn't even know why."

According to Daniels' telling, the match was genuine, albeit not a case of a fan plucked immediately out of the crowd and into the ring straight away. In his case at least, he raised his interest with the promoters and was given a few days to prepare. Dory Funk Junior witnessed the action and was suitably impressed, as he wrote years later:

"One Thursday night in Amarillo at the old Sports Arena, Adrian's challenger signed the release and stepped into the ring and peeled his shirt off. He was cut and weighed about 190 pounds. The first thing I noticed, this kid was no mark. I didn't know where he got them but he was wearing real wrestling shoes.

"Adrian as always took his time, feeling his opponent out. Sure enough, Adrian could out wrestle the kid. He slipped behind almost at will and took him to the mat. Each time the kid would move immediately to the ropes and the referee would break the hold. On about the third time when the kid went to the ropes, Adrian slid to the floor. The kid was on his back as the referee called for the break.

"Adrian cut loose with a blind side punch to the chin. As soon as the punch landed, the kid was on the floor looking Adrian right in the eye. The rules had been broken and now this kid was free to fight like he had been trained, a Golden Gloves Texas State Champion. The damnedest bare fist fight you ever saw in your life erupted. They fought right through the fans to the back row of ringside. The match was counted out and the two fighters were separated.

"The return match the next Thursday night in Amarillo sold out. Adrian Adonis vs Terry Daniels, with special referee, Dick Murdoch. There is another unwritten rule in pro-wresting, 'Never let a mark get the best of a wrestler.' Murdoch laid down the smack and let both men know he would stand for no bare fist punching.

73

> *"Adrian being a good wrestler won the match. That was the end of the 'Thousand Dollar Challenge.' Adrian came out of it fine, and his drawing power remained throughout the rest of his stay in the Amarillo territory and so did his pride and respect among the boys."*

The return match the following week was delayed, ostensibly as the heelish Adonis played for more time to prepare for his foe. There was no second one-on-one encounter but instead a tag match, four weeks after the original match, with Dick Murdoch indeed serving as referee.

The official word from the September 2, 1978, *Amarillo Daily News* had it thusly:

> *"Terry Daniels, Amarillo fan, gave Adonis a spirited battle in the trying to win a $5,000 Golden Challenge match. Both men were counted out at 1:46."*

Days later the same paper reported that Adonis had accepted a rematch from the spirited 20-year-old fan, although Adonis, the true heel that he was, backed out on the night claiming he wanted to focus on a tag match instead.

That would be the culmination of the feud. On Thursday, September 28, 1978, back at the Sports Arena, Daniels teamed with the area's top star, Terry Funk, to down Adrian Adonis and Dennis Stamp in nine minutes and five seconds in front of guest referee Dick Murdoch – future partner of Adonis. Daniels continued:

> *"It (shocked people). I never even talked with him afterwards, I never really heard anything else after that. I heard that it kinda embarrassed him. Next thing I know, Terry Funk comes up and now he's asking me if I want to be his partner against Adonis and Dennis Stamp and I'm like ok, you know who's going to turn down an invitation like that? This is Terry Funk!*

> *"So anyway, we tagged up, we went against Dennis Stamp and Adonis and that went over pretty well, I don't remember a whole lot about that but after that, Dennis is the one who came up and asked me if I wanted to learn how to do that, so Dennis Stamp is the one that trained me in the business, and that was pretty cool."*

With that, Terry Daniels embarked on a wrestling career of his own. Adonis' mentor Stamp took the young hopeful under his wing and began training Daniels for the ring, eventually helping him to get booked in other territories. While still in Amarillo, Daniels was put through his paces by tough local wrestler "Cowboy" Larry Lane. Lane, intriguingly, was an accomplished amateur who at one time during his career also did the 'fighting crowd members' gimmick, and teamed with Dory Funk, occasionally billed as the Funks' cousin due to a vague similarity.

74

Daniels ended up following Adonis from Amarillo to Southwest Championship Wrestling to the WWF, years later going up against "The Golden Boy" in Madison Square Garden.

Ted DiBiase, the future "Million Dollar Man" in the WWF, was the man to bring an end to the "Golden Challenge," as Adonis rounded out September and October with fierce feuds opposite DiBiase and Terry Funk. Funk, as noted in the September 17 edition of the *Canyon News*, took up against Adonis when the man from New York insulted the honour of his late father by claiming his own superiority in a local specialty match:

> *"Funk, with an eight-pound advantage over the 250-pound Adonis, has posted $5,000 for Adonis if the New Yorker can beat him in a Texas Death Match. Adonis recently won a similar match and laid claim to the title 'King of the Texas Death Matches,' a title held by the later Dory Funk Senior."*

Funk failed to beat Adonis in a Golden Challenge on August 17, 1978, despite having the pin, due to the referee being knocked out of the ring. The callous Adonis refused to give Funk a rematch. As the *Amarillo Daily News* of August 31 reported:

> *"Adonis will pay $5,000 if Funk pins his shoulders in ten minutes. If not, the Texas Death Match goes on until one of the men no longer can continue. Funk failed to pin the shoulders of Adonis in ten minutes on August 17. Funk had the pin, but the referee had been knocked out of the ring. Adonis refused to give Funk another chance. Now Adonis claims Funk tricked him into signing a contract for a Texas Death Match. Adonis thought he was signing to meet a fan in a $5,000 Golden Challenge match. Adonis says he will teach Funk a lesson."*

Adonis won their Death Match on August 31 when Funk fell off the top ropes to the floor outside the ring and was counted out, albeit only as an appetiser to their eventual blow-off. In a major card on September 21, 1978, at the West Texas State Fieldhouse, alma mater of the Funks and DiBiase, crowd-pleaser Terry Funk was victorious in his showdown with Adonis, allowing him to avenge the insult. In addition to the Daniels tag match, the pair also tussled a month later in a Russian Chain match in Lubbock, with Funk again the victor.

The slender DiBiase, who would go on to become one of the most memorable stars with Vince McMahon's WWF a decade later, was also in the midst of a big babyface push and had the upper hand throughout his two-month tangle with Adonis. A homegrown star and high school football standout, DiBiase was trained and debuted in Amarillo by the Funks and he had been presented as a rising star ever since making his bow in 1974, the same year as Keith Franke.

The pair first tussled in a gruelling 60-minute two out of three falls match on September 22, 1978. With Adonis' challenge gimmick starting to run out of steam, both thanks to Daniels and the audience's familiarity with it, DiBiase put it out of its misery. On a special card to mark a decade of promoting by Funk associate Jerry Kozak, DiBiase pinned Adonis within ten minutes to claim the Golden Challenge, as well as winning a battle royal later the same evening. Adonis was repaid for putting the young star over with a victory the following week in a New York Street Fight at the Amarillo Sports Arena, the first in a series of gimmick matches they faced off in.

Another meeting of the two took place on October 23, 1978, in Farmington, with *Farmington Daily News* staffer Bruce Williams in attendance to interview fans for their reactions on the matches, including *"the battle between arch-rivals Ted DiBiase and Adrian Adonis, the highlight of the evening as far as the fans' rooting and getting involved was concerned."* Among those he spoke to were regular attendees Barbara and Bob Foster. Neatly summing up the strange appeal of Adrian Adonis, Barbara told the reporter:

> *"I wanted to see Larry Lane, Ted DiBiase, and Adrian Adonis – because I can't stand Adrian Adonis."*

The feud culminated in a final New York Street Fight on a card in Odessa for Halloween evening. DiBiase, the babyface, went over, this time with the great Haystacks Calhoun as guest referee. Adonis got some measure of revenge to restore his character, defeating Calhoun two nights later at the weekly Thursday night Amarillo show.

DiBiase joined the WWF in May 1987 and missed the departing Adonis by two weeks, though the Funks briefly worked under the same on-screen tutelage of Jimmy Hart with Adonis in the WWF in 1986. They were not the only personalities from Amarillo who crossed paths with Franke down the line. Headliner Dick Murdoch, a Texan in every sense of the word, and Adonis, had a brief programme in November in Amarillo, with the more experienced "Captain Redneck" generally going over.

One such match-up included a draw between the two on a major Western States card on November 4, 1978, in Odessa, co-headlined by NWA champion Harley Race defending against Wahoo McDaniel, and a battle of the Funk and Von Erich brothers. Five years later Murdoch and Adonis formed one of the most effective and underappreciated tag teams in WWF history, holding the tag titles for nearly nine months in the run up to the first *WrestleMania*. Mid-carder Bob Sweetan and announcer Steve Stack meanwhile joined Adonis in San Antonio-based upstart Southwest Championship Wrestling in 1983, where he was also briefly reunited with mentor Dennis Stamp.

76

In November 1978, towards the end of Adonis's six months in Amarillo, the promotion was sold to Dick Murdoch and Blackjack Mulligan, two performers with local roots, for $20,000, and it was clear to many observers that the territory was not long for this world. Reporter Williams noted in the December 5, 1978, *Farmington Daily News* that crowds were dwindling:

> *"Approximately 500 people showed up for the evening's matches, the smallest attendance of the three professional wrestling on in the area since October. This was also the most unruly and inconsiderate crowd yet."*

Despite the downturn, Adonis was still doing his job to perfection, as Williams added: *"Adonis probably drew the most verbal abuse from the crowd."* By 1980, ticket sales were in steady decline, and viewers were tuning out of the Western States Sports hour-long Saturday afternoon show on KFDA-TV. The promotion closed the following year.

Adonis did his old friend Stamp a favour on his last night in the territory, going to a draw with the veteran on December 14, 1978. One final frantic Thursday night at the Amarillo Sports Arena, and once again it was time for Adrian Adonis to move on.

Chapter 7: Portland

"I promise you people this is the last time in Portland that I will let you people down,

and I'm deeply ashamed of myself."

- *Adrian Adonis, 1979*

As 1978 ended, audiences flocked to cinemas in their droves to see *Superman: The Movie*. Despite only being released on December 15, it was eventually ranked as the second-highest grossing movie of the year. The film saw Christopher Reeve, Marlon Brando and Margot Kidder bring an air of maturity and respectability to comic books never before thought possible. It has been repeatedly recognised as one of the most important and influential superhero movies of all time, and signalled a change in how the genre was viewed. As the curtain fell on the 1970s, a similar sea change would affect the world of professional wrestling, and the way it was perceived by mainstream audiences.

Clark Kent was not the only person taking flight during the festive period of 1978. Three weeks after the movie debuted, Keith Franke re-emerged in the Pacific Northwest, this time as "Golden Boy" Adrian Adonis. During his previous time in Portland in 1975 and 1976 Franke made sporadic appearances for Don Owen's group as part of a talent exchange while working for the nearby Vancouver territory, his 'main' residence. For the last year of the 1970s however, Portland would be his home, and another important turning point in his transition from regional mid-carder with lots of promise to national star and one of the best in the business.

The wrestling world of the late 1970s was slow to realise the changes Vince McMahon Junior had planned for the World Wide Wrestling Federation, still technically his father's company for another three years. One change that no one could miss however took place in February 1979 when the company dropped the "Wide" in its name to become the World Wrestling Federation (WWF). Under the WWF name and with McMahon Junior at the helm, the company would achieve its two most successful periods of business in its history, from 1984 to 1988, and from 1998 to 2001. Some, like the Funks in Amarillo, sensed something was coming. Others across the wrestling fraternity had no idea; comfortable, complacent, and satisfied with their protected lot, few predicted how quickly McMahon's plans would steamroll all in front of them.

Often a slow and plodding place for much of the 1970s storyline-wise, the WWF was a comparative hotbed of action in 1979. Inaugural Intercontinental champion

Pat Patterson turned babyface and dumped his manager The Grand Wizard in a notable angle. In November, the rising star of Hulk Hogan graced the WWF for the first time, heading towards a feud with Andre the Giant. For the NWA, Harley Race continued his dominance as heavyweight champion, while fans were treated to the first ever issue of *Pro Wrestling Illustrated*.

By 1979, Portland Wrestling under Don Owen was entering one of its most famed periods, thanks to two men in particular. While originally starting out as allies, "Playboy" Buddy Rose and Roddy Piper were to set the territory on fire for months with their brutal blood feud. Adrian Adonis, playing a babyface for one of the only times in his career, played a key supporting role in this dynamic. A stellar roster of talent played their part for Portland including former WWWF heavyweight champion Stan Stasiak, The Kiwi Sheepherders (prior to their WWF run as The Bushwhackers), Ron Starr, Rip Rogers, "Killer" Tim Brooks, Rick Martel, and others.

The raucous action from this array of colourful characters helped Pacific Northwest Wrestling maintain its status as one of the NWA's most important territories, at least until it faded from view like many others in the early 1980s. From its base at the Portland Arena, the group's weekly television programme, '*Big Time Wrestling*,' was shown in syndication throughout the Pacific Northwest, building a dedicated fanbase.

Workers enjoyed the Portland region too. Promoter Don Owen, and his brother Elton, ran a relaxed and respected show, albeit one within a poor climate that many found hard to adjust to. Another recurrent element in tales of the old Portland days is the wrestlers' fondness for passing the time by playing gags on each other. None more so than the mischievous Adonis.

Rip Rogers worked for Owens early in his career at the same time as Adonis and Piper, and described the relationship between Portland and Vancouver territories:

> "At the time there was sort of a working relationship, like on a Monday night we'd go [to Vancouver] and work their show, I can't remember if it was Cloverdale if that's what it was but it's like Buddy Rose would get a van and it'd be like me and the Bushwhackers, and Buddy would go up and he'd take some heels.

> "So I remember I had to fly up there one time and I hated it, because I remember Adrian was up there, Roddy went up there a lot, Martel went up there a lot, but it was Gene, Gene Kiniski, he ran up there and a lot of guys would go for the territory , like, some guys they would like homestead like in a certain place and then you might live in Vancouver, but you'd work there a year so you'd want to go down to Portland to have a break for like six months so you don't have the same old shit all the time."

Rogers had colourful memories of Don and Elton Owens, whom Piper and Adonis enjoyed their share of fun with too. He said:

> "Now Don [Owens], I never in my life heard a bad word about him. And he didn't ask much of you. He was sort of comical, like a keystone cop kind of character, thinking about the silent movies, and he treated you with respect, I never heard him yell at anybody, and he was always good to his word and everybody loved to work with Don Owen. It was like yin and yang, it was like Abbott and Costello [comparing Elton to Don]. And Elton was an old boxer, he was comical without trying to be, so it was like Laurel and Hardy, Don was the babyface and Elton was really the heel."

In the ring, Adonis' star continued to rise thanks to a combination of his ever-developing mat skills and his effectiveness in the babyface role. Still only in his early 20s and decked out in a casual sports jacket, footage from the era shows Adonis as the prototypical good guy, fair-haired and friendly. Dave Meltzer recalled watching Adonis from afar during his Portland run and being suitably impressed:

> "When he was "Gorgeous" Keith Franks in LA he was a good wrestler, but it wasn't like he stood out to anyone. But when he was Adrian Adonis with Ron Starr, those two guys were a great tag team. I remember Adrian never worked San Francisco but we got Portland television for about a year in San Francisco, when Roy Shire shut down he used the Portland tapes and so Adrian and Ron Starr, Roddy Piper, Ed Wiskowski, Buddy Rose, George Wells, that era. I remember watching this and saying 'Damn this guy's great!' and I found out who it was, it was Keith Franks - in those days news didn't travel fast."

A nine-month run in Portland that finally primed Adrian Adonis for his long-awaited rise to the national spotlight started on January 6, 1979. Given his years of experience and improvement, Franke's second run for Don Owens was far more high profile, as yet another group saw the sense in making the young brash Adonis a central point of its weekly wrestling show.

Unlike those other promoters, Owens brought Franke in as one of his promotion's top babyface acts for the new year. Alongside Jonathan Boyd, "Rotten" Ron Starr, and Dutch Savage, Adonis took up the good fight against the villainous headliners who comprised the Rose Army. Long-time Portland headliner "Playboy" Buddy Rose, Roddy Piper, "Killer" Tim Brooks and Ed Wiskowski (the future Colonel DeBeers) formed a formidable unit built around the inimitable Rose. Generally considered one of the most underrated workers in the wrestling business, the parallels between Paul Perschmann and Keith Franke are almost eerie.

Both were superlative workers with great technique; skilled and confident talkers; surprisingly athletic and agile despite poor physiques; and a particular talent for selling offence. Like Franke, Buddy Rose died before his time, his passing at the age of 56 in 2009 attributed to natural causes following a years-long struggle with his weight, as well as diabetes.

In 1979, Rose was on top of the world, or at least Portland. When the decade was done, he had drawn more money for the Portland group throughout the 1970s than any other wrestler, capturing the local Pacific Northwest heavyweight belt eight times while he did so, as well as twelve tag team titles. In addition, *Ring Around the Northwest Newsletter* ranked him as the region's best wrestler in both 1980 and 1981, and half of the best tag team (with Wiskowski) in 1978.

Rose was an important influence on many of those who came through the territory, and Adonis was no exception. In much the same way that Franke absorbed the teaching of Terry Funk in Amarillo, he borrowed heavily from the Rose's hard bumping style, and perhaps took some inspiration from Rose in later years when he had his own larger physique to manoeuvre around the ring.

Rip Rogers was another man who would align himself with Rose in 1979 in Portland and learn from his influence. Two years into his career he journeyed to the Pacific Northwest which was quickly developing into a hotbed of wrestling action, enjoyed by fans and workers. Reminiscing on Twitter in 2016 he noted:

> *"What a territory Portland was when I was there; Piper, Buddy [Rose]; [Rick] Martel; Ron Starr; Adrian Adonis; Col DeBeers; Johnny Mantell, Ice Man [Parsons], Sheeps [the Sheepherders]."*

In a short space of time the area hosted much top regional talent, many of whom would go onto become major names. Jesse Ventura passed through Portland in early 1979. Ventura was another who would play a significant part in Adonis life. The two crossed paths briefly in Vancouver in 1975 when both were not long out of their rookie year. Whereas Franke took up the role of roaming, rolling stone picking up a new trick in each territory, Ventura stayed with Don Owen's group through to the late 1970s.

The decision to stick with Portland was took its toll on Ventura, as he explained in a 2012 interview:

> *"Don [Owen] worked me harder than anyone ever did in the business, I worked 63 consecutive nights in there once without a day off, and there's guys that can beat that. We were selling out a lot, absolutely, for that era."*

It paid off and Ventura had notable feuds in Portland with Jimmy Snuka and Dutch Savage, capturing the local title twice and the tag team title five times (twice with Buddy Rose). By the start of 1979, Ventura was burnt out with wrestling and had plans to quit and open a gym. A final two-week run for Owen in February 1979, working the same cards as Adonis, was agreed before a chance encounter with Verne Gagne pulled Ventura towards the big-time of the AWA.

After a few weeks of wrestling in ad-hoc tag-teams with Dutch Savage and others, Adonis was teamed up on a permanent basis with "Rotten" Ron Starr. A Vietnam veteran a couple of years Franke's senior, Ron Starr was a prolific traveller of wrestling's territory system. Starr's 2016 autobiography gave a brief account of his time teaming with Adonis, and provided some insight into his propensity for causing mischief outside the ring. He wrote:

> "While working in California I was now working mainly as a singles wrestler, in the Pacific Northwest they paired me up with Keith Franke – aka Adrian Adonis – in a tag team. We were put in a programme working against a heel faction that included Buddy Rose, Roddy Piper, Ed Wiskowski and Killer Tim Brooks, who was working at the time as "Bad News" Brooks. The promotion gave us a nice push and after only a few months working as a team, we went over on Piper and Brooks on April 3, 1979, to become the new Pacific Northwest Tag Team Champions.

> "I really liked working with Adrian and he was a fun guy to be around. Adrian was also one of the biggest ribbers I ever knew, and he would do anything to get a laugh and anything to get under Buddy Rose's skin. Between the two of us, we drove Buddy completely berserk. One time, Adrian even managed to hot-wire Buddy's car and drive it into a hotel swimming pool!"

Renewing his rivalry with Piper inside the ring, and solidifying their friendship outside of it, Adonis and Starr went over Piper and Tim Brooks for the Pacific Northwest tag titles. They held the belts for nearly four months to the delight of the Portland fans before dropping them to the Sheepherders. The heightened exposure in a hot territory worked wonders for Adonis, and the increased screen time allowed him to fine-tune his interview style, often delivering passionate and compelling mic work like never before in his career.

While Adonis and Starr were popular with the crowds, playing the good guy did not come naturally to Adonis and at times he struggled to hit the right tone. One such example was on the weekly Portland TV show on April 14, 1979. As Starr showed off unflattering photos of three women he claimed were Buddy Rose's girlfriends, Adonis joined the 'fun' by belittling Piper with a bizarre pop culture reference:

> "Ron I just want to make a little correction here. I don't mean to be, y'know, stepping in, but just this picture right here is a picture of little Roddy when he was young, y'see he started off his uncle brought him to

the ring as a little pig. But he got too big and he decided to try out for the part of Arnold Ziffel on 'Green Acres' but he couldn't make it because he had too many pimples on his face, so they canned him right away."

The reference relates to the pet pig of a family on a now long-forgotten US sitcom, which even in 1979 had been off the air for nearly a decade. The spiteful, snide remark is far more heel-ish than you might expect from a good guy and was largely out of keeping for the more standard babyface fodder Adonis espoused elsewhere in Portland but gave a preview of what was to come. If this is what came most naturally, it is little surprise he never worked babyface again for remainder of his career.

As the summer shone on 1979, *Rocky II* was wowing movie audiences, with its female lead Talia Shire as Adrian Balboa perhaps giving Franke a wry smile that he had hooked himself to the right wagon by picking a name tangentially linked with what had grown into a monster franchise. Years later, franchise spin-off *Creed* (2015) would even give Michael B. Jordan's title character the forename 'Adonis' in an amusing coincidence.

For the team of Adonis and Starr things were going great. The duo turned back all comers in their role as the territory's top babyfaces, a status they retained until a certain Roddy Piper turned face. Backstage, Adonis' quirky demeanour was starting to manifest itself in traits that would become more pronounced over the next decade and which litter all recollections of Franke by former colleagues.

Rip Rogers started his career in the territory in late 1977 and was still considered a rookie when Franke arrived. Thirty years later when Rogers took to social media to regale his followers with a pair of anecdotes about Adonis' hijinks during their time together, both included excrement. The first took place in the showers after a gruelling street fight between Adonis and Buddy Rose in Salem, Oregon. When Rose asked his rival to soap his back, Adonis obliged, albeit not with soap.

The second tale occurred as Adonis was leaving the territory for the AWA. Rose, by this point weary of being the target of Adonis' pranks hid in his motel room until he was confident Adonis was gone and the coast was clear. Striding cautiously out of his room and reaching to lock his motel door, Rogers and others heard a cry of "He got me!" as Rose learned too late that Adonis had left his adversary a leaving gift...smeared on the door handle. Ron Starr confirmed a similar story in his autobiography with some added detail:

"It got to the point that Buddy became so paranoid about what we'd do next that while on the road, he'd try to sneak into the motel or hotel under our noses, hoping to avoid us and our ribs. I remember when on one occasion we had checked into this one hotel that used to give the wrestlers a special rate because we stayed there a lot. Adrian asked the female desk clerk if Buddy had checked in yet. When the clerk replied

"no," a devious grin began to spread across Adrian's face. The wheels in his mind were turning, and that was never good for Rose.

"Adrian sometimes dated this clerk, so he told her to make sure that Buddy was given a certain room and that when he asked if we had checked in yet, which he was sure to do, she should answer "no." Following Adrian's lead on this one, we then went upstairs and unscrewed all the lightbulbs in the hallway that led up to Buddy's room. I then started walking in the other direction towards a window at the end of the hall only to look back and see that Adrian had dropped his pants and was taking a dump on Buddy's doorknob.

"Adrian then joined me over by the window where we could see everyone who was entering and leaving the building and finally we spotted Buddy. Then we turned and watched in the direction of the elevator. Although we waited in the dark for what seemed like forever, it was probably only about five minutes later when Buddy exited the elevator. Our patience was rewarded less than a minute later with the sound of Buddy's anguished voice: "Arrgghh!!! Shit! They got me again! Adonnisss!!!"

Starr's offhand reference to Franke's apparent extracurricular activities with the hotel desk clerk showed how common such occurrences were for wrestlers on the road travelling from town to town. Success in the ring allowed Franke to display his true self to his peers, not all of it completely palatable. His cocky interviews, prank-pulling, disgusting habits, and more hint at a man prone to getting carried away. For now, he was able to curb these influences without them impinging on his career.

Rogers shared another abiding memory of working with Adonis, this time in an interview with the Portland Wrestlecast in July 2019, shortly before the anniversary of the van crash which claimed Adonis' life. In it he sheds some light on Franke's relationship with rookie wrestlers, as well as another indication that Franke struggled to play babyface. He said:

"Oh, Adrian was really fucking talented. He was quirky and he was a bully too, I remember, because I wasn't in their league. This guy was trained by Fred Atkins, he was from the east coast so he was an obnoxious asshole. He could be funny as shit, I remember Piper used to have to tell him to shut the fuck up and let Rip call the fucking match. He has to learn how to do this. But Adrian was so fucking talented. He weighed about 235 when he was in Portland, but Adrian was really good."

Matt Borne, son of wrestler "Tough" Tony Borne, debuted alongside his father in the Portland territory in December 1978. The younger Borne quickly found himself in the group of rookie wrestlers that received the 'Adonis' treatment. In a shoot interview prior to his death, Matt Borne spoke about the negative reception he got from the more experienced Adonis. He recalled:

> *"[Roddy] Piper smartened me up to who was wanting to mess with me; like Adrian Adonis, he had a problem with me. There was one time when I was really young in the business and he had this reputation for being a shooter....and he was kind of a tough guy for his time but he was nothing outstanding. But there was one night in Eugene, Oregon, where Dutch Savage - him and my dad had problems - and he pulled Adonis aside and told him to mess with me, to hurt me in the ring. So, we went out there and had the match and he tried to shoot on me. Well, it didn't work, he couldn't beat me."*

It was a jarring experience for the rookie, and he recounted there always being some ill-feeling between the two, including when their paths crossed again in 1985 when Borne briefly joined the World Wrestling Federation as an undercard talent. Rogers, on the other hand, was more conciliatory about his experiences as an up-and-comer sharing a locker room with Adonis. He said:

> *"You got to remember, a lot of wrestlers, they stay in character, whether you're a good guy or bad guy. Just like, I lived with Randy Savage, I saw him break character once in the four years I was with him. So, it's like you expect Sylvester Stallone is Rocky all the time or he's Rambo all the time, you know what I mean. But, [Adrian] liked to rib, he was rather devious. Where he lived at he had a fish tank and he had some baby piranhas in there, so he'd tell you just go in there and try to grab one and he'd try and bite ya and shit."*

After winning the tag belts Adonis and Starr played a role in one of the most significant events in Portland's illustrious history. Days after winning the tag titles, on April 7, 1979, the pair were on one side of a raucous eight-man elimination match alongside George Wells and Hector Guerrero. A mix-up between Wiskowski and Brooks led Piper to suspect Wiskowki and Rose of sabotage, chasing his two erstwhile partners out of the ring to protect Brooks.

Almost immediately, Piper became the most popular man in town. Rose and Piper went on contest one of the most popular and profitable feuds in Portland wrestling history, marking the period out as a high point in the territory's lifespan. In reality, it was Rose who had talked Piper into leaving California for the bigger paydays of Don Owen's territory at the end of the previous year. Piper arrived in November 1978 a matter of weeks before his old friend Adonis.

Starr and Adonis moved onto a feud with the Kiwi Sheepherders, Luke Miller and Butch Williams. The team lost a non-title match to the new arrivals, solidifying their claim to a title match the following week. On Portland TV on July 14, 1979, the champions gave an interview from the 'Crow's Nest,' the platform above the

86

studio that wrestlers used to cut promos, placed tantalisingly close to the audience. Taking the blame for their non-title loss, an inconsolable Adonis admonished himself and told interviewer Frank Bonnema:

> *"Everybody, I let everybody down, I let my partner down, I let myself down, yes I did, and I want to apologise, and let me tell you something, there's always, every day of the week, and I'm gonna have my day of the week next Saturday [raising voice] and I promise you people this is the last time in Portland that I will let you people down and I'm deeply ashamed of myself and Ron Starr I want you to give me a beating because I deserve it but next week I swear, I swear, this title match that they're going to go down, they're going to go down just like everybody else."*

An overwhelmed Adonis tailed off before he could finish, in tears and apparently caught Starr off-guard for real, who consoled his young partner. They would ultimately fail to live up to Adonis' prediction and a week later, Starr and Adonis dropped the Pacific Northwest tag belts to the Sheepherders, bringing an end to their successful reign and partnership. Adonis succumbed to a piledriver for the decisive pinfall. Starr moved on from the territory within days, leaving no opportunity to pursue the issue of the dethroned champions in the ring.

The pair never teamed or worked in the same company again, but Starr wrote glowingly of Franke in his book and recalled attending his funeral and speaking to Bea. Summing up his former partner, he noted:

> *"Adrian was a very good tag team partner and a lot of fun to be around. While he was a character, always pulling ribs and doing silly shit, he was actually a half-decent shooter."*

Starr continued wrestling at an independent level until 1997 and died of a collapsed lung twenty years later, at the age of 66. A consummate professional and underappreciated talent, Starr represented a class of wrestler left behind by the flashy, muscle-laden rise of the neon 1980s era of wrestling. Though he worked many territories and held a variety of regional titles he never rose to national stardom. In a profile of Starr following his death, Dave Meltzer wrote:

> *"No offer ever came after the WWF expanded. It was the era of big bodybuilders and not smaller talented workers. Starr was a very good promo, but not in the WWF way. But as one person after another that he worked with, from Adonis to Rose to Piper to Honky Tonk Man became stars there, particularly Honky Tonk Man, he was bitter that nobody put in a good word for him."*

Adonis did not move immediately into another programme, instead partnering with former WWWF champion Stan "Crusher" Stasiak in a series of throwaway tag matches. One newspaper review during this period noted that Adonis had taken to wearing a New York Yankees sports jacket on a regular basis to emphasise the Big Apple roots of his character. Postcards from Franke's time in Portland also exist promoting "The Italian Stallion" Adrian Adonis, as the Buffalo native remained loyal to his Italian American roots.

He also filled his time with occasional performances for his old stomping ground in Vancouver, as well as turning out for occasional Cow Palace show back in San Francisco, a financially astute night's work.

As the summer ended, Franke once again started making plans to move onwards and upward, this time to the relative major leagues of the AWA in Minnesota. Before he did so, it made good sense to put over the top heel on his way out of the territory. Adonis did just that and started a short but explosive series with Buddy Rose on September 1, 1979, with a disqualification victory. The following week Adonis repeated his feat, beating Rose in a match with an additional stipulation; namely that Rogers would be chained to Adonis' second, Steve Pardee, to level out any interference in the course of the two out of three falls match. It was all or nothing now for the pair, and a 'Loser Leaves Town' match, that staple of the wrestling territory days, was set for September 18, 1978 Promoting the match, Adonis told Bonnema:

> "Playboy Buddy Rose...For the last two, three years he's been in here, he's been a bad hombre, he's hurt a lot of people and ladies and gentlemen you have to agree with me; that he's been vicious. His deeds are very dastardly and each and every one of you has seen it here on Portland, one time or another. He's put a lot of people out of here, Bull Ramos, Jesse Ventura, Roddy Piper. He's also beatin' and cheatin' and that's how he does it.

> "Ladies and gentlemen, since I came here, January 10, I hope each and every one of you has your money's worth watching me in action because I give 100% in the ring always. You people are very, very great wrestling fans in this area. But let me have the chance to prove to you that I can destroy Buddy Rose, that I can get rid of Buddy Rose. Now you have to be with me now. Everybody, because I can't do it on my own. I'm going to put the 90% you're the other 10% but I'm going to beat him. Now you people are you with me, I want to know, that's all. September 18, Buddy Rose, Tuesday, this Tuesday, get yourself a car tune up because you're going."

Adonis acknowledged his birthday in the promo, his twenty-fifth he claimed, apparently confirming a September 1954 birthdate, at odds with government records. Rose in a responding missive sneered at Adonis for agreeing to the match having just "bought a home" in the area, with a pregnant wife. It was in fact true that Bea was pregnant at this point with the couple's first child.

Buddy Rose was the victor in the 'rubber' match of course, and Adrian Adonis's short but impactful time in Portland was over. Three days later he arrived in the AWA and within weeks he formed the East West Connection with Ventura, a team which raised the profile of both men immeasurably.

Franke said goodbye to Portland having firmly placed his mark on the area. This went both for wrestlers and fans, such as the young Art Barr, teenage son of Adrian's colleague Sandy Barr, who loved his time around his dad's colleagues so much he embarked on his own, ultimately tragic, career in the squared circle. Sadly, he picked up both good and bad examples from the many wrestlers he met.

More positively, Adonis picked up the Wrestler of the Year award for 1979 from the *Ring Around the Northwest* newsletter, a fitting end on his brief but eventful Portland run.

Chapter 8: The AWA

"I'm gonna be a Veg-O-Matic on you, I am gonna slice you,

"I am gonna dice you, and for no extra charge I am gonna turn you into a Julienne French Fry."

\-   *Adrian Adonis, 1981*

As 1979 drew to a close, Keith Franke was more than five years into his wrestling career and a change was in the air. Now a seasoned professional with a provocative character, not to mention a budding marriage, making a living as a rolling stone moving through territories six months at a time would not cut it anymore. In line with the thinking of others in the wrestling business as the 1980s dawned, it was time for Adrian Adonis to go national.

The Adonis character had been birthed in Georgia, refined in Amarillo, and prospered in Portland. On route Franke had picked up the local styles in Vancouver, Florida, the Carolinas, and California to boot. With the exception of one-off appearances for the WWWF, and an undercard run with Georgia Championship Wrestling, Franke could not yet claim to have wrestled in any significant capacity for one of the industry's major territories. That would change upon leaving Portland.

The Minnesota-based American Wrestling Association (AWA) was founded in 1960 as a breakaway from the NWA by Verne Gagne and Wally Karbo. Gagne was a well-known former amateur wrestler who formed his own promotion after being thwarted from his ambition of becoming NWA champion when industry politics worked against him. With a firm belief that real pro wrestling was built around sound technical mat skills and eschewed flashy gimmicks, the AWA grew throughout the 1960s and 70s to become one of the most successful and popular territories.

In 1979, business was good and the AWA was enjoying a healthy rivalry with the NWA and the newly-named WWF. As noted by George Schirc in *Minnesota's Golden Age of Wrestling*, wrestling's popularity was on the upturn as the 1970s ended – although very few people could have predicted how things would turn out for the AWA, and the industry as a whole, by the conclusion of the following decade. He wrote:

> *"Crowds in the Twin Cities and all over increased at an incredible rate, and those fans were made up of younger fans. Many factors contributed to the attendance increases, but the primary reason was a new breed of*

wrestler. Hulk Hogan and other colourful characters like Jesse Ventura, Jerry Blackwell, and Sheik Adnan El Kaissey were major draws."

Hogan didn't join the AWA until August 1981 following a lengthy stint in New York, but one muscle-bound attraction who did join the company in the final year of the 1970s was Jesse Ventura. Minnesota native Ventura joined the AWA in March 1979 after cancelling plans to retire and open a gym after a chance encounter with Verne Gagne, as he explained in a 2008 shoot interview. He worked as a singles wrestler for the first several months, feuding with fellow bodybuilder Paul Ellering over who had the nicer physique, before Gagne put him in a tag team with the incoming Adrian Adonis. Ventura explained:

"I worked single for a while and then Adrian came in and Verne right away saw, these two young guys let's put them together. I was from Minneapolis but they didn't dare have me be a villain from Minneapolis, so I was always from San Diego and Adrian of course was from Buffalo originally but New York City so Adrian and I came up with the 'East West Connection'. 'You're the east coast, I'm the west coast, let's call ourselves the East West Connection.'"

Three days after losing to Buddy Rose at the Portland Sports Arena, Adrian Adonis debuted for the AWA, defeating Chris Curtis at the Milwaukee Auditorium on September 21, 1979. Less than three weeks later, the East West Connection was born, going over Ellering and Steve Olsonoski on October 9 in St Paul. With Ventura's chiselled physique and natural ability behind the microphone coupled with Adonis' in-ring prowess, the pair were an instant hit with the fans of the AWA. Wrestling journalist Dave Meltzer concurred:

"The deal with Ventura was he was a great talker, Adrian was a good talker, I watched a lot of their matches with the High Flyers and they were really good because Adrian was so good, he was so talented. I thought they were a very, very good team. It would've lasted longer but both got called to go to the WWF."

It has often been observed that the East West Connection complemented each other perfectly as partners, with Jesse's capacity to enrage fans with his smarmy smart-talking interviews and arrogant posing, while Adonis took care of business in the ring. While this is an assessment which downplays Adonis' appreciable verbal dexterity, Ventura agreed:

"Oh, Adrian was phenomenal, Adrian was a great partner in the ring, mechanically he could work, he had the timing, he could talk, Adrian had the whole package and I kept him in shape. He was like me, he was a natural I think, Adrian was very good, he was a good bump man, plus I didn't like to take bumps so it was good to give me a bump man. And I

was probably the better talker of the two so we filled in the gaps, I didn't like to take bumps and I was a better talker so it worked good that way."

Adonis' own verbal prowess was considerable by the standards of the AWA at the time. While substance misuse clouded his verbal clarity and delivery in later years, Adonis's promos could employ a fascinating yet baffling style, crammed with bizarre stream of consciousness similes, and offbeat cultural references, as he did in this 1981 in-character interview:

"I hope you get this down, clowns, because this is how they operate. Now the way the Connection's gonna operate, it's gonna be black and blue daddy. It's gonna be torn cartilage, it's gonna be a lotta bumps and bruises, and it's gonna be all delivered to the High Flyers, at the hands of the East West Connection.

"You fans out there you wanna see a brutal attack? Well, you're gonna see it, daddy, because all stops are gonna be pulled out. You're gonna see a New York City Floor you've never seen before, daddy. Gerry Cooney don't have nothing on me daddy. And I'm gonna tell you something right now when 'The Body' gets the Body Crunch on 'em - either one of them - it's lights out, daddy, it is lights out."

The East West Connection, Ventura in particular, embodied a new breed of star permeating professional wrestling as the 1970s evolved into Ronald Reagan's inwardly focused go-getter 1980s. Ventura became a wrestler after more than five years in the US Navy and has acknowledged many times the debt in style and persona he owed to "Superstar" Billy Graham.

Graham, WWWF champion for ten months in 1977-78, revolutionised pro wrestling with his muscular physique and arrogant, charismatic interview style, creating a template that would change wrestling forever when it was picked up and sophisticated by others to varying levels of success, none more so than Hulk Hogan. Decked in feather boas and tie-dyed t-shirts stretched across his rippling torso, "Superstar" Graham was a sign of things to come; in 1979, the wave washed into the AWA in the form of Jesse Ventura, as he has freely admitted:

"It was during my tenure with Verne that I became Jesse "The Body" Ventura. In fact, Verne named me that. He had lost Superstar Billy Graham a couple of years earlier and he asked me; "Can you do Superstar Graham?" I told him I could do Superstar Graham better then Graham, because Billy was my hero.

"There would not have been a Hulk Hogan or a Jesse Ventura if there was no Superstar Billy Graham. Verne said to me that's what we want and it was Verne that actually thought of it. He said I want to call you Jesse "The Body" and I want you to pose and do all that stuff that

93

Graham does and that's where the birth of Jesse "The Body" came from."

It was common during this era for wrestlers to live in close proximity to each other, and this was the case for Adonis and Ventura during their run as the East West Connection. The pair lived in neighbouring apartments in Burnsville, south of Minneapolis. Wives Bea and Terry Ventura became friends, and the pair's eldest children would often play together in the formative years, as Adonis' daughter Angela Perides recalled getting into a little trouble on at least one occasion. She said:

"[My parents] lived in Minneapolis, they lived right by Jesse Ventura. I guess Jesse Ventura's son and I wandered off one time and they couldn't find us, but [eventually] they found us."

With Verne Gagne as promoter, and his reliance on wrestlers with amateur backgrounds similar to his own, the AWA had a reputation as an 'old school' show. Eventually, in the face of the onslaught from the rising stars of the World Wrestling Federation, this dependence on ageing stars would be the AWA's undoing. With Gagne booking himself and contemporaries such as "Mad Dog" Vachon, The Crusher, Baron von Raschke and others in top positions well past their prime, it was not difficult for the two brash newcomers to catch the attention of the audience of 1979. Against such a dull background, stars such as Billy Graham and the East West Connection moved the wrestling world from black and white into glorious technicolour.

The cultural clash was subtle and did not reach its full climax until the emergence of Hogan as WWF champion in 1984 under the guidance of Vince McMahon Junior. Until then, many territories continued on in wilful ignorance that anything would change, plodding along as they had done for many years with technically-sound, no-frills wrestlers able to put on engaging matches.

In the WWF, 1980 saw young star Bob Backlund as champion, while former top dog Bruno Sammartino faced off against Larry Zybszko in the 'Showdown at Shea' mega-card. The group's monthly Madison Square Garden card was shown for the first time on the rechristened USA Network. This began a relationship which went full time in 1983, at the cost of Southwest Championship Wrestling, and persists to this day.

The start of the decade also marked the tenth and final time Verne Gagne would book himself to win his company's version of the world title, toppling long-time champion Nick Bockwinkel at the AWA's July super-show at Comiskey Park in Chicago.

Business-wise the AWA was healthy, expanding into other territories and promoting bigger shows, while Gagne retired holding the title, which he had won at the age of 54. Gagne also entered 1980 as one half of the AWA tag-team champions alongside Vachon, a comparable spring chicken at just 50 years old. The pair eventually dropped the tag titles to the team of Adonis and Ventura – but not without making them sweat for it.

On July 20, 1980, the East West Connection were awarded the AWA tag team titles two days after Gagne won the heavyweight belt at Comiskey Park. The fans were given the storyline reason that Gagne had forfeited the lesser title after winning the big belt, and the AWA 'championship committee' had handed the belts to the Connection.

It was right, of course, for Gagne to refrain from holding two belts but many have questioned why this change could not have been done in the ring. With a feud already in progress, and the impressive new tag team on the rise, Gagne declined to give the East West Connection the undoubted career boost they would have gained from pinning an established star such as himself or Vachon. Instead, more concerned with not losing the tag title in an in-ring scenario, Gagne simply relinquished the belt and fans were told he had missed a connecting flight. Ventura recalled:

> "That was an angle because Verne wouldn't do a job. They knew they wanted to give us the straps but he wasn't about to get pinned in any way shape or form. So, they tried to make it he'd missed the plane and didn't show or some BS like that, that's all it was about, nothing more.

> "In fact the night they were supposed to drop them to us we were on a small plane and Crusher had left early and we got on the plane, Crusher said 'Well did you beat 'em for the title,' I said 'No, Verne wouldn't do the job,' Crusher said 'are you kidding me' I said 'No,' and then they did this shmozz where they forfeited the titles."

The promoter's egotistical manoeuvring did not harm the momentum of the East West Connection. With street-tough New Yorker Adonis exuding a no-nonsense, hyper-masculine style and taking care of business in the ring, Ventura thrilled fans with his California surfer slick vibe, posing up a storm and delivering his captivating promos in a style which would serve him well during his political career.

Adonis later went on to wear outlandish attire of his own; not just in his 'Adorable' phase, but his earlier sporting of diamond-studded chokers with leather jackets. For now, it was Ventura who took the eccentric apparel to another level, with feather boas, capes, gowns, multicoloured tights, and a feather-festooned beret all part of the act. Drawing on the influence of Gorgeous George, and more contemporaneously, "Exotic" Adrian Street, Ventura was happy to push the boundaries – and enrage the male-heavy crowds – with his somewhat suggestive trappings.

On more than one occasion in the AWA and WWF, Ventura wore a t-shirt for Plato's Retreat, a New York swinger's club. Ventura has claimed he made an exploratory visit with his wife to the well-known 80s establishment and picked up the t-shirt to wear in front of fans as he knew it would stir up controversy.

In a 2008 interview with Howard Stern, real-life Ventura rival Hulk Hogan disputed this version of events and claimed that the future Governor frequently attended the notorious club to indulge in wife-swapping, as well as various drug taking exploits, allegations denied by Ventura. During his on-air revelations, Hogan name-checked Adonis into the mix. Specifically, Hogan recounted how the pair often smoked pot in Adonis' hotel room.

Whether one visit to the swinger's club or many, Ventura was certainly successful in stoking reactions from crowds geared for nothing but aggressive heterosexuality. The gay undertones of the East West Connection were limited compared to what Adrian Adonis later embodied, but fans routinely chanted the f-word gay slur towards the pair, for daring to wear such a thing as a feather boa. Adonis for his part only went as far as sunglasses and a fedora, but clearly felt the power that could come from 'antagonising' a crowd in such a way.

Fans were not the only ones sitting up and taking notice of the loud, brash bad guys taking the AWA by storm. Up until their respective runs in the AWA, both Franke and Ventura had been restricted to largely local coverage of their exploits, generally confined to the newspapers of whatever towns they were working.

Details of their activities in the Minnesota territory made good copy and both men snagged their first wrestling magazine cover stories in 1980 while members of the Connection, captured posing up a storm in multiple issues of *Major League Wrestling* magazine, the AWA's official programme.

From featuring prominently at the AWA's big Comiskey Park 'Superbowl' show in July 1980 in front of 12,000 fans (albeit with Jerry Valiant subbing in for the absent Ventura); or christening AWA interviewer Gene Okerlund with the "Mean Gene" moniker with which he would become synonymous, the Connection was all over the AWA.

Switched on to the benefits of publicity as the 1980s dawned, Adonis and Ventura befriended a young wannabe journalist backstage at AWA shows. It was a relationship that would sustain them both for the rest of Adonis' life, as Fumi Saito recalled:

> *"We first met in 1982, he was still in the AWA, I'd been living in Minnesota. Way back in the summer of 1979, I was a high school*

exchange student in Minnesota and I didn't go back to Japan right away, and I started going to college in Minnesota and I stayed another five years there. While I was there I started working for wrestling magazines in Japan. I wrote a letter to the editor, I was a 19-year-old kid, I told him I live in Minnesota, I can do this, I can do that, go to shows, take pictures, interview things, because I was a wrestling fan all my life.

"You've got to understand, the AWA was a veteran's heaven, Mad Dog, Crusher, Larry Hennig, Bockwinkel. Jesse Ventura and Adrian Adonis were young champions. When I went to Minneapolis for the first time in the summer of 1979, Jesse Ventura and Adonis were not a tag team yet, they were working the first-second match. Then formed a team, the famous East-West Connection. They became stars in the AWA.

"When I started, Ventura and Adonis were the first ones who would sit down and talk to me, very friendly. Verne Gagne had a complete kayfabe attitude, 'who is this kid?' They don't believe you, they think you're just a fan. They were about the only guys that were friendly and would talk to me. I was still not quite a journalist yet. They were very real, that's when you first find out in wrestling, bad guys are the actual good guys, and good guys are the not so good guys!"

The spotlight continued with some television coverage in July 1981 for Adonis and his colleagues from Minneapolis. Gagne negotiated a valuable spotlight for the AWA, technically its parent company the Minneapolis Boxing & Wrestling Club, in an episode of the popular long-running network talk show, *The Phil Donahue Show*. Gagne hoped the valuable attention would help convince network executives that pro wrestling, and more specifically the AWA, was a viable option for a high-profile airing.

The show featured in-ring action, questions from the audience, and most importantly from Gagne's perspective, the debut of his newest acquisition in the closing moments of the show, when Hulk Hogan sauntered to the ring, fresh from his 18-month jaunt in the rival WWF. Hogan joined Ventura for a pose down, with the Gagnes, AWA Champion Nick Bockwinkel, Adonis and Brunzell also sharing the ring with their host.

The episode was recorded in Minnesota with an audience drawn from both wrestling enthusiasts and non-fans, some of whom debated the merits of the pseudo-sport, as Donahue played his part as the suitably bemused host. In addition to losing an athletic exhibition match to Greg Gagne, Adonis took part in a Q&A session with members of the audience, fielding questions while he sat on a stool in the middle of the ring alongside Gagne, Judy Martin and Joyce Grable. In response to one non-believer, Adonis responded in character, typically scathingly, and gave some insight into how seriously he took his profession. He explained:

"Well first of all how would she know about athletic ability or injuries, after all your main injury is dropping the supper dish on your big toe. Listen, my shoulders are as wide as the World Trade Center in New York City, daddy, and it takes a lot of guts to get in there in the ring especially to be number one like I am. Now first of all, I have dislocated my shoulder I have broken my nose it looks like the Youngmann Expressway. I have scars on my forehead, I am not just another pretty face. I am a talented young man, and you have no business telling us that it's flashy."

As well as detailing his history of injuries, he also refuted suggestions from one audience member that the 'soft' ring made it easy to fall on:

"Well, there's canvas and that's it, and plywood, and let me tell you something my vertebras are out in my back and I wish it was foam rubber. Believe me it'd be a lot easier."

Away from the talk show circuit and back on more familiar territory, the East-West Connection became embroiled in a feud with long-term AWA babyface tag-team, Jim Brunzell and Greg Gagne, son of Verne. The older Gagne had paired Ventura with Adonis to take advantage of the muscleman's physique and mic skills without exposing him in the ring, and the combination worked well against the fan favourite team of Brunzell and Gagne.

In a 2008 shoot interview with RF Video, the younger Gagne remembered Adonis as *"a fabulous worker, among the best ever."* His father, co-hosting a 1999 AWA Legends retrospective dedicated to Adonis' memory joked:

"I guess they wrestled as good as they talked, at least one of the two wrestled very well I'm not gonna say which one! And of course [Ventura] was complemented by the ability of his tag team partner Adrian Adonis. I wrestled them also and they did win the world titles at one time and anybody that can do that has got to be very, very tough."

Adonis and Ventura dropped the tag belts to the athletic pair, somewhat unexpectedly on June 14, 1981, in Wisconsin after a near year-long reign. The switch, while built up in the traditional way with multiple matches beforehand, was Verne's way of taking the belts off the Connection when he caught wind that both men would soon be departing, intent on building on the higher profiles they had established.

For the final three months of 1981, Ventura and Adonis both undertook the unusual step of splitting their time between the rival promotions of the AWA and WWF, journeying back and forth from the northeast for monthly WWF tapings and working in Minnesota in between. In their final appearance for the AWA, on December 13, 1981, the one-time headliners lost to the jobber tag team of George

Gadaski and Kenny Jay. It was the final time that the East West Connection would wrestle as a team on AWA television.

Having his outgoing stars lose to two no-name wrestlers in their final appearance gave the Gagne some pleasure. It was also a way of not-so-subtlety telling any fans who saw them turn up in WWF shortly afterwards that these two men are not the stars they seemed – a futile effort to undermine their mystique as they went to work for a rival promotion.

The ending of the match was uncharacteristically chaotic for the AWA, as cheating by the heels led to a mass brawl, with officials and other wrestlers dispatched to break things up. Authority figure Wally Karbo, incensed by the dastardly Ventura and Adonis, announced mid-ring that the pair were 'through' with the AWA due to their actions - thus explaining their upcoming absence to fans.

Franke's final AWA appearance of 1981 ended his longest uninterrupted stay in any territory throughout his career, at just under two and a half years. The influence that the East West Connection had on other wrestlers who followed was notable and has been remembered across the industry, providing an entertaining counterpoint to Ventura's later political achievements.

Also notable is that two of the team's AWA appearances remain some of the only Adonis matches to feature on a WWE DVD releases (as part of '*The Spectacular Legacy of the AWA*,' 2006). Ventura would later return to the AWA and form a short-lived team with Japan's Masa Saito, the amusingly named Far East-West Connection.

Though Adonis and Ventura's in-ring relationship did not give way to a longstanding personal friendship, Ventura was made it clear that both men played a pivotal role in the other's career – though clearly not enough to merit Adonis' inclusion as a character in the hastily-created 1999 TV movie of Ventura's life.

Ventura has spoken in interviews about the pair's differing lifestyles outside the ring, and coming to feel like a babysitter for the Buffalo native, ensuring his tag partner navigated his way from arena to arena in spite of his night-time proclivities – a familiar story among many tandems of the era. That tension never dimmed Ventura's respect for Adonis, as he would often show by name-checking his former comrade years later.

He did so famously in his 1998 gubernatorial election victory speech, and also while working as a colour commentator for WCW at the *Halloween Havoc* 1992 pay-per-view:

> "*When I teamed up with Adrian Adonis, the East-West Connection, we didn't always see eye to eye outside the ring but we when we stepped*

inside the ring, we knew at that point it was business, and it's the business of winning."

At home the Frankes welcomed their first child, Angela, born in March 1980, two years into their marriage. With another mouth to feed, the time was right for Adrian Adonis to take to the biggest wrestling stage of them all. Finally, it was time for the boy from New York City was to light up the New York territory.

Chapter 9: New York, New York

"This man has all kinds of ability, you may not like his effeminate nature,

or some of the things he does in the ring, but he can put it on you."

- *Vince McMahon, 1981*

On October 13, 1981, Adrian Adonis and Jesse Ventura made their surprise debut appearances at a WWF television taping at Agricultural Hall in Allentown, Pennsylvania. Adonis worked two matches, the first of which aired on the Federation's *Championship Wrestling* show the following Saturday, the second for the following week. Ventura worked three times that night, and both men made the short trip to the WWF's other regular taping venue, the Hamburg Fieldhouse, the following evening to record three weeks' worth of WWF *All-Star Wrestling*.

Vince McMahon Senior, majority owner and booker of the popular northeast territory, employed the same tried and tested approach for both men which had worked successfully for him in the past. Splitting up the East West Connection, Adonis and Ventura were pushed as singles stars from the outset, with convincing wins over jobbers, promo time to explain their characters to a new and largely unfamiliar audience, and the same on-screen manager, "Classy" Freddie Blassie. Fans were in no doubt that these new arrivals meant business. Bob Backlund, reigning WWF heavyweight champion, recalled their arrival in his 2015 autobiography. He wrote:

> *"This was typical of how things worked in the office at the time. Every three of four months Vince Sr. would bring in a fresh group of new heels from the NWA territories, the AWA or Japan. He would have the [Madison Square] Garden dates in his book six to nine months in advance, and once he got a look at the new heels at the television tapings, he would determine how many title matches he wanted each to get at the Garden, figure out how to get the new heels over with the fans by putting some heat on them, and then build the cards around that in a never-ending effort to draw fan interest and sell tickets."*

In storyline, Adonis and Ventura were acknowledged by Blassie as incoming tag partners, with their new manager claiming he had split them into singles as part of a strategy to dethrone Backlund and claim the WWF title for his stable. With both men going after Backlund on different nights, he predicted, one would soften Backlund up, allowing the other of Blassie's charges to get the job done. For the next two months, the pair switched back and forth between the WWF and AWA while they finished up their dates for Verne Gagne, returning to the northeast for WWF TV tapings every three weeks.

Blassie looked back on a lengthy career in wrestling in his 2003 autobiography and had fond memories of his days managing Ventura and Adonis. He noted:

> *"I thought that Adonis was an excellent worker, and a nice, decent guy. He appreciated the role that I'd played in the business and acted very respectful towards me. It made me sad, later on, when he put on a tremendous amount of weight and was turned into "Adorable" Adrian Adonis...but even then, he remained one of the best bump takers in the business, twirling himself upside down and bouncing high while selling his opponent's moves. His death was one of wrestling's great tragedies.*

> *"Because Adrian was such a stellar bump man a lot of people said that he did all the work while Jesse's flamboyant personality drew the crowd. I'm not so sure about that. Adonis was pretty flamboyant himself."*

Their final WWF appearance of 1981 came at the December 8 and 9 tapings, during which Ventura got some ring time with Backlund in the form of a dark match, early preparation for their Madison Square Garden clashes to come in the new year. The Connection made a final AWA appearance on January 7, 1982, dropping a cage match to old foes the High Flyers – their first outing for Gagne since losing to jobbers Kenny Jay and George Gadaski on December 13. With that, the East West Connection was done with the AWA. With 1982 on the horizon, the biggest match of Adrian Adonis' career was right around the corner.

While a strong, sustained commitment from McMahon Senior was a great benefit for any new arrival hoping to become established as a convincing bad guy, Franke was well aware that he could not rely on the push from the office alone. Being placed high on the card, prepped to face the champion, and making small work of enhancement talent will only get you so far unless you bring your own personality into the proceedings, something Franke learned from his time touring the territory network over the previous seven years. He had earned this opportunity to headline the world's premier venue for professional wrestling, and he was determined to make it count.

As soon as he arrived in the WWF, Adonis debuted a new finishing manoeuvre with which he would become synonymous. The sleeper hold, while tame by modern wrestling standards, was built up as a devastating move as Adonis put one low-card talent after another 'to sleep' to win matches by effective submission with his opponent's 'out cold.' More closely associated by later WWF fans with "Million Dollar Man" Ted DiBiase, Adonis made the sleeper hold his own more than five years before DiBiase turned up in the Federation.

Just as memorable to many was the *name* of Adonis new finisher – *"Goodnight, Irene."* At a time when finishing moves, like the wrestlers who performed them, were not the flashy and extravagant events they would later become, fans were used to matches concluding with nothing more frivolous than a knee drop or a power slam. In a nod to the delight he took in confusing and confounding people, as well as his propensity for music and film, Franke named his hold after a little-known blues record. Much like the 'Go To Sleep' finisher employed decades later by KENTA and CM Punk, the name forgoes a more obvious description ('powerbomb,' 'superkick') and has some fun with the convention of naming a signature move.

Adonis continued to build his persona for the WWF crowd with his strong promo work, relishing the opportunity to shine on his own without Ventura hogging the microphone. A month after his arrival, on the November 14, 1981, episode of *WWF All-Star Wrestling*, he appeared with show co-host Pat Patterson for a pre-match interview, decked out in shades and leather jacket, personalised with the phrase "I [heart] Adonis." Asked by Patterson about his legitimate amateur wrestling background, Adonis embarked on a sprawling promo the likes of which doesn't exist in wrestling anymore:

> *"Let's just talk about the beginning of time, the beginning of a style, about a man that was moulded...I'm talking about a kid from birth that was left on a doorstep in Manhattan, that worked his way out of the gutter, Jack. Worked at the docks at 17 years old, and I'm talking about taking on people and I'm talking about knocking them down one-by-one.*

> *"And then I'm talking about going into big-time football and then I'm talking about the Junior Olympics. I'm talking about scholarships to ten major colleges, turned them down, you know why? Because the teachers were prejudiced, they didn't like my attitude. Can you imagine somebody not liking Adrian Adonis' attitude?"*

Adonis made the most of the valuable spotlight with his exhaustive, meandering speech, delivered with a passion that few could match then or now. As well as making the standard threats to Federation babyfaces Backlund, Tony Atlas, and 'Ricky' Martel, Adonis insulted Patterson, dismissed the societal contributions of truck drivers and schoolteachers, claimed to be in the Guinness Book of Records for "covering 60 sewer caps down in Manhattan in 11 seconds," referenced 70s cop show *Baretta*, and made multiple references to New York City – both the World Trade Center, and "the man that owns the clam stand at Mulberry and Hester." He bragged about his "soft and silky" Italian skin, gave a nod to his past with a $10,000 challenge to all comers, and still had space for O.J. Simpson, the Buffalo Bills, and Elliot Ness.

At one point he crowed: *"[They] say all the bad people are in the cemetery...Here's one right here daddy, in living colour."* The scattergun approach had the desired effect and fans rightly despised the sneering, sarcastic Adonis as he pouted in the leather jacket that would become his trademark.

Leather jackets were a small but crucial part of the look that first emerged when Adonis joined the WWF in 1981. Jackets and boots adorned with the insignia of the New York Yankees baseball team were a feature of Adonis' ring attire dating back to at least Portland two years prior, and he had experimented with a fedora in the AWA. When he made the jump to New York, Adonis realised he needed something to emphasise to this crowd, many of them actually from the big city that Adrian claimed to hail from, that he was one of them.

Following the example of the big screen tough guy template set by Marlon Brando in *The Wild One* and Peter Fonda in *Easy Rider*, film buff Adonis leaned on the biker/street brawler motif, partly inspired by his own teenage years, more than ever before. While simply claiming to be a New Yorker may have thrilled fans in Portland or Vancouver, moving into the Big Apple itself required Adonis to underline just how much of a New York City villain he really was.

The look was likely influenced by the rebellious 1950s 'greaser' sub-culture which was experiencing a revival in the form of hit film and TV characters like the T-birds in *Grease* (1978) and the Fonz in Happy Days (1974 onwards). It is possible Adonis was also conscious of the media hysteria around 1979's *The Warriors*, a movie about vicious New York street gangs, and was keen to leverage fans' nervousness to enhance his character.

A more direct lineage of Adonis' biker character might be traced to Dusty Rhodes. Similarly named after a baseball player, Rhodes was a charismatic talker whose dexterity in the ring belied his unathletic shape, who matched Superstar Graham in his wearing of extravagant garb in the late 1970s – often robes, but also biker caps and leather jackets. Interestingly, one of the hight points of Rhodes' early career was his tag team with Dick Murdoch as part of the Texas Outlaws. Murdoch would later win the WWF tag titles with Adonis.

In some interpretations a leather jacket is the ultimate sign of male masculinity; see James Dean in *Rebel Without a Cause*. Most men are not James Dean though and possess neither the confidence nor physique to pull off such a look. Adrian Adonis needed little work on his confidence and did even less on his physique. For many, another correlation was drawn from the showy leather garment; namely, homosexual undertones.

Some fans heard alarm bells simply because Adonis – like Ventura, Graham, Rhodes, and others – had the gall to depart from the traditional wrestler's outfit of plain black trunks into something so unmanly as lavish clothes. A more specific comparison at the time may have been drawn with Glenn Hughes, the original 'Leather Man' character within the Village People, which had a string of hits from 1977 onwards. The group's characters lampooned traditional masculine stereotypes and macho fantasies, something which would have a significant impact for anyone attempting to employ one of those fantasies in its original, two-dimensional nature, such as Adonis.

Indeed, some modern social media comments on Adonis' 1981 leather jacket get-up remark that he looks *"more gay"* than he did when playing the 'actual' gay character he would later take up. Fans in 1981 picked up on this, and more than one appearance of Adonis (and Ventura) in the WWF took place with screams of *"Adrian's a [f-word slur]"* in the background.

Someone else who paid close attention to Adonis' appearance was Vince McMahon Junior. The younger McMahon had been working for his father as a television announcer since the late 1960s. In 1980 he and his wife Linda formed Titan Sports, the parent company which he then used to purchase the WWF from his father and other shareholders in 1982. As far as fans were concerned the younger McMahon was simply a commentator, although his true power became apparent as he grew into a significant on-screen character in the 1990s.

In 1981 he was the company's lead commentator, well-placed to sell fans on characters, storylines, and directions that his father wanted the audience to pick up on. Hyperbolic and repetitive, McMahon could grate on fans' nerves, but he was great at his job of putting over the right wrestlers. As soon as he was in charge of the company, McMahon Junior – a recreational bodybuilder – set about normalising the presence of weightlifter physiques on WWF television in the tradition of Superstar Graham. From Ventura to Snuka to Ivan Putski and Tony Atlas, the northeast quickly became the area of the muscle-bound meathead. As far back as 1981, Adrian Adonis did not fit in.

It started off subtlety enough, during Adonis' first match on October 24, 1981, as he quickly put away Steve King. McMahon remarked: "He's a cocky son of a gun. Can't say too much for at least the looks of his body but he seems to be able to do a great deal with what he has."

Babyface 'straight-man' commentators feigning dismay at the bad guy is nothing new in wrestling, but McMahon used his seat at the announce desk to make it clear what he thought of Adonis' "peculiar-shaped body," and "flabby mid-section," in later appearances.

McMahon's apparent preoccupation with Adonis' unspectacular – but far from obese at this stage – physique in 1981 continued throughout his first run with the company, even into his most high-profile match. Throughout his own career, it became no secret that McMahon placed a substantial premium on muscular physiques. While Adonis disrobed to prepare to face WWF Champion Backlund at Madison Square Garden, McMahon made the following observations, ostensibly to pile heel heat on the challenger:

> *"A good look at the body, the physique, of Adrian Adonis. There is no doubt some fat about the mid-section of Adonis, a very peculiar-shaped physique. But as you will see momentarily Mr Adonis is in a class all by himself."*

During other matches, McMahon Junior employed language similar to that which he later used when describing Dustin Rhodes' Goldust character, decrying his "most unusual personality," this "eccentric individual," with his "very peculiar style."

On November 14, 1981, perhaps a way of acknowledging the loud homophobic chants from the crowd to the audience at home, Junior noted: "You may not like his effeminate nature, or some of the things he does in the ring, but he can put it on you." Junior never forgot the chants that night. More than four years later, he would facilitate Adonis returning to that 'effeminate nature' like never before.

The younger McMahon did Adonis and Ventura much good too, opening doors to mainstream media attention for his dad's colourful new headliners. While with the WWF, the pair appeared in an extended feature within the pages of the May 24, 1982, edition of *People Magazine*, garnering national attention that most wrestlers could only dream of at the time.

The article was written by Jim Jerome, a rock station DJ and frequent writer for the prestigious magazine, generally on culture and music. He would later go on to ghost-write autobiographies for Kathie Lee Gifford, the Mamas and Papas' John Phillips, Marilu Henner, and others. The pairing of Jerome and the East West Connection made sense, with Ventura's rock star aura and served as something of a precursor to the famed 'rock and wrestling' era, which saw Hulk Hogan appear on the cover of *Sports Illustrated* two years later on his way to becoming an international celebrity.

The article was released days before Hogan's well received appearance in *Rocky III*. While Ventura did kayfabe the inevitable 'is it fake' question, the article included the real names and backgrounds of Adonis and Ventura, a rarity at the time for anyone within the wrestling industry. About Adonis, readers were told:

> *"Adonis' battles began early in life. Born on Manhattan's Lower East Side, he was raised in the Buffalo area by his adoptive parents, Kenneth and Kay Franke. The Golden Boy, then known as Keith Franke, hated schoolwork, had the grades to prove it, and engaged in gang fights every day after school.*

"Giving up on school during his senior year, he played semipro football in Canada before setting off to learn his trade as a wrestler. For several months the migrant muscleman offered $5,000 to anyone in arenas in Texas who could pin him in under 10 minutes. He never lost. His pursuit of glory finally took him to Portland, Oregano, where he met the equally hungry Ventura."

Readers received some insight into Adonis' opinions of wrestling's popularity *("Money's tight," he says with a shrug. "People need to take out their frustrations. The American people are sickos who love violence and the sight of blood"),* and the impact it has had on him as a person, both physically and mentally *("five nose breaks, battered vertebrae and torn knee cartilage. "One thing is sick with me," he concedes. "I'm starting to squeeze my stitches. I'm beginning to enjoy the pain.")*

Elsewhere in the article it was revealed that the partners were living close to each other at the time in southern Connecticut, convenient for the WWF circuit, but the Frankes had settled with their young daughter in Bea's native Bakersfield. Adonis' interests were listed as rock music and the violent films he'd catch on cable TV – quite evident from the references littering his promos. Ventura even in 1982 was keen to make clear the two were very different personalities away from the ring:

"Each is married, has a young child, and works out daily in a local gym. But East and West rarely connect socially. 'We have our ups and downs,' says Jesse. 'And different lifestyles.' Besides, says Adrian, 'We see enough of each other on the tour.'"

On the question of what they would do without wrestling, Adonis' answer is equally eery *("If I left the contact of the game, I'd end up a maniac on the street or in a bar.")*

The first meeting of Adrian Adonis and Bob Backlund took place at Madison Square Garden on January 18, 1982, broadcast on the MSG Network, in front of 18,301 fans, some way short of a sell-out. Adonis won by referee's decision due to excessive blood loss from Backlund, defeating the WWF champion after almost 31 minutes of gruelling action.

While the title did not change hands, it capped a remarkable rise for the young man from Buffalo who made his debut in 1974. Surely the apex of his career, and one of the highlights of Backlund's often hum-drum title reign, the young world champion was grateful to be able to work with someone who could make him look as good as Adonis did.

"Although Adrian and I had not spent any time in the ring together before, something just clicked with the two of us. Adrian was a very skilled worker who could get up and down really well back then. He was

flexible and acrobatic, with a good knowledge of chain wrestling, and he was a bump machine...Vince Sr knew right away that he had something in Adonis, and when he brought us together for our pre-match discussion, he had a sold out house waiting for the match. Accordingly, Vince Sr called for a blood stoppage – and asked me to put over the sleeper as convincingly as possible to sell the possibility that Adonis could take the title in the rematch."

Prior to their encounter at the Garden, Adonis cut a promo on Backlund on a January 1982 episode of *WWF All-Star Wrestling*. Adonis was interviewed at ringside by Pat Patterson, after making short work of Barry Hart. Again, he gave a baffling yet enthralling sermon. Perhaps on the assumption that a certain Mr Gagne might be watching, Adonis even found space to bash Minnesota, hometown of Bob Backlund:

"The man comes from milk and cookie land, Minnesota. They only got stagecoaches there, they have no electricity, just a little generator in the backyard. They've never seen no crime, they've never seen any street fights, they've never seen people laying on the docks begging for a buck because they don't have a cent to their name.

"Well Mr Backlund we come from two different backgrounds, and the background that always prevails is the most hungriest and the most meanest, and the most terrifying. Terrifying, brag, trash, vulgarity, that's where I come from daddy, and I made a name for myself through that.

"And violence - That's a banquet from which I feed, daddy"

Despite the backing of McMahon Senior, the thrilling Garden debut, and the strong working relationship he quickly formed with Backlund, a longer-term marriage was not to be. The rematch, a Texas Death Match refereed by Ivan Putski, took place on February 15, 1982, at MSG with Backlund victorious in an enthralling match to the delight of a red-hot crowd.

There were rave reviews there would be no third, blow-off match between Backlund and Adonis at the Garden in the spring of 1982, but they did face each other in big markets such as Boston and Philadelphia, as well as a scintillating Lumberjack match in Landover on March 28. Dave Meltzer noted:

"In Landover, Maryland – that was one of the best matches of Backlund's career, that match was fantastic. Adrian in that run with Backlund he looked really, really good. In the northeast territory it was really about bodies and the one negative about Adrian was he didn't have a good body. It wasn't about work because he was a fantastic worker. People don't really remember Bob Backlund and Adrian Adonis but in the ring,

that was probably, I think that might have been the best Backlund match he had in his whole run, the Adrian Adonis match in Landover."

Backlund moved on to face Ventura at the Garden, while Adonis slipped down the card to face Intercontinental Champion Pedro Morales on March 14. The following month he beat jobber Pete Sanchez, which would be his only clean victory at the Garden during this stay with WWF, albeit against lowly opposition.

Once tangling with Backlund was done, Adonis and Ventura had essentially served their purpose and were thrown back together as a tag team for the remaining months of their stay in the northeast. While largely exclusive to the WWF during this period, they did appear on one Maple Leaf Wrestling card, defeating Tony Parisi and Dominic Denucci on January 17, 1982, in their sole match in the area as a team.

The following month they made an even more unexpected appearance for Mid Atlantic Championship Wrestling. Returning to Adonis' old stomping ground in the Carolinas for one night only on February 7, the East West Connection wrestled twice in a one-night tournament, losing to eventual finalists Ray Stevens and Pat Patterson. Adonis and Ventura returned to Maple Leaf Gardens as singles to partake in the one-night $27,000 Maple Leaf Cadillac tournament, with Ventura losing to Jimmy Valiant in the final, and Adonis falling to Ricky Steamboat in the first round.

As in the AWA, fans and co-workers alike were impressed with the team of Adonis and Ventura, and they are often misremembered as former WWF tag team champions, an accolade Adonis did not achieve until teaming with Dick Murdoch. Rick Martel, a young babyface tag champion in the Federation in 1981, recalled his impressions of the pair in a 2014 interview:

> *"Adrian was amazing. You look at his body and say, you know, but the way he moved and everything. And Adrian liked to have that personality to shock people, the way he would talk and the way he would do things, he was somebody who would try to shock you by doing different things, he had that personality. You'd say how can you do that, and he used to get off on it. So, in the ring when he and Jesse teamed up it was great, they really complemented each other, and I could've predicted these guys' success right off the bat."*

The next Garden show on June 5, 1982, saw the sole appearance of the East West Connection in action at the world's most famous arena, losing in tag team action to the Strongbow brothers. Interestingly, Adonis put his foot on the ropes during the pinfall, a sign of his reluctance to take the fall, poor ring etiquette which cropped up again later in his career when unhappy with a finish.

109

The match was also the final ever appearance of the East West Connection, as both men finished up eight-month stays with the WWF and went their separate ways. While Ventura returned the following month to the AWA, Adonis embarked on the first of several tours of New Japan Pro Wrestling. Adonis and Ventura crossed paths again, in the WWF circa 1985-86 when colour commentator Ventura often acknowledged his history with the "Adorable One." For now, their stay with the Federation was over. The East-West Connection was history.

Adonis undertook his first three-week tour of Japan in July and August 1982 for the Summer Fight Series II, alongside Murdoch, Greg Valentine, Rick McGraw, Len Denton, and young Calgary-based grapplers Bret Hart and Dynamite Kid. Enjoying his relative freedom after nearly three years tied to the WWF and AWA, Adonis also made a brief return to Los Angeles for an NWA Hollywood card promoted by Mike LeBell.

On August 6, 1982, a day after they had both appeared in Japan, Adonis pinned McGraw while revisiting another old favourite, the $5,000 challenge. The card also featured Backlund, Valentine, and former tag partner Black Gordman, but is more notable for being the first and only time Adonis ever worked the same bill as "Exotic" Adrian Street. The ailing territory was eking out an existence due to its vague connection with the WWF, the flyer for the event noting an agreement with promoter Vince McMahon to air Madison Square Garden matches in the area.

Adonis also returned to the AWA for a three-month solo run between August 26 and November 7, 1982, providing fodder for the rising babyface sensation Hulk Hogan, red hot after his appearance in the summer blockbuster, *Rocky III*. In one newspaper clipping Hogan picked up the theme from McMahon's WWF commentary earlier in the year, teasing his upcoming opponent as "pudgy" and questioning his sexuality, something he did far more of when they were paired together for a WWF house show run in 1986. In reality, Hogan and Adonis became firm friends during their time in the AWA and New Japan.

During the second of his three AWA tenures Adonis tangled with aging stars Larry Hennig and Baron von Raschke and shared a ring with Andre the Giant in several battle royals. Andre, Hogan, Adonis and several others formed the foreign contingent for another New Japan tour, in November and December 1982, competing in the Madison Square Garden Tag League.

The side of the world Franke was working on was not the only thing changing. A huge shift in the wrestling landscape was afoot by 1982. Vince McMahon Junior had purchased the WWF from his ailing father and journalist Dave Meltzer launched the *Wrestling Observer* newsletter, both moves which would impact and influence Franke. The *Observer* was a big supporter of Adrian Adonis in its early months, naming him its Most Improved Wrestler of 1981, and Most Underrated of 1982, with more praise to follow.

December 26, 1982, saw the closure of NWA Hollywood, just a year after the end of Big Time Wrestling in San Francisco. The Amarillo territory was likewise out of business. In Portland, long-time Portland announcer Frank Bonnema died at just 49 years old. Everywhere he looked, fragments of Franke's wrestling past were disappearing rapidly as a new wave emerged.

Chapter 10: Southwest Championship Wrestling

"Adonis is here to stay, in the big state of Texas.

"At least they think they're big down here."

- *Adrian Adonis, 1983*

Southwest Championship Wrestling (SCW) was formed in 1978 by Joe Blanchard, a wrestler and former professional football player who actually did spend time in the professional Canadian Football League (unlike Keith Franke, as some rumours would have you believe).

Blanchard found his biggest success in the squared circle in Hawaii and Texas, retiring in San Antonio after a 25-year career in the ring, and set up his promotion in the same town. For the first few years of its life, SCW was a standard wrestling territory for the era, showcasing the high-energy, violent Texas style that fans in the region were used to, building on working relationships with the AWA and Paul Boesch's Houston office.

Unlike most territories of the time, Southwest never became a member of the NWA, which made it barely conceivable to fans and non-fans alike when the group snared a national television slot in the form of a deal with the fledging USA Network.

On December 5, 1982, Southwest Championship Wrestling began airing at 11am on Sundays, becoming only the second wrestling promotion with a nationally televised show following Georgia Championship Wrestling on TBS. The deal struck by Blanchard with USA Network president Kay Koplovitz was remarkable for its boldness, even if it did call for payments from the promotion to the station of between $3,000 and $7,000 per week.

Months earlier the USA Network had been rebranded and started operating a 24-hour schedule, filling its timeslots with talk shows, children's cartoons, old movies, and cheap sports coverage – such as wrestling. The show started strongly and did well in syndication across the country. The group boasted a number of stars familiar to Texas crowds, including Gino Hernandez, Bob Sweetan, and the promoter's son Tully Blanchard.

Jumping aboard within weeks of the first show airing on USA, Adrian Adonis relished the chance to continue building the profile he had enhanced so effectively in New York. Tully Blanchard recalled:

"My dad promoted San Antonio, Corpus Christi, the Rio Grande Valley, and Austin, and in conjunction with the Dallas office and then as we grew, we had our own office and we ended up having our own territory, our own TV show, we were the first wrestling show on the USA cable network and Adrian was our first world champion.

"We got a lot of good people because my dad paid very well so people liked to work for him and Wahoo McDaniel was our first booker and we had a lot of good talent that worked hard every night because everybody worked hard and it was a team thing and Adrian came down and worked. He was working for Verne Gagne at the time and came in and out for us."

After spending Christmas Day at home with Bea and Angela, Franke debuted for Blanchard's group at a television taping on December 29, 1982, defeating his old acquaintance, Terry Daniels. Three days later the company held a one-night, 16-man tournament for the vacant Southwest Heavyweight title, the promotion's premier singles belt at the time. Doing its best to pull in some notable names, SCW roped in Jerry Lawler, Baron von Raschke and Mike Graham from Memphis, Minnesota and Florida, respectively.

Despite this, the event, as with the promotion in general, was short on star power for a national level. Adonis put in a good showing, going over Steve Olsonoski and Ricky Morton before succumbing in the semi-final to Bob Sweetan, who himself lost in the final to Tully Blanchard. Adonis formed a short-lived tag-team with Blanchard and the two waged war against fan favourite Sweetan for the first few months of 1983.

Keeping his options open, Adonis continued to tour New Japan, spending most of March competing in the NJPW Big Fight Series tag league, teaming with future WWF and AWA ally Bob Orton Jr for the first time. A hectic period followed as Adonis returned to the States in late March and promptly relieved Sweetan of the Southwest title on April 15, 1983 in Austin.

The company had bigger plans for Adonis which meant his first title reign in the Southwest territory was a brief one, and he dropped the belt back to Sweetan five weeks later. He did still find time to pop up on a pair of WWF cards in Los Angeles and San Diego on April 23 and 24. The WWF was keen to revive Southern California as a viable market having moved in after the collapse of Mike LeBell's territory the previous year. The roster for the two nights in April read like a veritable Adrian Adonis appreciation night, featuring old Portland pals such as Buddy Rose and Steve Pardee, ex tag partner Black Gordman, and even Mil Mascaras.

The occasional appearances in Southern California followed the Frankes relocation to Bea's native Bakersfield. With Keith constantly on the road as Bea raised young Angela the couple agreed it would be easiest on all concerned if she moved back to Bakersfield to be with her family, especially with a two-year-old. Mother and daughter settled in Bea's hometown in 1982, with grandparents, uncles, aunts, cousins, on hand to support them while Adonis roamed the ring.

In addition to popping up for local WWF cards in the area when time allowed, Adonis made a habit of visiting backstage at other local shows. One of these was promoter Antone "Ripper" Leone's Western States Alliance, a short-lived 'outlaw' promotion that ran shows outside the auspices of the National Wrestling Alliance. According to wrestler Tom Hankins, Adonis often visited the dressing room on Saturday nights when Leone was running shows in Bakersfield if he was in town, although he never worked for the promotion.

Interestingly, Bakersfield in the early 1980s was briefly home to one of Adonis' favourites, "Dr" Jerry Graham. The colourful Graham had mostly retired from the industry after a lengthy career but kept his hand in as a heel commentator for Leone's show, keeping his acidic sense of humour on full display. No doubt Adonis and Graham crossed paths during this time, ahead of Adonis paying unwitting tribute to the platinum-haired, large-framed Graham years later in the WWF.

The bed-hopping antics of spring 1983 hint at Adonis lacking faith in Joe Blanchard's bold move to national television. It is possible he was already seeking an out by reconnecting with the WWF and AWA and testing the waters for a return. Adonis' stock was higher than ever, largely thanks to his escapades with Bob Backlund.

The *Wrestling Observer* was particularly effusive in its praise of the "superb" Adonis's all-round work during this period, featuring him as its cover star in April 1983 and noting the following month that he *"continues to be among the world's elite."* In the revered newsletter's July 1983 summer ratings for wrestlers across all territories across the globe, Adonis was ranked third behind only Flair and Brody (*"more wrestling ability than any big man – deceptive agility."*)

The following month Blanchard attempted to entice Adonis to stick with San Antonio by promising him the one thing neither the WWF or AWA were ever likely to give him – a run with the company's very own world heavyweight title. To capitalise on the national exposure the group was receiving via the USA Network, Blanchard decided to demote the Southern title, with its unhelpful regional connotations, and create a new and 'undisputed' world heavyweight title for the promotion, hoping this would enhance the image of SCW and whoever held it.

To add even more prestige, the announcement was made by on-screen commissioner and legitimate all-time wrestling icon Lou Thesz on March 27, 1983. In addition to the new title belt, Thesz announced, the winner of the upcoming tournament would be personally awarded by Thesz his original NWA heavyweight title which dated back to 1938, albeit only as a symbolic 'bonus' prize. As Tully Blanchard recalled, it was his father's relationship with the legendary NWA champion that brought Thesz into the proceedings. He said:

> *"My dad had a very good relationship with Lou Thesz and I did also, and Lou was a great choice to be there, there was no greater champion than Lou Thesz in the NWA and he was just a great guy."*

The real belt which would be worn to the ring and represent the championship was a replica of the NWA's famed 'domed globe' belt with the 'National Wrestling Alliance' wording removed. This version of the strap had previously been created by Terry Funk as a replica for himself when he won the NWA title and had been used in an angle with Dick Slater in Jim Crockett Promotions in the late 1970s. With trademark infringement almost unheard of in wrestling in 1983, SCW happily passed off a counterfeit version of the NWA's belt for its big tournament. Thesz's belt has a storied history of its own and was later awarded to Nobuhiko Takada in Japanese shoot-fighting promotion UWFI in 1993.

SCW claimed its title to be "undisputed" though it was nothing of the sort. With national wrestling titles contested by the WWF, NWA and AWA, and others further abroad, the pronouncement was just another promoter's trick to entice people into thinking the product was a bigger deal than it truly was. The group sent letters to the big three organisations inviting their champions to participate in the tournament, which they proudly displayed copies of on their weekly television show.

Of course, none of the opposition groups responded and Blanchard used that as justification for calling his new world title "undisputed." After downing Sweetan, Wahoo McDaniel and finally Bob Orton Jr in a one-night tournament for the new belt on May 21, 1983 (24 hours after dropping the Southern title), Adonis called out the opposing champions by name in a memorable promo:

> *"Now a lot of people say, 'Adrian are you the undisputed champion?' Well, I'd say so. I understand that there was a lot of invitations sent out, Mr [Nick] Bockwinkel, Mr Bob Backlund, who I have great respect for, a very talented individual, and also Mr Ric Flair, Woo! Woo!*

> *"And also, that night a little bit of history came down, a lot of history came down. Mr Lou Thesz, who was the undisputed champion at one time, gave me his belt. Well, I guess, I guess everybody had their chance, some showed up, and some didn't. But ladies and gentlemen that proves*

that I am the man, that I am a single - that I stand by myself as the undisputed world champion."

Finally, after nine years in the business, taking in almost a dozen territories and headlining Madison Square Garden along the way, Keith Franke was a world heavyweight champion – of sorts. Perhaps the reign comes with an asterisk against it, given that it was for a small promotion with a newly created title which did not last, but maybe it does not matter.

Adonis celebrated with a night on the town. He was joined in his festivities in downtown Houston by Tully Blanchard, Abdullah the Butcher, who also wrestled on the card that night, and the legendary Lou Thesz, in what must have been a personal highlight to be toasted by one of the all-time legends of the business. Wrestling journalist Dave Meltzer attended the show in person and recalled speaking to Thesz about Adonis:

> *"I was at the world title tournament and he had a good match with Orton, he was outstanding that night. When they decided to go with a guy and he was an interesting pick but he was the best one. And Thesz really liked him too because I was there with Thesz. I don't know what [Adonis'] background was but it was always said he was a good amateur."*

The tournament final itself was a bruising 15-minute affair, as Orton and Adonis both did everything they could to get the new title over and deliver a match worthy of the great Lou Thesz, looking on at ringside. The encounter was included years later on a DVD box set entitled '*Wrestling Gold*,' a 2000 production that compiled various gems from the territory days. Meltzer and fellow wrestling historian Jim Cornette recorded original shoot commentary for each match. During his voiceover, Cornette made a number of observations of Adonis in general:

> *"[Adonis and Orton] both had reputations with the wrestlers in the locker room across the industry as two of the finest technicians in the game. When they got the chance to lock up not only were the fans paying attention, the eyes of the wrestling world were on this match.*

> *"You can judge for yourself – the fact is this guy could do things that he had not only no business doing at a guy at his size but that were incredible, that were phenomenal. And Adrian Adonis both as a psychologist in the ring and an athlete in the ring he was just phenomenal.*

> *"Of course, Adonis had been a life-long wrestling fan and that just shows the value of being a fan of this business. Nobody wants to have a bad match in front of Lou Thesz. He's the man who basically spearheaded this business. The greatest wrestler of modern times.*

"Jokes were made about Adonis and he didn't deserve them. This guy – what a tremendous performer and a hard worker. Tell me where he can get that kind of stamina at that bodyweight and that conditioning. He's a physical marvel. As you can see Orton is breathing just as hard if not harder than Adrian Adonis."

Meltzer, for his part, noted that Terry Funk was expected to win the tournament given he was the biggest name announced to take part. Instead, that honour would fall to Adonis, who was *"almost in this period of time considered close to the level of Ric Flair,"* according to the editor of the Wrestling Observer.

Not long after, Adonis delivered a blistering promo in front of announcer Steve Stack (or "Jack Stack," as Adonis often called him in much the same way the East West Connection renamed Gene Okerlund). Similar to the challenges made to the champions of other wrestling groups, Adonis took the opportunity to issue another unsolicited ultimatum which would go unanswered, this time to heavyweight boxing champion Larry Holmes. Sadly for Adonis, he in fact issued the challenge to NFL player Ernie Holmes, who likewise never took up the offer. He bragged:

"I challenge Ernie Holmes, the heavyweight boxer of the world to put his belt on the line against me. Anyplace, anytime. It could be June 18 in St Louis, it could be the Summit in Houston, wherever, I don't care where it is. It could be in Central Park in front of every violent criminal in town. I want to make it right now as the baddest person in the world. Now if I have all those titles, I am going to be history, I am going to be a bigger name than Lou Thesz. I am going to have a bigger name than Buddy Rogers, I am going to have a bigger name than Strangler Lewis.

"I am going to be the man, and may the Great Gama roll over in his grave, Jack. Because I'm telling you, I deserve it, I came from the gutter, I rose up, and I took the bull by the horns, and I brought him down. No brag, just fact, Jack, and plus that I am good looking. Remember this folks: they should've stopped me at Houston because I'm just like Hitler, I'm moving on from Munich. And remember, you spell wrestling A-D-O-N-I-S. Take it to the bank, you're gonna get the highest interest in town."

The Hitler reference, jarring in a modern context, bludgeons a line from 1972 movie *The Godfather ("You know you got to stop them at the beginning, like they should have stopped Hitler at Munich")* which Adonis was fond of reusing in promos over the years. With his visceral, volatile delivery, Adonis could convince even the most hard-nosed non-believer that Southwest was the real deal, wrestling wasn't fake, and he was here to stay in San Antonio. He wasn't, of course.

The tournament itself could not be considered much of a success, despite Blanchard's best efforts to hype it up as much as possible. As noted in the Observer's end of year review, local wrestling followers were not convinced:

> "[The tournament] drew 1,700 fans as the local fans were apparently turned off by Blanchard and company's extravagant claims about the tourney and refused to turn their back over then-popular promoter Paul Boesch."

It did not get much better for the company from there. The very next night, Southwest Championship Wrestling debuted in Fort Worth, home territory of the legendary Von Erich wrestling clan, and struggled to pull in even a fraction of the audience that had turned out for the title tournament. The Observer noted:

> "Southwest's first foray into the heart of Von Erich territory with a line-up that included Adrian Adonis vs Terry Funk, Gino Hernandez vs Tully Blanchard in a cage and Bob Sweetan vs Bob Orton drew only 300 fans. Southwest's next two shows in the [Dallas] Metroplex did almost as well, pulling in 125 and 31 respectively."

Meltzer provided a logical reason for this in his commentary on the Wrestling Gold DVD. Simply put, Blanchard's outlaw outfit was no match for the bigger, better established Texas territory of the Von Erichs. He remarked:

> "Southwest was a big 'blood-and-guts' territory and they could not compete with the production values and the rockstars of the Von Erichs, and Ric Flair coming into town."

Nevertheless, Adonis' promo work developed a harder edge during his second stay in Texas. He had been convincing behind the microphone since his time in Portland. Now misanthropic tendencies started to emerge in his promos, his general disdain for humanity and desire to shock people for the sake of it became very clear.

For Adonis, he straddled a line between bizarre, meandering and menacing in his vocal delivery which would differ, seemingly, dependant on his mood. On his day, he could be both amusing and interesting, as in this snippet shortly after relinquishing the Southwest world title around September 1983:

> "I'm gonna tell you something right now ladies and gentlemen, these promoters, these 9-to-5'ers, these guys with the wingtips and the clamdiggers, they don't like me. I don't go to church on Sunday - big deal! But I listen to Jimmy Swaggart. Big deal I believe in the National Enquirer, it is the gospel, Jack."

Bizarre nonsense for sure, but just penetrable enough that the audience could grasp his point. If Adonis is this unhinged behind a microphone, fans may have asked themselves, what would he be like in the ring? Adonis was counting on that air of intrigue and invitation while legitimately distancing himself from the fans.

During his months in Texas Adonis treated fans to a cornucopia of pop culture references he picked up from his love of music and late night cable TV; President Truman, the Manhattan Transfer's 1981 cover of "The Boy from New York City," Dallas villain J.R. Ewing, *M.A.S.H.*, Dirty Harry movie *Magnum Force*, blues singer Tom Waits, 60s game show *Video Village*, and Bertie Higgins' "Key Largo", which references the Humphrey Bogart film of the same name, all featured in his colourful soliloquies while in SCW.

He was also fond of emphasising the Big Apple gimmick wherever he could, offering to take to the streets of New York against challengers, from Central Park to Jackson Heights, to the corner of "42nd and 7th."

In a promo on May 29, 1983, after winning the title Adonis was sure to make a renewed challenge to Flair, again mocking his trademark "woo!" catchphrase. While setting up his actual match, an altogether less exciting clash with Bob Sweetan, Adonis rambled:

> *"Hey daddy, [I] buried a lot of people. Remember Crazy Larry, the baddest man in town? Crazy Larry went to sleep, right on the Hudson River. Crazy Larry goes and gets coffee, but he forgets the cream and sugar. What good is he? A mental midget, yes sir."*

His empty-arena promo, largely ad-libbed as was the style at the time, featured a similarly curious proclamation: *"I lost a home in California, floating in the ocean but hey, it's only paper that's all it is man, we come in with nothing and we leave with nothing."*

In the same speech a suddenly more lucid Adonis addressed Ivan Putski who was also now in the Southwest territory. Referencing the "Polish Power" acting as referee for the second Backlund MSG match, he called Putski *"a man that cost me a world title in New York,"* bemoaning the missed opportunity at the WWF belt – or, as he called it, the "granddaddy" title.

When not busy shoe-horning easter eggs into his verbiage, Adonis could be both amusing (ingratiating himself to local fans in January by refer to the town as "Goat-whooper City" and "Downtown, Redneck") and memorable ("Violence, it's a banquet on which I feed on.") He even borrowed a page on at least one occasion from Graham and Ventura, bragging about his "python-like arms," a line which would gain greater fame associated with Hulk Hogan.

Using Southwest as a training ground to develop a more unpredictable interview style – likely doing so in a drug-induced state – was not the only thing Adonis picked up in the region. While teaming with Tully Blanchard he came into contact with a young Bert Prentice.

A relative rookie in the wrestling business in 1983, Prentice went on to work for several years in a number of roles in wrestling as both a promoter and on-screen manager, making a name for himself in Memphis and later as a host for TNA in the 2000s. At the start of his career in Southwest he spent several years as Christopher Love, an effeminate, ostensibly gay "panic" character undoubtedly lifting much of the style of Adrian Street, with less of the panache.

Adonis was in close proximity with Love via their shared associations with Blanchard, who had Love as his on-screen manager while tagging with Adonis. The future 'Adorable One' no doubt picked up on the hatred the tough Texan crowds had for Love and may have even drawn a correlation between those thrown at Love and the anti-gay chants he had already received earlier in his career for simply wearing leather jackets. Did Adonis see in Love a chance to harness what was already coming his way, for his own ends?

On June 13, 1983, Blanchard faced Sweetan for the Southwest heavyweight title. Adonis (world champion at the time) joined Steve Stack on commentary for the match and heard loud and clear when Stack questioned the sexuality of Christopher Love at ringside.

When Blanchard successfully wrested the title from Sweetan, he joined the new champion and Love in the ring for the celebrations, but not before showing yet another string to his bow with his accomplished and insightful performance at the announce desk. An unexpectedly literate and clear colour commentator, Adonis' love for professional wrestling shone through.

Adonis was adept playing the heel commentator role that Roddy Piper perfected in Georgia and Ventura revolutionised in the WWF. Throughout the match Adonis obviously favoured Blanchard but was savvy enough to give Sweetan his credit where necessary, putting both men over, and explained the psychology on show to advance the storyline for the benefit of those at home.

As the summer approached, Adonis once again got itchy feet. He was gone from Southwest almost as soon as they handed him their new, theoretically most prestigious title. Despite promoting their champion with his own t-shirt, Southwest regularly had to allow for several of its stars, including Adonis, to wander elsewhere. All of July and the start of August were again spent in Japan for Adonis, teaming with Murdoch on a trip which also included Brian Blair, Paul Orndorff, and the British pair of Dave Finlay and Pete Roberts.

Adonis returned to Southwest Championship Wrestling only briefly after his lengthy tours of Japan, effectively only doing so to drop the title and move on. He did this in a match with future tag partner Dick Murdoch on a San Antonio card which took place on August 20, 1983. The Wrestling Observer wrote several months later:

> *"Dick Murdoch pinned Adrian Adonis on a flop of an outdoor card which drew 800 in a match where the Southwest version of the World Title was declared vacant because Murdoch hadn't signed for the match. Adonis promptly left the area and mercifully the title was done away with."*

The belt was in fact handed to Scott Casey, with fans fed the story that Casey had beaten Adonis in an un-filmed match in St Louis in August. In truth no such match took place, with Joe Blanchard opting for a "phantom" title change to get the belt back from Adonis, who had left the territory.

Adonis did acknowledge dropping the belt in a promo for St Louis television in September, although he made it clear he was stripped, making no mention of a match with Casey. He told Steve Stack:

> *"Stripped, they take it away from me right, for what? I don't know. Did I get beat? No, I didn't, no."*

Adonis wrestled two more spot shows for the WWF in California, on August 28 and 29, 1983, proof once again that both sides were keen to keep the lines of communication open after his departure the previous summer. After returning from Japan Adonis also wrestled a handful of times in the famed St Louis territory, by this point another fading icon of wrestling's past. The area played host to a civil war of sorts, which Adonis a minor player.

In 1982, long-time St Louis promoter Sam Muchnick retired and sold the St Louis Wrestling Club to his Kansas City counterpart Bob Geigel. Muchnick's right-hand man and mentee Larry Matysik initially worked with Geigel's crew but by February 1983 split away. Matysik started his own independent promotion, drawing fans away from the traditional St Louis group with him. The NWA had a long-time association with Geigel and refused to recognise Matysik's upstart group, so he instead created an informal partnership with Southwest.

Matysik's St Louis group went so far as to (briefly) recognise Adonis as its own undisputed world champion, in much the same way that NWA member promotions all recognised the same NWA world champion. Adonis wrestled a few times for Matysik in St Louis during August and September, including one notable tag match in which he teamed with Nicolai Volkoff against Jerry Oates and his old Amarillo foe, Bruiser Brody – the second and last time the two men ever worked together.

Blanchard senior had more important things to worry about for his promotion. Southwest was beset by financial difficulties. With Blanchard regularly missing payments to USA, and the network dissatisfied with what it viewed as excessive violence on some shows (including a particularly bloody battle between Tully Blanchard and Eric Embry in June 1983), Southwest's show on the USA Network was cancelled in August. Having only lasted eight months, the group was replaced by Vince McMahon Junior's expanding WWF the following month. Tully Blanchard reflected:

> "[Joe Blanchard] was a bit of a visionary, unfortunately we jumped before anybody else would like to jump and we didn't have enough money personally to make it work and, so we were paying them $7,000 dollars a week to be on the network and that was before television was the product, and so we owed them a lot of money and Vince paid it, and he got the TV time."

As well as cementing the WWF's relationship with USA Network, 1983 was an important year for Vince McMahon Junior as he worked to attain the breakthrough that would come his way the following year. In addition to formally withdrawing the WWF from the National Wrestling Alliance once and for all, he solidified his strategy of syndicating his television shows in areas run by other wrestling promoters and targeting their markets, later picking up the 'Wrestling at the Chase' time slot which had been a St Louis mainstay for years. A war was brewing.

Chapter 11: Japan

"He was at Bakersfield airport waiting for me with his red corvette."

- *Fumi Saito, 2021*

Adonis made his first tour of New Japan Pro Wrestling (NJPW) in the summer of 1982, shortly after finishing up his first run with the WWF and still fresh off his acclaimed run of WWF title matches with champion Bob Backlund. WWF booker Vince McMahon Senior most likely provided the connection which saw Adonis make his Japanese wrestling debut, given the Federation's alliance with NJPW in the late 1970s and early 80s.

In 1978 New Japan negotiated a talent-sharing agreement with the WWWF as it was at the time, with NJPW booker Hisashi Shinma given the on-screen title of Federation "President" until being replaced by Jack Tunney in 1984, one of a number of token gestures the American promotion made to solidify the relationship. The deal primarily related to the Japanese company's junior heavyweight division, and saw the revival of the WWF Junior Heavyweight title, which in turn helped establish a young Tatsumi Fujinami as a star in his home country.

Adonis was far from the first foreign wrestler, or gaijin, to tour Japan. Stan Hansen first made the trip in January 1977 through the booking of McMahon Senior after a period in the WWWF. After Hansen's first tour proved a commercial and critical success, other wrestlers followed his lead, and when he returned in the September of that year, he was joined by the likes of Blackjack Mulligan, Sonny King, and Adonis' old friend, Roddy Piper.

Over the five years that followed, more and more wrestlers from North America journeyed to Japan to wrestle in the tournaments of New Japan and its competitor All Japan, which would usually last just short of a month from start to finish.

Tours to Japan became a staple in the careers of many American pro wrestlers in the late 1970s and early 1980s for a number of reasons. The gimmicks and stunts typically associated with American pro wrestling were less prevalent and the language barrier meant promos, often a hurdle for many even when talking in their native tongue, were not an issue. Wrestlers could get on with what many of them signed up for in the first place and display their in-ring wrestling skill in front of a discerning and appreciative audience.

Throughout the 1980s and 90s multiple US wrestlers gained superstar status in front of Japanese audiences who appreciated the stiff, bracing style of wrestlers such as Big Van Vader, Steve Williams, and Terry Gordy. Adonis fit nicely into this category. Most importantly, the trips paid exceedingly well, as Dave Meltzer explained on an episode of *The Lapsed Fan* podcast in November 2015. He said:

> *"New Japan was the number one wrestling promotion in the world at this point in time, and we're talking late 1983, it generated more money, it paid better than anybody else. They were number one. And Hogan and Andre the Giant were their two big foreign stars and they were making $10,000-$15,000 a week. So, people think [Hogan] was in the AWA and he was, but it was the AWA in between Japan tours. He made more money in Japan than he ever made in the AWA."*

The financial incentives for working in Japan were huge for other US-based wrestlers too, as Meltzer explained further:

> *"In that era if you worked on top for New Japan or All Japan that was the best paydays in wrestling. They paid so much better than the US. They cherry-picked Adrian, Hogan, Murdoch, they were making a lot of money there. Adrian had to overcome [the body] but he was on that rung with Masked Superstar, Murdoch, kept strong. In that era, he wasn't the top heel but he was that second rung, in that era that was one of the best jobs in wrestling."*

Adonis displayed a believable, hard-hitting style. Like many of his compatriots he quickly won over Japanese fans who appreciated his propensity to fly around the ring for and against his opponents. He retained his leather jacket, tough guy, biker stance but largely dispensed with the erratic promos, and gradually received increasing coverage from Japanese wrestling media (including one press conference where he publicly challenged heavyweight boxer Larry Holmes – not confusing him with namesake Ernie on this occasion).

This welcoming atmosphere extended to the close friendship that had developed with Fumi Saito, the young Japanese wrestling journalist whom Adonis first met in Minnesota. In July 2018, Saito reflected on the anniversary of his late friend's passing on an episode of the Portland Wrestlecast with host Jim Valley. He recalled:

> *"We first met in Minnesota back in 1979. He'd say 'I'm going to Japan, do you know any good nightclubs?' He was wanting to kind of sit down and chat, very friendly. The AWA had a lot of old guys, and they were young guys back then. I guess they had fun, 'Hey sit down,' ok I was able to sit down and talk with them. He went to New York, he went to Japan, and I started working more and more with New Japan Wrestling magazine and they recognised my photos and articles in the magazine; 'okay, you must be okay,' right."*

126

Reflecting on Adonis' status in Japan on his early trips, he added:

> *"He in the early 80s was one of the best wrestlers in the world. He was an instant hit when he made his first appearance with New Japan Pro Wrestling – was that 81 or 82? It slipped my mind but very early 80s that was the summer with the original Tiger Mask, Sayama Tiger Mask was still around and New Japan Pro Wrestling was on fire and Adrian headlined a tour as a newcomer. Not the blonde hair Adrian but black hair Adrian with black leather jacket and NY 'New York' logo on his back. That was his prime, that was right off his New York WWF run. That was in his prime."*

Saito made his way back to Japan around the same time Adonis started touring. The Buffalo native was happy to see a familiar face, Saito recalled:

> *"WWF also had a business partnership with Inoki, so after their run most wrestlers did tours with New Japan. Ventura first, match with Inoki, Adrian came next. Jesse not so successful. In Japan no promo or much storyline, you had to be able to work – Adrian could. I went back to Japan Summer 82, 83, and I worked full time on magazines, spent time with wrestlers and Adrian was happy to see me back – someone who spoke English."*

Adonis first wrestled in Japan from July 16 to August 5, 1982, spending three weeks with other US-based workers including Greg Valentine, Dick Murdoch, fellow party animal Rick McGraw, Dynamite Kid, and a young Bret Hart, for New Japan's Summer Fight Series. On the second day of the tour Adonis teamed with Murdoch for the first time in his career as part of a three-man combination with McGraw. Two weeks later, on July 31 ,1982 they wrestled as a duo for the first time.

The pair were a good fit, as Adonis's athletic style meshed well with Murdoch's brawling sensibilities, doubtless reminding some older fans of the burly Texan's previous tag combination with Dusty Rhodes as part of the Texas Outlaws. Both men returned in December 1982 for New Japan's Madison Square Garden Tag League, alongside Hulk Hogan, Andre the Giant, Dino Bravo, Rene Goulet and the Masked Superstar.

While Hogan teamed with hometown hero Antonio Inoki to win the tournament, Adonis teamed with Bravo and came third from last in the rankings. These early appearances solidified Adonis' reputation as a superlative worker to Japanese onlookers. Surrounded by other great talent Adonis rose to the occasion, particularly catching the eye in a pulsating solo encounter with Tatsumi Fujinami on July 30, 1982, which ended in a disqualification when Fred Blassie, along for the ride, interfered on Adonis' behalf.

The presence of Blassie on Adonis' early tours of Japan is a minor but important detail. Blassie was hugely respected in Japan during his time as an active wrestler. Despite being in his early sixties and working predominantly as WWF on-screen talent by this point, Blassie made the trip to help the likes of Adonis and Hogan get over in this new frontier. The *Wrestling Observer* wrote in 2003:

> *"He was Hogan's teacher on how to handle himself in Japan, as Blassie knew the ropes and taught Hogan to act like such a big star that he would never have to pay for anything in Japan, and long before his status in the US reached that level, Hogan was regarded in the category with Stan Hansen, Terry Funk, Bruiser Brody and Andre as the top foreign drawing cards in the country.*

> *"There is little doubt being paired with Blassie gave both Adonis and Hogan a major rub to the general public in Japan, who didn't know either of them at first, but by this point all had heard the stories, exaggerated by the years, of the night Blassie hit Rikidozan."*

Hogan first travelled to Japan to wrestle in May 1980 and experienced huge success with the local crowds well into the 1990s, headlining the Tokyo Dome on more than one occasion and battling top stars during his visits. In May 1983, while Adonis was wrestling for Southwest Championship Wrestling, Hogan made waves by defeating Inoki in the first IWGP League tournament, forerunner of the G1 Climax.

Adonis did not make that particular tour, but time spent in Japan would strengthen the bond between himself and Hogan, as well as other frequent fliers including Murdoch, Andre the Giant, and Don Muraco, as their paths intertwined frequently before they later all converged in the WWF. Muraco recounted one particular extracurricular activity he enjoyed alongside Hogan and Adonis on one of their Japanese excursions:

> *"Hulk Hogan was a big supporter of Adrian, he'd tell us stories about…if you've ever been to a strip club, they took us a couple of times, they took us to strip clubs in Tokyo, and those places, you know like Singapore, Puerto Rico, you know you've heard about the biggest whore houses in the world, but in Japan it's like a Broadway production.*

> *"I mean, no less sleazy, but they do it so well, the music, the dancing, they have booths where they flicker the lights. I mean, we were [young] so we never really took part, or watched them take part, but Hulk will tell stories about oh the girls finish dancing and stuff, and after that they flicker the lights and after that Adrian would come all soaped up covered in bubbles and dive naked and slide across the stage. That's kind of a thumbnail of where he would go. You've got to laugh."*

For the Big Fight Series 1983, Adonis teamed with "Cowboy" Bob Orton Junior, who would later act as his on-screen bodyguard during the 'Adorable' phase in the WWF, and again in the AWA. The tour lasted three weeks in March 1983 and also featured the likes of Bad News Allen and Chris Adams.

While Adonis' tag teams with Ventura and Murdoch are far better known in the States, the short-lived pairing of Adonis and Orton made something of an impact on a number of Japanese fans. Fumi Saito described the brief alliance in glowing terms in a 2020 article for Tokyo Sports:

> "Once upon a time, there was a regular foreign wrestler in New Japan Pro Wrestling who fascinated fans despite the short-lived tag team formation. Thirty-seven years ago, on March 4, 1983, the "Manhattan Combination" Adrian Adonis and Bob Orton Jr. formed a tag team at the "Big Fight Series" that opened at the Sagamihara Municipal Gymnasium in Kanagawa.

> "The two, who had teamed up in San Juan, Puerto Rico, showed good teamwork and demonstrated various combination techniques using corner posts in this series. At that time, fans were overwhelmed by the number of moves they saw for the first time."

The June 1983 edition of the Wrestling Observer concurred:

> "Adrian Adonis and Bob Orton Jr. both looked incredible as a team here in March. Adonis, perhaps 20 pounds heavier than in the States, is like a bumblebee. Aerodynamically there is no way he can get that ill-conditioned frame to do some things, but nobody ever told him that. So, he just does it."

Despite their chemistry, Adonis spent his next tour teaming with Murdoch and Brian Blair, often in six-man tags, as his long-term marriage to "Captain Redneck" started to set. The Adonis and Murdoch pairing became permanent later that year, as the two entered the MSG Tag League 1983 tournament together, putting in a string of impressive performances and finishing third in the rankings.

Both men saw the potential in the union after bettering their performances the previous year; as Adonis had faltered in his ill-matched pairing with Bravo, Murdoch had finished fourth in 1982 alongside the Masked Superstar. While Murdoch and Adonis did not come out on top on this occasion, they played their part in a scintillating round-robin tournament. This included a rousing eleven-minute showdown with eventual winners Hogan and Inoki in front of more than 12,000 fans at Kuramae Kokugikan. Days earlier the fledging team of Adonis and Murdoch scored a shock count-out win over Hogan and Inoki but could not repeat their feat in the final.

The winter 1983 Japanese tour proved a pivotal one in the careers of several wrestlers, not least of all Adrian Adonis. The relationship between New Japan and the WWF played a role in kickstarting the New York promotion's bid for dominance of the wrestling world, taking Adonis and Murdoch with it. When Hogan made plans to capitalise on the babyface stardom he had found in 1983, and his cameo in *Rocky III*, Japan played a role – as did a wedding.

Hogan last wrestled for the AWA on November 14, 1983, defeating Jerry Blackwell in Phoenix, Arizona. But for months prior, the blond muscleman had grown tired of the machinations of booker Verne Gagne, who demanded what he saw as unreasonable percentages of Hogan's Japan earnings, while declining to put the AWA world title on Hogan. Conscious of his growing star power, Hogan opened up a channel of communication with another man looking to build something bigger in the world of wrestling – Vince McMahon Junior.

McMahon Senior travelled to Japan in December to meet Hogan in between matches in the Tag League tournament. The younger McMahon took the lead in negotiating with Hogan, who subsequently backed out of a verbal agreement to renew his deal with the AWA and sent his notice to Gagne. McMahon agreed to Hogan's demands, which included that the WWF also sign his AWA colleagues Dave Schultz and Gene Okerlund – as well as a sustained run with the WWF championship.

While in Japan, McMahon Senior rekindled his fondness for Adonis who had torn the house down for him with Backlund a little under two years earlier. The elder McMahon finalised a deal with Adonis to return, this time in the form of a tag team with Murdoch, so impressed he was with the work of the no-nonsense combo. The pair became the final major talent signings ever made by Vince McMahon Senior who died from cancer five months later, in May 1984.

The tour ended on December 10, 1983, and the contingent, Inoki in tow, flew back to the States with another important engagement lined up – but not a wrestling card. On December 18, Hogan, under his real name of Terry Bollea, married Linda Claridge at the eye-catching Church of the Blessed Sacrament on Sunset Boulevard. Footage of the union remains online today (as a result of being taped for a Japanese news segment at the time) and serves as a who's who of the wrestling landscape with Vince and Linda McMahon, Keith and Bea Franke, Terry Funk, Inoki, and others all present.

Not known for the accuracy of some of his statements over the last 30 years, Hogan has claimed online that he and Adonis "went straight back to Japan" after the picture was taken. Possible, but if they did so, no matches took place, and both were back wrestling in a WWF ring on December 27. A misty-eyed Hogan posted a pic of the Frankes at the wedding online in 2018 and told followers how much he missed his late friend.

In the same interview with Jim Valley, Saito added an endearing note about the bond between Hogan and Adonis, and how it has quietly endured:

> "Adrian and Hogan were close. They were working against each other in the ring during the New York run and on New Japan tours, they were pretty tight. They came to Japan on a lot of tours together, they spent three weeks touring together, they ate together, they went to the gym together, nightlife, Japanese bars together, they were friends, very good friends. Even to this day in Hogan's home living room there's a photo of Adrian on the wall. A small photo, kind of like your high school wallet sized photo."

The formation of the North-South Connection, as Adonis and Murdoch would come to be known, was another seminal relationship in Adonis' life and career. In veteran brawler Murdoch, Adonis gained another partner who would complement him perfectly in the ring, and curb some of Adonis' enthusiasms outside of it, not dissimilar to the relationship he had with Ventura.

Though the pair first linked up on trips to Japan, they gained their highest profile as a team in the World Wrestling Federation, holding the world tag team titles for nine months from April 1984 as the company sat on the brink of national and international exposure.

Generally remembered as the North-South Connection, the team had a different moniker in Japan little known by North American fans. Here, Adonis and Murdoch were Super Violence, or the Super Violence Combination, a name mainly bestowed on them by local wrestling publications. Murdoch even once made a fleeting, jumbled reference to the name on WWF television. In a pre-match promo before the team faced the Wild Samoans at Madison Square Garden on August 25, 1984, 'Captain Redneck' instructed Gene Okerlund:

> "That's right, we don't have the nicknames the American Violence for anything, the North-South Connection."

The name would be refined and reused a few years later for the team of Terry Gordy and Steve Williams, who took All Japan Pro Wrestling by storm in the early 1990s as the Miracle Violence Combination.

There can at times be an underappreciation in the West of little-known, perhaps apocryphal nomenclatures applied to gaijin wrestlers who worked in Japan – at least as it pertained to Adonis. A variety of short-lived monikers, however poorly translated, show the appreciation Adonis was held in by Japanese wrestling fans and publications of the time.

At least one source ascribed him the nickname 'Runaway Wolf,' an apparent reference to biker culture. More references can be found to Adonis' localised finisher, the inverted Atomic Drop, a move which has ever since borne the name the 'Manhattan Drop' due to Adonis' supposed hometown. Lastly, references can be found to Adonis and Orton as the 'Manhattan Combination,' and Adonis himself as the 'Manhattan Rider.'

Whatever their name, Adonis and Murdoch hit great heights in Japan as a tandem just as they did in the WWF. The pinnacle came when the pair reached the final of the annual end of year Tag League tournament for 1984, losing to Inoki and Fujinami in an epic 34 minutes.

The Connection also wrestled earlier in the year for New Japan during a three-week tour in March, and five weeks in May and June, the latter of which saw them permitted by the Federation to leave the US for over a month despite reigning as WWF tag champs at the time.

The May-June 1984 Japan tour also featured a rare match between Adonis and Andre the Giant, with Adonis doing strong work to make the creaking Giant look mobile, and a one-on-one match-up between partners Adonis and Murdoch. In this May 24, 1984, encounter, won by Murdoch in eleven minutes, Adonis had already gained a significant amount of weight compared to how he appeared in his last trip to Japan.

Adonis' waistline was not the only thing changing. In September 1984, Vince McMahon Junior made his first trip to Japan to participate in a press conference at Keio Plaza Hotel alongside Hogan, Inoki and Seiji Sakaguchi. The event heralded the signing of a renewed booking agreement for 1984-85 between the WWF and NJPW, signed on August 22, 1984.

According to the *Wrestling Observer* newsletter, the new deal outlined a big increase in New Japan's payment to Titan Sports, as the Japanese group was anxious to have certain US-based stars visit its shores. The WWF meanwhile, riding a Hogan and MTV-shaped wave, was in a far superior bargaining position than it had been when previous deals had been struck.

Tellingly, McMahon's new deal did not promise to send Hogan to work for New Japan, or to feature WWF Title defences, both sure signs that the WWF had tired of the relationship. The following August, Titan Sports and New Japan failed to reach a deal and it would be years before the companies worked together again.

After finishing up with the WWF for a second time in January 1985, Adonis spent nearly three months in Japan between March and June. The North-South Connection participated in the Big Fight Series of 1985, one of the final cards co-promoted by New Japan and the WWF during the groups' association.

The trip also saw the team lose the WWF International tag-team titles (by count-out) on May 24, 1985, to Fujinami and Kengo Kimura. The titles, defunct since

1971, were resurrected briefly as a result of a business agreement that McMahon had with New Japan booker Sakaguchi which called for a certain number of appearances in Japan by WWF champions.

With growing success in the States and internationally, McMahon's interest in a link-up with the once red-hot New Japan waned and sending 'legitimate' WWF title holders to Japan was no longer a priority. To satisfy contractual demands, a placeholder title was created, with recent Federation departures Adonis and Murdoch enlisted to do the honours.

The pair were awarded the belts in early April 1985, defended them a handful of times solely in Japan, and then passed them onto the Japanese duo. The belts lasted until October 1985, when the partnership between the WWF and New Japan was terminated. Shortly after losing to Fujinami and Kimura, Adonis and Murdoch wrestled their final match together for nearly three years, against the same opponents, on June 13, 1985, ending in a double count-out.

Despite his relatively short time spent in Japan, Adonis made a significant impression. Murdoch and Adonis had the privilege of being the featured subjects of "wrestling album" volume 44, a 1984 scrapbook full of colour photos of the pair such was the esteem they were held in locally. There was an even more special feature in another Japanese wrestling magazine the following year, thanks to Fumi Saito. He recalled in 2018:

> *"[Adonis] started coming to Japan regularly and one summer he invited me over to his Bakersfield home. I flew to LA, then switched planes to this scary looking commuter plane that only carries six to eight people, then went to Bakersfield. He was at Bakersfield airport waiting for me with his red corvette. Oh, he was going like 75, 80 miles per hour just what you would imagine from this real cool heel. That was the summer of 85, 84 or 85."*

Saito played the role of live-in photojournalist with the Frankes for several days in Bakersfield, for an "at home with Adrian Adonis" photo spread which featured a few months later in a Japanese wrestling magazine. The piece featured Adonis at home with Bea and Angela, both in kimonos, showing off his hot-tub, fish tank, colour tv, red corvette, and other fruits of his labour. Five years old at the time, Angela Perides recalled the visit in a 2020 interview:

> *"I actually remember that, the reporter came and stayed at our house for three nights and spoke very limited English, and I remember having to hurry up and clean my room."*

Saito further recalled the colourful circumstances of Adonis' home life in 2020:

"He had a big fat joint; sunbathing, swimming pool; satellite dish at back of house; 'I get 200 channels,' stayed up all night and watched movies, relaxed and talked. He had to have cookies because he was hungry and crabby. He cooked a big salmon steak on barbeque grill, he was so proud of it."

More pertinent details on the trip, and Adonis' general state of mind about his lot in life during the summer of 1985, were offered by Saito in a July 2017 article for the Nikka Spa! News website. In the article, Saito painted a picture of his friend as a sullen, distant man hiding a deeper sadness.

His host was keen to show off his hi-tech satellite dish (*"You can watch anything on sports, movies, MTV, CNN. You can watch about 200 channels,"* Adonis boasted), but struggled for fulfilment. One dinner time tantrum from Adonis, who wanted to eat in front of the TV and not at the table, led Bea to remark that she had "two babies in the house," while Saito recounted:

"He was an awkward man, but he had a strong desire to show himself, always dreaming of 'somewhere else, not here.'"

Shortly after the visit, Adonis was recalled to Vince McMahon's rapidly expanding World Wrestling Federation, in June 1985, as a stand-in for another wrestler. Adonis stopped visiting Japan, to the disappointment of his friend Saito. They would be reunited, briefly, when Adonis made one final tour of Japan in May 1988. Keith Franke never forgot Japan, and many who were wowed by his style in those early tours never forgot him. Considering the brief impact Adrian Adonis had on Japanese wrestling culture, Saito concluded:

"He liked to be called Adrian rather than Keith, real nice guy but had wrestler's ego. At his house, he was being Adrian Adonis more so than Keith. Superstar wrestlers are just as insecure, almost fragile.

"[I'll always remember] the fact that when I was still a rookie, Adrian and Jesse were nice to me. And he had a strong desire to be someone too, said come over here and sit down.

"You remember wrestlers for the time you shared with them – Adrian Adonis shared more time with Japanese fans, on Japanese TV all the time, had real good matches every week, they remember him fondly. It's a good example for how people should remember your wrestlers."

Young Keith Franke with his junior football team, the Tigers.

Copyright Paul Neiss

As a teenager with his Ellwood Fire Company-sponsored hockey team.

Copyright Paul Neiss

Photographed in spring 1982 by Bill Apter for Pro Wrestling Illustrated.

Copyright PWI/Kappa Publishing Group

The new Southwest Championship Wrestling heavyweight champion, May 1983.

Copyright PWI/Kappa Publishing Group

At home with the Frankes, summer 1985. Copyright Fumi Saito

A Japanese influence, summer 1985. Copyright Fumi Saito

138

Bea, Keith and Angela, summer 1985. Copyright Fumi Saito

The family home in Bakersfield, summer 1985. Copyright Fumi Saito

Jan 30 1987, vs Roddy Piper, Nassau Coliseum, with Andre the Giant as guest referee.

Copyright PWI/Kappa Publishing Group

Chapter 12: The North South Connection

"We stroll through Central Park with $1,000 dollar bills hanging out of our back pockets taking on all comers.

"There are no comers. If there were, there'd be no men left."

- *Adrian Adonis, 1984*

When the history of the World Wrestling Federation is recounted, much is written about the company's purchase of Georgia Championship Wrestling in 1984. The event which precipitated the industry's "Black Saturday," has grown in infamy among fans in the years since. Less discussed is the Federation's forays into other territories during this time as Vince McMahon Junior finally got the chance to stretch his legs as company owner outside of his father's auspices.

One of those earlier excursions took place in St Louis. In September 1983, local station KPLR ended its relationship with the faltering St Louis Wrestling Club and the time slot was soon snapped up McMahon, who had a policy of paying to snag airtime in regions outside of his traditional markets. *Wrestling at the Chase* first aired in 1959 and was steeped in history and respect from wrestling fans. The WWF retained the moniker for its show on the station and taped the first few shows from the same location, the impressive Chase Park Plaza Hotel. The first of these tapings took place on December 27, 1983, and the WWF came packed with reinforcements.

The US debut of the North-South Connection took place at these tapings, as Adonis and Murdoch won a pair of squash matches, recorded to air on episodes of WWF's syndicated *All-Star Wrestling*. They didn't come alone, accompanied by their short-lived on-screen manager 'Mad Dog' Managoff.

Managoff, real name Jerry Jaffee, was one of a handful of experiments WWF attempted in their efforts to replace the recently deceased "Grand Wizard" Ernie Roth to fill out the trio of heel managers which also included Fred Blassie and Lou Albano.

Jaffee was a journeyman wrestler who usually competed as Jerry Graham Junior and got the opportunity through his relationship with George Cannon, one of McMahon's regional promoters at the time. Managoff also managed "Big" John Studd at the same taping. While his promo work was passable, the signing of a certain "Rowdy Scotsman" made him expendable and he was not kept on.

Jaffe recalled his brief tenure in the WWF years later:

"To be honest [Adonis and I] first met at The Chicago Amphitheater and used to have friendly dressing room chats. We went on a WWF tour of Kuwait [before] I managed him one night in St Louis Chase Hotel, he was teamed with Dick Murdoch. Other than that, we never socialised in any way, and I only wrestled him once.

"I will not talk ill of the dead, but John Studd didn't want me for his manager. Adrian and Murdoch were fine with it. Of course, I was disappointed being let go by the WWF but it's a tough business and I always had work somewhere."

Some other new (or nearly new) faces at the tapings made more of an impression, it's safe to say. The same show featured the returns or debuts of Hulk Hogan, "Dr D" David Schultz and announcer "Mean" Gene Okerlund, all plucked from the AWA. A week later, at a *WWF Championship Wrestling* taping, this burgeoning crew was joined by "Rowdy" Roddy Piper, fresh from Mid Atlantic, initially as a manager. The massive sea-change about to engulf the industry was in full effect and Adrian Adonis was very much a part of it.

Adonis and Murdoch were immediately pushed as major heel contenders to the babyface tag team champions, Rocky Johnson and Tony Atlas. The company had hopes for a long, successful title reign for the popular Soul Patrol but off-screen disharmony between the two made it impossible. Adonis and Murdoch were considered candidates to take the belts, but some signs pointed towards their fellow heel team the Moondogs being primed for a title run.

Adonis and Murdoch's continued excursions to Japan may have given the McMahons some hesitancy, with the pair not appearing in the Eastern part of the organisation until a March 27, 1984, Allentown taping win over SD Jones and Tony Garea. The pair didn't feature on WWF television, aside from the St Louis show and on syndication for *All-Star Wrestling*, until their first appearance on the flagship *WWF Championship Wrestling* in early May.

Making up for lost time, Adonis and Murdoch defeated Atlas and Johnson for the tag titles at the Allentown tapings on April 17, 1984. Such was the nature of the WWF's dizzying TV schedule at the time, the title change did not air nationally until May 26. Writing in the *Wrestling Observer*, Dave Meltzer noted at the time:

"Although [Adonis and Murdoch] have looked tremendous in their St Louis and Japan bouts plus West Coast appearances, the title change makes little sense only because they will be in Japan May 11 to June 14."

Rocky Johnson wrote in his autobiography in some detail about the discord between himself and his erstwhile tag partner. As he described it, Atlas had a volatile temper that would argue with pretty much everyone, not least of all the younger McMahon, as the new owner was assuming full control from his ailing father. After one shouting match too many, McMahon Junior made the call to take the belts off the 'Soul Patrol,' with Adonis and Murdoch the beneficiaries. Johnson wrote in 2019:

> *"Vince then brought Tony, Murdoch and Adonis in to discuss the finish. When Vince told them the belts were going to change hands, Tony had nothing to say. I had a strong suspicion that since he planned to fire Tony, Vince wanted him to do the job. I knew that would lead to an all-out war, not to mention the possibility of Tony walking out, so I said, 'Let them take the fall on me.' Vince thanked me later that night because he knew why I did it."*

That is exactly what happened, as Adonis rolled up Johnson for the win and the titles. A follow-up feud with the dethroned champions was cancelled when Tony Atlas quit the company abruptly in early May 1984. Ageing legend Bobo Brazil was drafted in at short notice to cover Atlas' bookings. A few weeks away from his 60th birthday, any thoughts McMahon had of teaming Brazil with Atlas for a longer run were dropped when everyone saw him in action.

Instead, Adonis and Murdoch moved on to a feud with the Wild Samoans, who were in the process of a babyface turn. Adonis was still turning in top notch performances, but his inability to keep off weight was becoming difficult for onlookers to ignore, as he steadily gained more and more girth around his midriff throughout 1984. The Observer's summer 1984 ratings listed Adonis as the number 10 wrestler in the world – no mean feat – but a sharp drop from being in the top three a couple of years prior. The article opined:

> *"[Adonis] would be number one if he was in any kind of condition to wrestle in singles, but his 300-pound current frame limits him."*

The summer of 1984 was an eventful one for Adonis and Murdoch in the WWF as they maintained a high profile on several fronts. The North-South Connection faced the Wild Samoans at Madison Square Garden on June 16, 1984, Adonis' return to the mecca of wrestling for the first time in more than two years.

The following month, the champions defeated Sgt Slaughter and his young Cobra Corps recruit – a certain Terry Daniels – before going over the Wild Samoans by disqualification on August 25 at the Garden in a match which saw the Samoans' erstwhile manager Albano as guest referee. By this point, Adonis and Daniels were well acquainted; Daniels was also on the opposing team when the North-South Connection made their WWF debut the previous December in St Louis. Daniels recalled what it was like to bump into Adonis again years after their infamous encounter in Amarillo:

> *"I never talked with him any. But when we was wrestling, he was professional about it, he didn't try to take any revenge or do anything like*

that. In the one match with me and Slaughter against Murdoch and Adonis, he was a little stiff a couple of times.

"I got in trouble a couple of times in that match. I tagged too early one time. When I say that's when I got in trouble, when I got back in there with Murdoch he said, 'What the hell did you tag for?' But you know, it worked out real well.

"Towards the end of the match when they started taking over me and they started double-teaming me he threw a few shots that was kind of solid but I didn't worry about it, I didn't care."

Signs in June and July pointed towards Albano becoming manager to Adonis and Murdoch, something which had been par for the course for WWWF/WWF heel tag team champions since 1971. In the intervening years, Albano had taken charge of Luke Graham & Tarzan Tyler, Mikel Scicluna & Curtis Iaukea, the Valiants, the Blackjacks, the Executioners, the Samoans, the Moondogs, the Mongols, and Mr Fuji and Mr Saito. Adonis and Murdoch appeared to be lined up to join that impressive roll call.

Albano spoke appreciatively about the North-South Connection on the sofa of Vince McMahon's faux talk show, *Tuesday Night Titans*, on May 29, 1984, and subsequently deserted his charges, the Wild Samoans, turning them face in the process.

The June MSG show featured a backstage segment in which Albano was 'caught' in deep discussions with the Connection, an effort to create some intrigue about Albano's loyalties ahead of the match. Albano did join the pair for a short series of six-man tag matches in the months that followed, but the company stopped short of making the trio a permanent unit. Instead, the company wisely decided to capitalise on the profile Albano had built earlier in 1984 during his high-profile feud with Cyndi Lauper.

Albano wrote about his break-up from the Samoans in his 2008 autobiography and touched on his interactions with Adonis and Murdoch:

"Although Adrian didn't look the part of have a great body, he was a great amateur wrestler and a tough son of a gun."

When the Freebirds of Michael Hayes, Terry Gordy and Buddy Roberts briefly joined the Federation expansion project in July 1984, long-time fans salivated at the prospect of a tag title feud between two of the most interesting teams on the wrestling landscape. Sadly, this would not transpire as the 'Birds left the WWF almost as quickly as they joined, and Adonis and Murdoch instead continued to feud with the Samoans.

July was a particularly busy month for the Connection, even without the prospect of the Freebirds to face. On July 7 at the Philadelphia Spectrum the pair defeated the makeshift team of Brian Blair and Bob Backlund. Backlund, yesterday's man since the arrival of Hulk Hogan, was making his final appearances for the Federation for nearly eight years, his standing in the company now light years away from what it had been when he and Adonis faced off two years earlier.

The following week, Adonis and Murdoch made wrestling history as the first wrestlers to compete, alongside their opponents SD Jones and Nick DeCarlo, on the WWF's version of the popular *World Championship Wrestling* television show on TBS.

Vince McMahon's highly controversial move to procure the only other national cable wrestling airtime saw the WWF supremo grab the Georgia Championship Wrestling stakes of Jim Barnett and the Brisco Brothers, Jack and Jerry, giving the WWF the controlling stake in GCW and McMahon access to the Saturday night-time slot.

Fans had no knowledge of the wrangling and were stunned to find their regular stars usurped by those from the New York territory. McMahon promised exciting action but delivered mainly highlights from WWF house shows and syndicated programming. The first was the Adonis and Murdoch outing, taped on July 10 at the Maple Leaf Gardens.

The WWF was moving at a dizzying pace, and its wrestlers with it. Nine days after 'Black Saturday,' as it came to be known, the company aired a special event live on MTV, capitalising on the relationship the company had built with Cyndi Lauper and her manager David Wolff. Only the women's title match, which featured Lauper in a supporting role, aired on the network, while a full MSG card took place for the live crowd, including the North-South Connection's win over the Cobra Corps.

Another blink-and-you-miss-it aspect of this period for Adonis and Murdoch occurred at this point. On several occasions in spring and summer 1984, the team which was otherwise called the North-South Connection, was referred to without explanation as 'The Wrecking Crew.' The name is clearly inspired by the famous Minnesota Wrecking Crew, which featured various combinations of the kayfabe Anderson brothers dating back to the late 1960s.

While the Minnesota Wrecking Crew name had been dormant since 1981, wrestling fans would have immediately associated it with one Ole Anderson. Was the 'Wrecking Crew' name a very unsubtle dig at Anderson, the sole hold-out shareholder in the Georgia Championship Wrestling buy-out, or simply a coincidence?

During a handicap match against Andre the Giant and Hulk Hogan on July 15 in East Rutherford, commentator Gorilla Monsoon referred to the champions by the alternative name, something he repeated a month later during August's MSG show. On the latter, fans got the only ever spoken reference to the name from Adonis himself, as he dismissed the evening's opponents:

> *"But it's gonna be whole control and the Wrecking Crew, the Wrecking Crew is gonna wreck everything in our way. I don't care what it is daddy, we'll even take on trucks, we'll even take on a van, we don't care what it is."*

These were formative days for Vince McMahon's vision of a family-friendly, character-driven sports entertainment vision of pro wrestling, but later years have shown how opposed the future WWE chairman was to promoting wrestlers with names he did not create and own the trademark for. Perhaps this is an embryonic example of that same impulse. McMahon himself used the phrase months earlier, commentating on Adonis and Murdoch's title victory.

Something much easier to spot between Adonis and Murdoch was the chemistry shared by the unlikely pairing, in the ring and behind the mic. Several years Adonis' senior and almost a decade more experienced in the ring, Dick Murdoch was the adopted son (or stepson, or both), of Frankie Hill Murdoch, who found success wrestling across Texas in the 1950s against the likes of Dory Funk Senior.

The younger Murdoch followed in his father's footsteps and debuted in 1965. Fans started to truly notice Murdoch when he formed a hard-hitting tag-team with a young Dusty Rhodes. The pair teamed as the Texas Outlaws from 1968 to 1971, winning tag team titles in Florida, Dallas, Detroit, Australia, and the Buffalo territory, gaining admirers for their unorthodox style wherever they went.

The run set the path for their solo careers, as Dusty Rhodes soon turned face and went onto superstardom in Florida and beyond, built on his charisma and personality. Murdoch meanwhile gained acclaim in the Mid-South territory during his early 1980s run teaming with the Junkyard Dog, his 'Captain Redneck' persona drawing the cheers of white working-class fans in the area.

Parallels have been drawn between Murdoch's successive partners of Rhodes and Adonis', particularly due to their shared atypical physiques and propensity for the occasional leather biker cap. While there may be some truth to this, Adonis cannot claim to have the sheer magnetism or Dusty Rhodes, nor was Rhodes ever close to Adonis' in-ring capabilities.

Nevertheless, Adonis and Murdoch got in a groove teaming with each other in Japan, with the former's technical competence and quality selling meshed perfectly with Murdoch's southern brawling. It was the elder McMahon who signed the pair to the WWF, clearly impressed by the way they had got over with

Japanese fans, and the pair soon had the sombre accolade of being tag champions on the day the pioneering promoter died. In his place was his son, Vince McMahon Junior, who was less concerned about what the two wrestlers could do in the ring.

Everyone could see that Murdoch and Adonis were clearly gifted wrestlers. What McMahon Junior wanted in 1984 was characters. As heels, they were not grotesque, racial stereotypes (such as the Wild Samoans or Fuji & Saito), or colourful cartoons (like the Strongbows, or the Hillbillies that would later populate the Federation).

They certainly didn't fit the picture as Vince's preferred swoon-inducing poster-pin up babyfaces, a slot he envisioned at different times in the years that followed for the US Express, Can-Am Connection, and Strike Force. Adonis and Murdoch were men out of time. Five years earlier and they would have dominated. All was not lost, in McMahon's eyes, thanks to the 'odd couple' dynamic which presented itself; others agreed, as Jerry Brisco could attest:

> *"I'm surprised the combination worked so well because here's Dickie Murdoch, this old wild West Texas cowboy and here's Keith Franks, he's a city boy basically, a laid-back hippy and Murdoch hates being around guys who smoke pot, hates drugs, all that stuff, loves whisky and beer.*

> *"And those two mixing together was really the unique thing about it. I mean, you take a redneck and a hippy [laughs] with completely different lifestyles and you're different in age, but they were totally different culturally, but they blended again together in the ring because of that athletic ability that they both possessed. They became one of the top tag teams in the entire world during their run."*

This wacky relationship took centre stage on a pair of episodes of the WWF's wacky *Tuesday Night Titans*, in which each member of the Connection went to the other's home turf, to see how the other half lived.

First up, on July 31, 1984, Adonis, with "Mean" Gene Okerlund in tow, played chaperone to the redneck Murdoch on a hilarious tour of his 'old New York neighbourhood.' As onlookers stared in disbelief, Adonis aimed to prove that he "was "in the Guinness Book of World Records for touching sewer caps." Adonis proceeded to run into a busy New York road touching hubcaps, cartwheeling, barking at cars which understandably encouraged him to move. "This is my neighbourhood, not yours," he admonished one car. When Okerlund suggested he should have an affinity with the local residents, he retorted chillingly: "Ah, nobody's my people."

The vignette continued with Adonis and Murdoch checking out some new threads – and a leather whip for Adonis – before Adonis grabbed a bemused older

147

gentleman, declaring him to be a family member: *"Hey Uncle Joe, hey Uncle Joe. Uncle Joe! Dick, this is my uncle Joe I want you to meet him."*

The unscripted and chaotic nature of the trip is rarely seen in today's closely regulated version of pro wrestling and gives a window when viewed through a modern lens into what has been lost in terms of character development. After stopping off for a hotdog, Murdoch rode pillion passenger on Adonis' motorbike. "You know how to get to the Garden?" asked a nervous Murdoch. "Yeah, right through that wall right there," replied Adonis, laughing manically.

Two months later, on the October 2, 1984, episode of *Tuesday Night Titans*, it was Adonis' turn to visit Murdoch at his ranch in Waxahachie, Texas. Adonis was seen on a dirt track, lost, and bemoaning the absence of a subway or taxicab before hitching a ride on a passing truck. Once at Murdoch's residence, complete with its shrine to John Wayne in the front room of course, Adonis learned how to lasso a cow and unsuccessfully tried to mount a horse, leading to a pratfall not dissimilar to those he was famed for in the ring.

As the feud with the Samoans ended and 1984 drew to a close, Adonis and Murdoch moved on to work with the recently recruited Jack and Jerry Brisco. Both brothers had played a role in selling the Georgia group to Vince McMahon and joined as on-screen talent in September 1984. Popular and gifted wrestlers, particularly former NWA heavyweight champion Jack Brisco, neither were well suited to the growing circus which was Vince McMahon Junior's WWF. Nevertheless, in the absence of any other candidates, they were pencilled in as the next opposition to the North-South Connection, and thus the team most likely to relieve them of the titles. Writing in 2003, Jack Brisco recalled:

> *"Jerry and I were booked to work our program with Murdoch and Adonis in order to get established and to get over in the WWF, after which time we would move into a program with the current tag champions, Mike Rotundo and Barry Windham, who took the title from Murdoch and Adonis midway through our run with them. At least, that was the plan."*

The North-South Connection and the Briscos worked a number of matches between November and February, taking in most of the major markets. This included a thrilling 27-minute-long Madison Square Garden match which ended in a disappointing double count out. The feud did not reach its planned conclusion.

By now twenty years into a storied career, Jack Brisco at 43 was unenthusiastic about the prospect of life on the road as one-half of a mid-card tag-team act destined to get lost in the shuffle. After a disagreement about who was going over one night in February, compounded by poor weather conditions and a growing desire to retire, Brisco flew home to Florida, bringing an end to both his WWF tenure and career. His younger brother Jerry Brisco stayed in a behind-the-scenes capacity for decades and retold the tale in a December 2016 interview:

"We were ready to attack WrestleMania I with Murdoch and Adonis for the title and get the titles. That's when Jack [Brisco] said, I've had enough. I'm forty years old and I'm finished. And he quit. He was one of those guys that when he walked away, he walked away. He never came back."

While it is quite possible that McMahon had outlined a plan for the Briscos to dethrone the North-South Connection and enjoy a run as babyface champs, the suggestion that the four men may have done so at the first *WrestleMania* seems unlikely, at least from a timing perspective. Even before Jack walked out in February, Adonis and Murdoch were essentially done with the WWF and had dropped the belts the month prior. That's not to say it was not the plan months earlier however – just that Jack's departure would not have been what cancelled it. Jerry Brisco remembered the feud as an underappreciated gem in a 2021 interview:

"That series got us in contention go for the titles and everything like that, but my brother didn't want to take that step and that commitment at that time. I just think being able to go in there with, my brother and I if you think about it, we'd just come off that heel run down in North Carolina with Ricky Steamboat and Jay Youngblood, we were stone cold heels and then all of a sudden next time people see us on a national basis we're back babyfaces again, these two guys they can go.

"Our matches they had that natural chemistry to them where there wasn't any egos, when all four of us were in the ring we're willing to work with each other, because there was a big size difference and back then size counted a lot, my brother Jack and I weren't the biggest guys in the world but we could wrestle, we could work and we had people believing in us.

"We had a lot of fun but we knew it wasn't going to last so we put everything into it for two go rounds that we did and made it work and then they were able to make it work because all four guys were professionals out there. So, it was a lot of fun with them."

It is easy to view the lengthy title reign of Adonis and Murdoch as a sign that McMahon appreciated their work. Clearly, if he had a significant problem with them, they would not have held such lofty status. A more realistic take may be that their long run was simply a visible sign of the transition from Senior to Junior. As the younger man found his footing, he replaced the furniture – some quicker than others. In the same way that Ernie Roth's death brought with it opportunity, and Albano would be dispatched before long, the writing was on the wall for Murdoch and Adonis.

The nine-month title reign of the North-South Connection ended on January 21, 1985. Brothers-in-law Mike Rotundo and Barry Windham joined the WWF in October 1984 from Mid Atlantic, after successful runs in Florida and the

Carolinas. The pair were much closer to what Vince McMahon had in mind for his dream of a mainstream international wrestling promotion, especially Windham who bore at least a passing resemblance to Hulk Hogan, with his yellow trunks and flowing blonde locks. With little hesitation, the good looking, popular new arrivals were to be installed as the company's premier tag-team. The old-school, no-frills combination of Adonis and Murdoch were yesterday's news.

The U.S. Express of Rotundo and Windham won the titles on a house show at the Hartford Civic Center a little over two months after debuting in the territory. Title changes on house shows have always been a rarity in the WWF. That the match has never aired in its entirety on television has led some to suggest that the belts may have been taken from Adonis and Murdoch without their agreement – a 'screwjob' in other words. This is compounded by the somewhat abrupt nature of the switch, as the company was still so early in its work to build up the young newcomers.

This has never been confirmed, and the footage of the finish which has aired doesn't appear to show any real struggle, though wrestling has a history of double crosses dating back more than a century, as McMahon would have been well aware. Later in 1985 the veteran Fabulous Moolah relieved Wendi Richter of the women's world title without the champion's prior approval.

What is evident from the match, which ended when Windham pinned Murdoch with a sunset flip, is that it was filmed at ringside from a handheld camera, which one anonymous online source has attributed to a young Kevin Dunn; again, this is unsubstantiated rumour. Word was spreading that Murdoch had grown weary of the heavy WWF schedule and was planning to quit. McMahon always wanted to avoid one of his title holders leaving with the belt in the middle of a promotional war, and potentially showing up on a rival's television show with his company's title.

As such, the decision to change the title on the house show was made at short notice, hence the lack of camera equipment, and could be discarded if required as it was only witnessed by the live crowd and not the wider television audience. If Murdoch and Adonis stayed, they could stay champs and drop the belts at a more high-profile juncture. If not, it could be inserted into an episode of television, which is exactly what McMahon did, with overdubbed commentary by himself and Bruno Sammartino recorded from a studio days later.

Barry Windham recounted the scenario in a shoot interview afterward, commenting on Adonis as "a guy he didn't really understand," and that "he never really knew him well because Adonis didn't want to know him". His recollection was that a surly and unwelcoming Adonis refusing to put the newcomers over for the titles until he was convinced to do so by Murdoch. He added in a 2019 interview: "I can't remember anybody that really got along with Adonis or liked him."

A contemporary edition of the *Wrestling Observer* concurred that Adonis' attitude was a factor, which showed in his resistance to putting over Rotundo in a series of singles matches following the title change. Adonis put over Rotundo on a single occasion, at a Dallas house show in February 14, 1985:

> *"Adonis missed several dates rather than lose to Mike Rotundo so I'm assuming he's through. Murdoch is still around as I write this, just playing out the string losing to Windham but will be gone within weeks."*

Memories of Adonis from his tenure in the WWF from 1985 onwards increasingly paint the same picture of a distant, antisocial character whose only pleasure came from cynicism.

Adonis' hard partying lifestyle on the road was at odds with Murdoch's nature, and the Texan eventually tired of being Adonis' handler outside the ring and ensuring he reached arenas on time – much as Ventura had before him. After leaving the WWF, Murdoch returned to Mid-South in 1985 and criticised his former partner on camera to that effect:

> *"You know I was one of those world's tag team champions with the WWF and at one time I was proud to have held that title but I never knew if my partner was gonna show up. When he showed up we had a good team. We had to have, we were the champions. But I never knew whether he was gonna show up or not and that's one thing that happens when you belong to the WWF, a lot of wrestlers don't care if they show up or not."*

Murdoch himself was far from perfect. Multiple wrestlers have come forward over the years to claim that the 'Texas redneck' was an unapologetic racist and member of the Ku Klux Klan, although this has never been verified. What is true is that both Adonis and Murdoch are responsible for hateful racist slurs against opponents during their WWF run, labelling the Samoans "animals," insulting Johnson and Atlas, and mocking the (genuine and kayfabe) Native American heritages of the Briscos and Chief Jay Strongbow. Adonis particularly enjoyed terming the Briscos the 'Last of Hekawis,' an insult borne from merging of the '*Last of the Mohicans*' (the subject of a 1977 TV movie he presumably watched late one night), and the native tribe featured in 1960s sitcom '*F-Troop*.' It was a lot more routine in the mid-1980s for heels to mock the ethnicity of anyone and everyone, but something that makes for uncomfortable viewing today.

It is possible that Murdoch was uncomfortable with the subtle effeminate overtones of Adonis's character, although the pair were close enough to refer to each other on screen as "Dickie" and "Adie" – the latter being Adonis' affectionate nickname with the boys backstage during this part of his career.

Murdoch died from a heart attack in June 1996 at the age of 49. A year beforehand he made a final, unexpected guest appearance at the WWF's *Royal Rumble* pay-per-view, on January 22, 1995, ten years and one day after dropping the tag titles in Hartford. The fleeting appearance prompted one of the only on-screen acknowledgements of Adonis in memoriam by WWF owner Vince McMahon.

Chapter 13: Going solo

"I've been abused, I've been misunderstood by everybody in the United States."

- *Adrian Adonis, 1985*

The last match of the North-South Connection on mainland US soil took place on in February 1985, losing to the Brisco Brothers in what was also one of the final matches ever in the storied career of Jack Brisco, who went home shortly after.

Adonis and Murdoch teamed again a month later for Ata Maivia's territory in Honolulu, a favour for her son-in-law Rocky Johnson who, along with his brother Ricky Johnson, were their opponents for the evening. Two nights later, on March 29, 1985, the Connection was back in Japan participating in New Japan's annual Big Fight Series.

The pair were essentially on loan from the WWF, which still had a working relationship with New Japan Pro Wrestling, albeit one which would be curtailed by McMahon before the end of the year. After their first three-week tour was over, Adonis and Murdoch were back in action in early May, this time as part of the IWGP & WWF Champion series, a co-promotion as the companies attempted to breathe some life in to their faltering relationship.

Adonis and Murdoch entered the series billed as WWF International Tag Team Champions, title belts created especially for the region when McMahon found himself contractually obliged to send title holders for an appearance, but not wishing to interrupt the US bookings of the 'real' tag title holders. Within two weeks they had dropped the belts to Kengo Kimura and Tatsumi Fujinami, on May 24, 1985, in Kobe.

The tour also featured more singles matches for both men than they had worked in Japan in recent memory, and six-man tags alongside fellow wrestlers not currently being used by the WWF including Jimmy Snuka, King Kong Bundy, "Iron" Mike Sharpe, and the Masked Superstar. Hogan was also dispatched as a special attraction.

The tour ended on June 13, and with it the final outing of the North South Connection, again opposite Kimura and Fujinami, until a brief reunion nearly three years later. Aside from the one-off appearance at the Royal Rumble ten years later, Murdoch would never wrestle for the WWF again. The same could not be said for Adonis, who was recalled to the WWF within days.

McMahon found himself in need of a replacement for Ken Patera, who had just been sentenced to two years in prison for assaulting two police officers alongside

Masa Saito after working an AWA show in May 1984. Patera, who served around 18 months, was working for the WWF by this point and was sentenced on June 14, 1985, meaning all his bookings for the months ahead would need to be covered. Welcome back, Adrian Adonis.

At a Madison Square Garden show on June 21, Adonis subbed for Patera on the winning side of a six-man tag with Big John Studd and Bobby "The Brain" Heenan, going over George Steele and his old foes, the US Express. The following night at the Boston Garden he had his first solo match back, defeating the veteran Swede Hanson in bout which aired on *Prime Time Wrestling* on July 23, when many WWF fans would have first learned of his return.

By the time his return match aired on television, Adonis had been off WWF television for six months and much had changed. Uppermost was the impact made by the inaugural *WrestleMania*, and the WWF's continued surge of mainstream popularity. The successful super show laid down a marker in both the wrestling and television industry and cemented the WWF as a force to be reckoned with.

This built on McMahon's machinations of 1984 which had included his own chat show on the USA Network (*Tuesday Night Titans*), a kid's cartoons series (*Hulk Hogan's Rock n Wrestling*), action figures, and more. Adonis and Murdoch's decision to leave the WWF just as the company was going into overdrive may have been the wrong one financially, but it did not impede Adonis from receiving a decent push when he came back.

When the Hanson match aired on TV, commentators Gorilla Monsoon and Gene Okerlund were under orders to highlight a number of aspects of Adonis' appearance, making it clear that the decision had been made to lean into his 'unusual' stylings.

Monsoon and Okerlund were quick to point out Adonis' attire to fans, from his leather jacket, leather hat and choker, as Adonis returned to the biker chic which had proved successful for him in riling crowds circa 1981. As the pair commented on his visible weight gain, Monsoon noted that Adonis had been "out of the country, travelling worldwide." Adonis put his opponent away with an elbow drop – a favourite move throughout his career but one which would be quickly replaced as his finisher.

Days prior, on July 20, Adonis went over Gary Starr on an episode of *WWF Championship Wrestling*. He was once again decked out in his leather finery, plus fingerless leather gloves. This time he had two notable additions. With Bobby Heenan officially installed as his manager, Adonis was seen holding a briefcase, handcuffed to his wrist. In large letters on the side of the briefcase, "Relax with Trudi."

The commentary team of McMahon and Sammartino speculated that the briefcase must be ransom money, reference to a $25,000 bounty that Heenan had earlier put on the head of Paul Orndorff, who had recently turned face and broken away from "The Brain" to side with Hulk Hogan. The contents of the briefcase were never made clear and remained evermore a WWF/WWE mystery alongside who was behind GTV, and who blew up Vince McMahon's limo in 2007, other storylines started and never concluded. It does imply a possible feud with Orndorff was in consideration at one point, a fascinating prospect.

McMahon once again remarked on Adonis' dress sense, as he had all those years ago in 1981, encouraging viewers to sneer alongside him:

> "My goodness, look at the choker on Adrian, Bruno, look at his pipe sticking out of that. he's really into his leather, there's no doubt about that."

Adonis put his opponent away with his trusty sleeper hold. No longer labelled 'Good Night Irene,' the move was briefly referred to as the "Big Apple," another aspect of the character quietly dropped. Adonis officially confirmed his on-screen partnership with Heenan when the pair appeared as guests on the July 27, 1985, edition of Piper's Pit.

This appearance, taped June 21, featured Heenan holding one briefcase containing $25,000. Adonis meanwhile clutched a separate one, containing something other than the ransom, and not yet with 'Trudi' written on the side, in a distinct lack of continuity. When pressed by Piper for contents of his briefcase, "a secret" was all Adonis would confirm.

After confirming his international sojourn as the reason for his absence ("I've been all over the world, I've been to Japan, Saipan, I've been to Beirut,") Adonis made a statement of intent, and included his own vague dig at the departed Murdoch:

> "I've been abused, I've been misunderstood by everybody in the United States. I've had bad partners, I've had people try to take advantage of me ever since I've been six years old, but I've always got revenge. But now I have a man right here Mr Piper to look out for my interests, Bobby "The Brain" Heenan."

The easiest conclusion to draw, which many have, is that the briefcase held Adonis' new identity, namely the "Adorable" gimmick, which he would debut in January of the following year. What specifically that might be – ribbons and bows? Women's clothing? – people are less clear on. As with so many open-ended storylines in wrestling history, this has never been confirmed one way or the other, and the briefcase simply stopped appearing around October, leaving a decent gap of several weeks before Adonis' 'transformation.'

Either way, the use of a woman's name, similar to 'Irene' years earlier, was a deliberate way of silently coding to fans that there was something less than masculine about Adonis, with more to come. '*Relax*,' meanwhile was one of the most provocative phrases of the 1980s following the success of the debut single of that name by Frankie Goes to Hollywood.

Released in the UK in October 1983, the song eventually reached the Top 10 of the Billboard charts in March 1985 – just three months before the briefcase debuted. Its use by the WWF in relation to Adonis was deliberate, with everyone aware of the media panic around the song's suggestive lyrics, a thinly veiled celebration of gay love.

Closer to home, in August 1985, the Frankes welcomed their second daughter, Gena. For Keith this additional stability brought undoubted joy yet more pressure. Recollections from fans who interacted with Adonis outside the ring and wrestlers who shared a dressing room with Franke around this period point towards more erratic behaviour, and a man determined to distance himself from those around him.

That is not to say Adonis did not like being home – quite the opposite. Back in Buffalo, now a father-of-two, Adonis loved to surround himself with friends and family, even if he may not always have had the energy to entertain them as he did the crowds in the arena. Gena said:

> *"When he came home [off the road], he was all about us, my sister and I and my mom, he was a big family guy and he got a kick out of us, he thought we were the greatest."*

Elder daughter Angela also retold, second hand, an example of how her father could get irritable, with noise a particular bugbear. She noted:

> *"Well, my mom had also said like if we went out to dinner and somebody else's kid was crying, [he would say] 'Can't that shut that kid up' or 'Why'd they sit these people right next to us.'"*

Sociable and irascible in equal measure, it was around this time that Adonis built close relationships with two people with whom he would remain close friends for what remained of his life.

Originally from New Jersey, actor and comedian Joey Gaynor was based in Los Angeles throughout the 1980s and ran in the same circles as many fellow comedians on the circuit at the time. Gaynor and comedy partner Fred Asparagus employed a wrestling 'bit' on their shows, in which they played the loudmouth manager with his startling new find, lampooning years of television wrestling storylines.

156

Promoter Lester Kirschner was in the crowd one night and lapped up the pair's performance, inviting them to put their shtick on display at a venue he ran, namely the Olympic Auditorium. The chance encounter put Gaynor in Adonis' orbit – and not in a welcome way, at least at first. He recalled:

> "[Kirschner] said 'I would love to have you guys come down and do it but the wrestlers would probably kill you. Anytime you want to come down just give me a call.' So, every time the WWF comes in, we go to the Olympic Auditorium. This is when they were doing their shows in 1984-85, I think it's around March of '84.

> "A big card Adonis, Muraco, Bob Backlund, and when Adrian comes out he's in a black leather jacket, black hat, NY that he had made for him and he comes out and he's strutting around in this black leather outfit. In NY that's a tough guy in LA that's something else. So, I started to chant – now this is 1984 remember, a different era – I start chanting Adonis is a [gay slur] within 30 seconds or less 10,000 people are chanting Adonis is [it] and he's running around with his hands over his ears!"

Gaynor recognised Adonis as "Gorgeous" Keith Franks, whom he had watched years earlier tussling with the likes of Roddy Piper and others at the same venue. After the show, he visited backstage to thank Kirschner for the tickets, only to come face to face with the man he had moments earlier been verbally skewering from the audience. Gaynor recalled:

> "I gingerly walk up and say you were great. He says 'Thank you.' He looks like a kid that's lost. I say, 'Everything all right?' [He said] 'My ride's left and I don't know what I'm going to do.' Real New York, down to earth like the guys I grew up with. 'If you need a ride, I can give you one.'

> "[In the car] I say, 'Just so you know, don't hit me - I started the chant.' He drops his bags and looks at me. 'You started that?' He goes, 'Man, thank you, that put an idea in my head, you're not going to believe what I'm going to do with that. You got me over in this building bigger than I ever.' I introduced myself [and he said] 'Oh, the comedian!' All of a sudden, we're fast friends!

> "He comes to my friend's house in the Valley and hang out all night. My friend's buddy was going to Bakersfield the next morning, so he hangs out and spends the whole night talking about wrestling."

Adonis and Gaynor quickly became friends and spent time together whenever both were in the Los Angeles area, taking any opportunity to paint the town red:

"The first night we hung out we had nowhere to go so we went to mud wrestling at the Tropicana on Fountain in LA before we went back to the house. He bought us a round of beers at 1.20am and at 1.30am the door guy comes round collecting them. [Keith] said 'Take it from me', and the guy says 'No, you drink, big star here.' He realised who he was and thought I'm not going to mess with him!"

Gaynor's wider circle came to know Adonis, too. Sam Kinison was a former Pentecostal preacher who turned to comedy and became known for his wild, audience-baiting style- a tendency perhaps similar to Adonis' own. Kinison, who appeared several times on *Saturday Night Live* as well as in a handful of movies, was a rising star of the LA comedy scene at the time he and Adonis bonded over shared interests in the mid-1980s. Gaynor noted:

"They're in the Midwest and Keith and Sam hooked up somehow and wound up in the same hotel, you know the '80s the decade of the marching powder, which wasn't something I did.

"They were partying because Sam came into town a couple of days later, we were partying, and [Sam said] 'I met your cousin, him and Rick [Jones, Kinison's bodyguard] almost got into it!' [I said] 'Oh please, you're always starting trouble!'"

The tempestuous pair share more than just a similar demeanour, as Kinison also tragically died in his 30s in a car accident, killed as a result of a head-on collision in 1992. The time the pair shared had a clear effect on Adonis, who mentioned Kinison as one of his celebrity friends during arrogant promos in the years that followed.

Franke was also making friends closer to home. The father-of-two was in the habit of frequenting the Venice Beach Gold's Gym, a regular haunt of his close friend Hulk Hogan, in order to get in at least some kind of shape for his next run of WWF shows. It was there that he met Bakersfield native and professional bodybuilder Tom Touchstone.

Touchstone years later declined an offer from WWF head honcho Vince McMahon to join his World Bodybuilding Federation offshoot. But in 1985, he was a competitive bodybuilder coming off an impressive victory in securing the title of Mr. California. While the pair may have been quite a sight to onlookers at the workout bench with their differing physiques, Touchstone has fond memories of his friendship with Franke. He said:

"Adrian and I ran into each other in Gold's Gym and struck up a great friendship, he kind of knew me because Adrian and I were both from Bakersfield, meeting each other in LA. You'd see a lot of the other

wrestlers too, you'd run into Hulk, who was a mainstay. Back in those days, if you were at Gold's Gym – it was an experience.

"Adrian and I started on that note and struck up a real close and intense friendship that I think we both enjoyed. I think we pushed each other in the gym, it was easy to push each other. And one of the things I don't think a lot of people knew was how incredibly strong he was.

"Later when I came out with workout called 'Hundreds' we did it, and I think the first time we did it, Adrian threw up in the gym! It's kind of an innovative workout, the Hundreds or Century programme, high-intensity, one hundred reps. So, Adrian did it and the day after we did it, he couldn't walk!"

Bakersfield born-and-bred it is perhaps no surprise that Touchstone can wax lyrical about the joys of living in the city. Through this lens it is easy to see with the Frankes were comfortable with raising their young family in the place that Bea knew best – and somewhere that Keith could be at rest during his time off the road. Touchstone described his hometown in the following way:

"I told friends you've never been to a place more family-oriented, a little slice of a place you can still afford to own a house, we had three or four industries that would always support, you can raise a family, to this day, it's a great place, connection with community and Adrian had all that."

Friends far and wide, and a stable home life was all well and good. Without a tag team partner to act as his handler on the road and help curb his excesses, Adonis had even less reason to control his destructive tendencies.

Travelling to Japan had been a sanctuary for Adonis for years but that too was gone as Vince McMahon declined to renew his talent-sharing deal with New Japan. McMahon, with plans to expand into Japan's wrestling arenas without any outside help, pulled the plug on the agreement, pulling both Adonis and Andre the Giant from the end of year tag-team tournament in 1985.

On the surface, Adonis' summer 1985 return to the WWF was a simple resumption of his 1981-82 leather biker/street fighter gimmick, at the request of a McMahon who fondly remembered the remarks he made on commentary back in the day. That was only half the story.

Adonis was perhaps the first and finest example of a wrestling star from days gone by given the precious opportunity to return to wrestling's biggest company, albeit with a catch. In the years that followed, many performers were subjected to wrestling's version of a Faustian pact – that is, the door was always open for a return. On a condition. Often under a new name, usually with a cartoonish new character.

It was a formula employed when Tony Atlas was brought back as tribesman 'Saba Simba;' Rotundo as taxman 'Irwin R Shyster;' and Windham as gunslinger the 'Widowmaker;' among many others. The WWF, and wrestling as a whole, was full of characters and gimmicks prior to 1985, but none maybe so unapologetically gimmicky as "Adorable" Adrian Adonis, possibly with the exception of Hillbilly Jim and family. Something different was happening with Adonis – a salacious mid-80s twist on his late 70s street tough persona.

Almost as quickly as he gained Heenan as a manager, both he and stablemate the Missing Link were 'traded' to Jimmy Hart in return for King Kong Bundy. Bundy went on to headline *WrestleMania II* against Hogan, unsurprising as Heenan was a master at manipulating himself into positions alongside top guys. While fans may not have picked up on it at the time, those who could read the signs knew this was a demotion for Adonis. The sudden change also left the question of what was in mind for a Heenan-helmed Adonis between July and August before the decision was made to change track and put him with Hart in September.

As summer turned to autumn, Adonis' minor mid-card push continued. He picked up wins over underneath talent like SD Jones and Rick McGraw, the latter in one of his final matches before his own untimely death in November. He was victorious over George Wells on August 28, 1985, on the undercard of a show held at the Michigan State Fair before an estimated 30,000 people. There was no paid attendance for the show as it was promoted as part of the fair, but nevertheless the crowd was one of the biggest in WWF history at that point. It would be topped by several WWF cards in the next two years, and Adonis would perform on most of them.

On television, delighted commentators continued to draw attention to two aspects of the recently returned Adonis: his increased weight, and his 'mysterious' demeanour.

Twice in September 1985, against Jones in the Boston Garden and McGraw on the MSG Network, Gorilla Monsoon highlighted the additional weight Adonis has packed on "in the last six to seven months." Co-commentator Jesse Ventura, retired by now due to injury, acknowledged his previous tag team partnership with Adonis as part of the "infamous" East West Connection.

In the ring, Adonis' sleeper hold had reverted to its original name, but was not used as his finish. Instead, Adonis debuted a DDT. Monsoon, well known for his overly verbose descriptions from the announce desk, had clearly not been clued in and identified the new move as a "reverse bulldog" and, bafflingly, a "corkscrew brain squeezer."

Adonis first employed the DDT on television in the WWF in July 1985 in a match with Jose Luis Rivera, using it intermittently with other old favourites like the sleeper and bulldog, for around six months. He stopped using the move in

160

February of the following year which coincided with the time that Jake "The Snake" Roberts entered the territory.

While Roberts named and popularised the DDT in wrestling thanks to his profile in the WWF from 1986 onwards, the credit for its creation goes to another man. Black Gordman, co-holder of the NWA Americas tag title with Adonis in another life, has been documented as using the move as far back as 1977, and provides a logical clue for where Adonis learned the manoeuvre.

Perhaps keen to display his wide knowledge of mat-based holds as his increased size lessened his ability to bump as wildly as before, Adonis also became the first WWF user of the hold that would gain more fame as the 'sharpshooter' during these months.

The sasori-gatame, or scorpion hold, is credited to Riki Choshu, the *Wrestling Observer* newsletter Wrestler of the Year for 1987. Choshu and Adonis crossed paths during the latter's trips to Japan in the first half of the 1980s where he presumably noticed and learned the hold, debuting it on WWF television on October 15, 1985, to defeat Rene Goulet. Several other US wrestlers experimented with the hold as a finish (Ted DiBiase, Terry Taylor, and Ronnie Garvin among them), but not until Sting and Bret Hart began using the move in 1990 and 1991 respectively did it truly capture fans' imaginations in the States.

Shortly before the change of managers, Adonis and Heenan appeared on *WWF Tuesday Night Titans*, on September 6, 1985. Adonis' comments were relatively brief, aside from a foreshadowing reference to "changing with the times," and a refusal to expose the contents of his briefcase. In response to a question from McMahon, Heenan potentially pointed to off-screen incompatibility between the two, when he admitted the caustic Adonis was difficult to manage. He stated:

> *"I'll admit there are times when this man is off the wall and I have to sit him down and talk to him and we discuss things."*

He revisited the topic three weeks later on *WWF Championship Wrestling*, as he told McMahon:

> *"Adrian is a little bit hard to control sometimes, people think he's crazy, he's a little bit crazy that's why I like him."*

While these comments were purely in character, they correlate with some of the testimony to those who knew and worked with Adonis.

With Jimmy Hart in tow from late September onwards, Adonis was occasionally announced as a member of the Hart Foundation. The name solidified soon after around the tag-team partnership of Bret "Hit-Man" Hart and Jim "The Anvil" Neidhart, but for a short period all three were considered members of the Hart Foundation unit, with the stable's moniker synonymous with the manager

161

responsible for it, such as was the case with the later Heenan Family or Camp Cornette.

Hints continued that something was quite different about Adrian Adonis. Adonis competed twice on the WWF's debut pay-per-view offering, *The Wrestling Classic* tournament on November 7, 1985. He defeated Corporal Kirschner in the first round before succumbing to the Dynamite Kid in a match which wrestling purists would have salivated over three years earlier. But it was outside of the ring that the show was most significant for Adonis.

While still sporting his natural wavy brown locks and customary leather jacket, blond streaks appeared in his hair for the first time. The briefcase was also absent. More interestingly, when Okerlund addressed Adonis as "The Golden Boy," now a name of the distant past, Jimmy Hart was quick to correct him on two occasions. Viewers were told they were instead witnessing, "Adorable" Adrian Adonis.

Adonis had time for one more overseas jaunt before tying himself down to the gimmick that would come to define him. He joined a WWF crew featuring the likes of Junkyard Dog, the Killer Bees, and the Iron Sheik for a two-week tour of Australia in November 1985, one of the World Wrestling Federation's first ever international expeditions. The WWF group stayed at the now-defunct Brisbane Travelodge in Kangaroo Point for the duration, with Adonis taking the opportunity of some downtime at one point alongside Les Thornton and Tiger Chung Lee in the form of a ferry ride down the Brisbane River.

Seven days after *The Wrestling Classic* Adonis appeared on *Tuesday Night Titans* to flesh out the subtle change, slumped in a chair alongside Hart, looking sloppy and disinterested in his tracksuit bottoms and top. Prodded by McMahon about his weight, Adonis finally reacted with the passion of a man on a court room stand admitting his guilt: "I'm fat!" he shrieked to applause from the audience.

A month later, on a December 7, 1985, show aired from the Boston Garden, Adonis wrestled for the first time with a full hair of blonde hair (but still sporting the leather jacket), in a defeat of Lanny Poffo. Poffo had worked with a very different Keith Franke years earlier and was taken aback by how much his opponent had changed, physically and emotionally, in the intervening period. He said:

> "I didn't enjoy working with him [by 1985] and I looked at the booking sheet and I saw I had four more matches to go, and then I knew because if we got in a fight, he was criticising everything, blaming me for everything. But this was not the same guy. So, it was him on drugs.
>
> "And he even yelled at me in the dressing room. He says, "Come on, Poffo, we gotta do this, this, this and this" and I thought to myself "Oh, I'm not making enough money for this." But I was married at the time,

162

and I had a daughter and I didn't want to get fired because the money was good."

Seven days after his most recent, sprawling appearance on the WWF's in-house chat show, Adonis participated in a brief promo with "Mean" Gene Okerlund, which aired on December 21, 1985. It was the final time that the leather-clad, street punk Adonis would appear on WWF television, with many a not-so-subtle reference to make it clear that the transformation, teased for months, was upon us.

Okerlund acknowledged Adonis' new hair, allowing him to briefly revisit the colourful linguistic dexterity that the Buffalo native showed often in his early promos but little after his 1985 return to the WWF:

> *"Here's what I'll say right now, it's sort of like fried, dyed and laid to the side, sort of the new thing, sort of the new era around professional wrestling, sort of a new era with Adrian Adonis, you know I don't just change when I do something, I do it."*

Invoking a phrase associated with retro African American hairstyles (and used by Red Foxx on a 1973 episode of *Sanford & Son*) completely out of context, Adonis went on to mention some new attire Hart was acquiring that would some be "out of the box." The reference to 'coming out of the closet' as a synonym for declaring one's sexuality couldn't be clearer. Just in case that was too subtle, Adonis and Okerlund continued with their not-particularly-comedic double act.

Adonis acknowledged his recent tour of Australia and noted that the local men *"just lay on their back and wait for adonises to pin 'em."* Once Adonis had flounced off set, Okerlund got the last word and assured the viewer that he "always wants to be behind that man."

It was Adonis' final remark that succinctly set the stage for what was to come in 1986, as he gave the simple sign off: "I want to wish everybody a gay new year's." With that final phrase, Adrian Adonis signalled his intention to take the WWF, and the wrestling world, in a direction like never before.

Chapter 14: The Adorable One

"It was a curious gimmick."

- *Don Muraco, 2020*

After months of hinting, fans got their first proper look at "Adorable" Adrian Adonis when he appeared to face Jeff Grippley on the January 7, 1986, episode of *WWF Championship Wrestling.* New Yorkers got a glimpse a week earlier when he defeated Lanny Poffo on the MSG Network. It was a few days later when the world got the full low-down. There was no one better to be on hand to marshal important proceedings in the life of Keith Franke than his old running buddy, Roddy Piper.

Jimmy Hart appeared first on the set of Piper's Pit, by this point established as the WWF's premier interview segment, unveiling the "new" Adrian Adonis. Adonis sashayed onto the set complete with three coloured bows adorned on his startling new mane. Piper, still heel for now, was subtle is his disdain for what had become of his old friend. Nevertheless, in an era more accustomed to long-term storytelling, seeds were sown for what would come later in the year. Piper quizzed Adonis on the bows in his hair, and Adonis responded with pride:

> *"Well let me tell you something, I've been rough and tough and mean all my life, and I can wear exactly what I want. I did jump out of the closet and there was no brooms behind me. You understand, I'm from New York City, I can do exactly what I want. I feel so much like Adrian Adonis with all this in my hair."*

In a symbolic act, cementing transition to the new gimmick, Adonis handed over his trademark leather jacket to Piper. As he did so he told the world, *"The leather jacket is going to be retired. This is a hall of famer jacket."*

Another exchange of leather jackets involving Piper placed an incidental spotlight on Adonis years after both men had passed away. When Piper's friend and MMA fighter Ronda Rousey debuted at the *Royal Rumble* 2018, she did so in a leather jacket belonging to the "Rowdy Scot," borrowed from his son Colton. Some eagle-eyed fans questioned whether it was the Adonis jacket from 1986 but it was in fact a much later one that Piper wore in the 2000s. Piper became synonymous with wearing leather jackets from the late 1980s onwards, a trend he initiated as tribute to Adonis.

Adonis mimicked the Rockettes as he exited the set, blowing a kiss in Piper's direction, and the die was cast. From the outset, it was hinted that the "Adorable" character was gay – or the WWF's twisted interpretation of what a gay man in 1986 might be. It would be a little while until this was made explicit. Presumably keen to enrage and offend as many people as possible, not least of all gay people, Adonis liberally sprinkled in elements of transvestism throughout his sixteen months as "Adorable," disinterested in the fact the two are different things.

According to daughter Gena, Bea Franke was not bothered by the 'gay' gimmick that her husband undertook and supported him in his latest endeavour as any good wife might. She noted:

> *"[She] said the same thing about the gimmick [that it was fine]. She thought it was entertaining, it was not demeaning. It was a different time. They [even] shopped for dresses together!"*

A staple of heel wrestlers going back years, the bright blonde hair of this incarnation of Adonis is more pertinent than it first seems. First and foremost, any man who would care enough about his appearance to dye his hair such a lavish shade must of course be gay. At least that was the lazy, offensive message WWF sent to its audience without having to say as much.

It evoked Gorgeous George, the effeminate wrestling pioneer who Adonis emulated, as well as other 'blonde bombshell' wrestlers of the 1960s and 1970s such as the Valiant brothers, Austin Idol, "Superstar" Billy Graham, and many more. Bright blonde hair was an easy, unspoken shorthand for audaciousness and needless preening in an era when most babyface wrestlers displayed a no-nonsense, short-back-and-sides, plain trunks-and-boots approach, Bruno Sammartino-style.

For "Adorable" Adrian, it was Vince McMahon Junior who was ultimately responsible for the character, its conception and direction, likely with the assistance of his deputy booker and right-hand man Pat Patterson, whose own homosexuality was well known among the wrestlers. For McMahon, Adonis' new persona could have been the manifestation of the influence of another finely coiffured performer who even made Junior reach for the peroxide bottle himself once upon a time.

McMahon's admiration for "Doctor" Jerry Graham is well documented. McMahon has made numerous references in interviews over the years of his boyhood love of the patriarch of the kayfabe Graham wrestling family.

A well-trodden piece of wrestling trivia involves a tale McMahon told *New York Magazine* in 1998 in which he recounted sneaking around town with Graham and secretly dyeing his own hair blonde to mimic his idol, to the horror of his wrestling promoter father. A gifted but overweight wrestler who struggled with alcohol addiction and mental health issues, Graham in his prime was a red-hot heel who helped sell out Madison Square Garden on more than one occasion. A wistful Vince McMahon told *Playboy* in 2001:

> *"Damn, Jerry, he loved to drink. There was a time when I thought Jerry Graham walked on water, but he could be a mean drunk, and that turned me off."*

The McMahons both had a soft spot for Graham and made sporadic attempts to welcome him back into the New York fold, but the 'Doctor' always found a way to derail things.

In July 1975, Graham lasted two television tapings for the WWWF with a big push planned and the "Grand Wizard" Ernie Roth as his manager, before deciding to go drinking instead. Ten years later, the younger McMahon had designs on introducing Graham as a heel manager, one of many potential replacements for the late Roth. Graham appeared as a guest on *Tuesday Night Titans* in April 1985 and was introduced to the crowd at a Madison Square Garden show the following month. He had been set to start managing on the card but was recovering from a broken leg.

It was backstage at an MSG show around this time that a conversation took place between McMahon and Graham – with Adrian Adonis the unlikely subject. Graham was due to come in as the manager of his own "Golden Graham Wolfpack," comprised of three young wrestlers who would debut under the Graham 'family name.' One of those men, Tom Hankins, was to be part of the trio as "Mad Dog" Steele Graham, and witnessed the interaction. He remembered:

> *"Jerry was standing with Vince watching Adrian at MSG and Vince called Adrian a fat slob. Jerry spoke up and told Vince what he thought. Jerry would call guys fat all of the time, even though he was about 400 pounds himself. Adrian never reached Jerry's size, but he came close enough. McMahon then cancelled our coming in."*

Despite the falling out, McMahon evidently still carried a torch for his former favourite and kept his name alive on WWF in the months that followed. When discussing the identity of the incoming manager for Randy Savage in July 1985, McMahon speculated on air that Graham might be the man. Three months later on *WWF Championship Wrestling*, McMahon evoked Graham's name one final time on WWF television, when commentating on an encounter between Jimmy Jackson and Adrian Adonis.

While co-host Bruno Sammartino rightly noted Adonis' "great amateur moves," McMahon's mind was elsewhere. Adonis, he told fans, had "an unusual physique." As Adonis prepared to finish off Jackson with a knee from the second rope, he proposed that the mid-carder was *"Reminiscent in terms of his style and his physique about 1958-59, Doctor Jerry Graham."* Sammartino agreed, mostly.

"Quite similar," said the American-Italian hero, *"apart from Jerry Graham had blonde hair."*

With these comments McMahon struck upon an idea. If he couldn't have the real Jerry Graham, perhaps he could mould one of his existing wrestlers into a warped caricature of the big man he had admired so.

The motivations which resulted in the emergence of "Adorable" Adrian Adonis were numerous. From Gorgeous George to "Exotic" Adrian Street, to Adonis' own interactions with Christopher Love. McMahon, meanwhile, was always most enthused by well-honed, sculpted physiques. As shown by his comments towards the earlier WWF run of Adonis in 1981, he was not above critiquing the physiques of wrestlers on air under the guise of commentary; here, some have theorised, was a chance to 'punish' one for an unsightly weight gain in a most extraordinary way.

Also a factor was the desire to snatch Adrian Street's gimmick and create the WWF's own reheated version; lastly, a final symbol of the torch which once flickered for Jerry Graham. Perhaps even McMahon's famously twisted sense of humour detected an opportunity to achieve all these things while watching his friend and deputy Pat Patterson observe from the side lines as they pitched a 'homosexual' wrestler to the masses.

Franke, for his part, obliged. Various people have noted over the years that Franke hated portraying "Adorable" Adrian, though he was glad to be making money and doing so in an angle that the company was behind. The truth may be a more nuanced. Franke by now had been on the road without a significant break for over a decade. He had experienced the joy of marriage and two daughters, with glimpses of domestic bliss when home. Close friend Don Muraco gave his opinion:

> *"As far as I know, it kind of just happened. It fitted what they wanted going down for him, I guess. Piper might have had more insight, his daughter says it was his idea, and I have no idea.*

> *"It was a curious gimmick. He got it over, but it was so… it was a nasty person he was portraying, and he was kind of living that life. As far as him being gay or bisexual I would never have accused him of that, knowing him that well, he liked ladies, as far as I know, it was strictly a gimmick. Maybe it went deeper but I wouldn't think so, I think it was just an act."*

A similar sentiment was shared by former WWF wrestler and executive Jerry Brisco, who was working behind the scenes for Vince McMahon by the time Adonis' transformation took place. Brisco remembered:

168

"I thought he was absolutely insane for doing it! I didn't understand why, I really didn't. When I kind of asked him, he just said, 'you know, just changing the gimmick.'

"He had always been really good friends with Playboy Buddy Rose. Buddy Rose became a hero and I think that was his tribute to Playboy Buddy Rose, and he took it a step forward and put the dress on. You know he could make it work because he was such a damn tough ass in the ring and people knew that. So, I'm not going to give him too much grief about it, face to face. You know, he made it work."

Fumi Saito's informed opinion was that the gimmick was a deliberate attempt to "force [Adrian] out," pointing towards a trusted tactic of the WWF in later years of foisting unflattering storylines or outfits on talent until they quit out of despair. Dave Meltzer, on the other hand, gave the former WWF boss more credit. He opined:

"I think Vince always kept Adonis around, though he had a lot of problems in that era. He brought him back but he gave him a very humiliating gimmick in my eyes. But he got a push, I think in Vince's eyes that was all he [could do]. He could go but the stamina wasn't there. But he could still do amazing things in the ring.

"There were a few scattered but more subtle – the [original] Hollywood Blondes – they were and they weren't. Adrian Street was the first one. I had no doubt, Adonis was Street but, in their mind, Street was too short for their [WWF] territory. To be fair to McMahon I think at his weight he needed a certain gimmick to get away [with it] because that body."

Along with the platinum blonde hair and effeminate demeanour, the weight gain was unignorable. Adonis' unremarkable physique had been the subject of comment as far back as 1981, and steadily increased. By 1986, euphemisms such as 'portly' and 'stocky' were no longer apt. Adonis was well and truly overweight, if not obese. For many, it confirmed the suspicion that he had stopped caring. Today, weight gained due to personal issues or food addiction might be met with more sympathy, such as is this case in WWE remembrances of Rodney "Yokozuna" Anoa'i. Keith Franke was not so lucky.

Friend and training partner Tom Touchstone shed some light on a possible reason for Franke's weight gain which went beyond the usual theories of addiction or sloppiness. On some level, he explained, bigger meant better for his wrestling persona. Touchstone said:

"We did [discuss his weight gain] because a lot of the workouts were around getting stronger, and I think a lot of the wrestlers of the day were getting focused like today they've got a six-pack, but in those days the

only one that was in super-shape was Hulk. You had Roddy [Piper] and Bret [Hart] with more of a thinner build, not quite as big.

"For Adrian, I think he was looking at getting larger for a presence in the ring, and a lot of our workouts we went through two or three different cycles together. At points, Adrian and I would diet together or gain weight together and so when you were gaining weight, it really didn't matter what kind of food you would eat."

As Fumi Saito noted when he visited the Franke residence in Bakersfield, his host at times seemed irritable and unfulfilled. His enormous weight gain and recreational drug use also suggested a man perhaps despondent, if not clinically depressed.

As is evident from numerous anecdotes, Franke also enjoyed messing with people's expectations and taking any opportunity to confuse, confound, or dismay. Whether this was employing the traditional heel posture outside the ring of barking at fans who approached him for interviews, or receiving negative feedback on unpleasant grooming habits, endless tales attribute a 'bad attitude' to this version of Adonis.

To think Franke's life out of the ring was simply one of frustration and self-destruction would be an oversimplification. As Joey Gaynor found out, his new friend was a multi-layered individual with a love of family, a respect for his elders, and someone who liked to make time for his passions – particularly wrestling. He said:

"[Once in 1986] I picked him up at the airport, he missed the flight back to Bakersfield. No one was in town, so we go back to my house in Whittier [in California]. I was living with my mom till she passed away, one of those old Italian women from the old days. My mother was the biggest wrestling fan in the world. I said 'Listen, we have an overnight guest, my friend Keith is here.' She said 'Keith, I don't know Keith'. I said, 'Kind of you do.' She's looking at me going, 'You brought him here, I hope the living room's tidy.'

"Get up in the morning, he's sitting at the table having breakfast and all these family photos are out and he says 'You know I'm adopted? My parents' name was Caputo,' he says. 'And your mom is Caputo.' My mom goes, 'Doesn't he look like so-and-so.' He looked like everybody. The Caputo face is very Italian, classic Italian, with the nose and so we're talking, and I knew of some people related to my mom. And now we established we're related!"

Gaynor also noted Franke's love of television and video, specifically tapes of classic wrestling matches, which the Buffalo native would trade with others on the wrestling scene in the early 1980s to catch a glimpse of his favourite grapplers from years gone by. This checks out with a separate report in a newsletter years later that Adonis sold VHS tapes as well as purchased them, including one particularly popular item which featured a compilation of several contemporary music videos. Gaynor added:

> *"He told me a lot of [the wrestlers] watched their own videos. [He said] 'I like to watch Vic Christy, I like to watch [Jim] Londos, I like to watch those films.' He would watch the old wrestling films when he could get the tapes."*

One of the first men required to put over "Adorable" Adrian Adonis in January 1986 was Tony Atlas, whose stock had fallen greatly from the early 1980s when the musclebound "Mr USA" was one of Vince McMahon's favourite acts.

In a match aired on the PRISM Network for the Philadelphia audience, Atlas put his foot on the rope during the pin attempt initially. Once pinned, he immediately rolled out to the ringside and walked away, as commentator "Lord" Alfred Hayes acknowledged the rushed departure. Clearly annoyed at having to job to Adonis, Atlas was outspoken about his WWF colleague years later in his autobiography:

> *"Adrian Adonis was the nastiest man I ever met in my life. He was a sick individual. One time he stuck a cucumber up his butt, then pulled it out and ate it...he would even eat boogers."*

In a more serious allegation, Atlas recounted a tale of Adonis selling crack cocaine from his own supply to WWF staff members backstage, before telling management about the employee's indiscretion, for his own amusement. Atlas wrote in 2010:

> *"That was the last time anybody bought anything from Adonis. They didn't trust him. That was pretty low."*

Chris "King Kong Bundy" Pallies painted a similar picture, seconding the claims on Adonis' lack of hygiene, as well as recounting in one interview a time he witnessed Adonis approach young fans in an airport to tell them there was no Santa Claus.

Atlas himself followed in Adonis' footsteps in one regard, returning to the WWF years later with a preposterous (and short-lived) gimmick. In the late 1980s and early 1990s, stars from yesteryear were often given new opportunities in the "big time" of the WWF in return for agreeing to play colourful caricatures aimed at the Federation's younger demographic. Ricky Steamboat, Tito Santana and Mike Rotundo, were all among this number.

171

George Steele was another member of the 1986 WWF roster. Steele had a different take to Atlas in a 2012 interview with Sean Oliver, noting that the idea of giving his leather jacket away was Adonis' own. While Adonis took a lot of ribbing for the locker room for portraying the gimmick, Steele claimed, he loved the attention. It is not hard to see why.

For all the justifiable criticism of the "Adorable" gimmick, it gave Adonis the most-high profile run of his career; a manager, a bodyguard, an interview segment to host, a key part in the biggest feud of the year, a house show run with Hogan, an action figure, and more.

Many subscribe to the view that Franke was being punished by McMahon for his weight gain. While an element of that may be true, many wrestlers would surely love to be punished in a manner so rewarding – main events at Madison Square Garden, and very rarely losing on television. For as many people who certify the "Adorable" gimmick was a reprimand, and one Adonis hated, plenty of others say he enjoyed shocking people, or at least, didn't care.

On a professional level, it was also the most profitable year of Franke's career, by some distance. Payslips show he earned $15,000 for 18 days' work in Toronto while employed by the WWF during this time, with Tunney Sports sending his payslip care of Titan Sports made out, amusingly, to his ring name. That alone gives some indication to that oft-asked question, why did Adonis' do the 'Adorable' gimmick?

While the opinions of his fellow WWF wrestlers in the mid-1980s is split fairly evenly, one man who did enjoy Adonis' company was Bret Hart. Hart joined the WWF in 1984 and formed a tag-team with brother-in-law Jim Neidhart the following year, under the tutelage of the unrelated Jimmy Hart – also Adonis' on-screen manager.

Before the 'Hart Foundation' tag referred to the combination of Bret, Jim and Jimmy, it was used to refer to Jimmy Hart's stable, Adonis included. Off-screen, the young Calgary native was taken under the wing of Adonis and the select group of old pros he considered his 'inner circle.' Hart wrote in 2007:

> "Long before cliques in wrestling had become a major angle, the big clique was Don Muraco, Bob Orton, Adrian Adonis, Mr. Fuji, and Roddy. They didn't hang out together for "political" reasons but for comradeship. One night, after a Hart Foundation tag match, Roddy invited Jim "The Anvil" Neidhart and me up to a hotel room for a beer with the boys, and they let us into the fold.

> "It was a privilege to sit with these top stars, soaking up their advice on wrestlers, wrestling, psychology, angles and territories. The camaraderie

in those lonely hotel rooms provided some of the most insightful and significant lessons a young apprentice like me would ever get."

In his autobiography, Hart described almost bringing a tear to the eye of the mighty Andre the Giant backstage at *WrestleMania VI* by presenting him with a drawing of the WWF roster, complete with caricature of Adonis with angel's wings atop a cloud. Though Hart has given a different recollection at times, Jim Neidhart has credited Adonis' influence in encouraging the Hart Foundation to switch their ring attire from a drab turquoise to the more eye-catching pink they became synonymous with.

Jimmy Hart gave his take on Adonis' abrupt gimmick change in an interview with columnist and drag queen Pollo Del Mar for a 2014 *Huffington Post* feature on how wrestling had changed for gay people in professional wrestling. Hart agreed that the gimmick would have to come across quite differently in the modern era. He said:

> *"We didn't try to make him any particular character, one way or another. We just wanted to make sure he was flamboyant. What a draw, what a great person he was! Just by the way he curled his hair, had bobby pins and walked to the ring with a little swagger and threw them out there, people responded to him so unbelievably and packed the place.*

> *"He was still Adrian Adonis -- phenomenal in the ring. Now if they did a character like that, I don't think it would be so flamboyant. Times have changed, and people see things different nowadays."*

Another part of Adonis' on-screen entourage, as well as the backstage clique that welcomed the young Bret Hart, was "Cowboy" Bob Orton, who was added to the mix as Adonis' bodyguard, in a move designed to sow further on-screen hostility with Piper.

Orton previously seconded Piper but jumped to Adonis' side as the issue with Piper developed, complete with pink cowboy hat. Throughout the summer of 1986, Adonis took to referring to Orton, also known as "Ace," as 'Acey,' a girlishly affectionate pet-name which recalled 'Dickie' for former partner Murdoch; 'Pipes' for Piper, and 'Adey,' his own name with the boys backstage.

Orton considered Adonis a close friend but admitted that the partnership with Adonis – resumed two years later in the AWA – did not work as well as his previous association with Piper. In a 2018 shoot interview, Orton reflected:

> *"Oh, Adrian was fun to be around, but at the same time, even me, I couldn't follow up what I'd done with Piper because that clicked so well. When I went with Adrian it was good, but it was never as good as the original – I couldn't follow myself!"*

173

As "Adorable" Adrian, Adonis' first programme was with Junkyard Dog. It was during an appearance on *Tuesday Night Titans* to build the feud that Adonis made one of the most memorable declarations of his career and confirmed what a lot of people had been whispering about. Wearing a "Frankie Says Relax" t-shirt, an unsubtle clue for the viewing audience during the time of the media-fuelled HIV/Aids panic of the 1980s, he told Vince McMahon:

> *"You have no right to laugh at what I am, or what I like to do, or where I like to go, or where I like to hang out. And I'm going to say something right now and admit it right now everybody wants to hear it and I'm going to say it...Yes, I'm gay!"*

Standing up and posing with his hands on his hips for effect as he defiantly shouted the final words, Adonis came across with all the poise of a babyface, fired up and rightly rebellious at how he had been unfairly laughed and mistreated. Through modern eyes it is difficult to disagree with Adonis – accepting the fact that he was of course a straight man playing the role for boos and jeers.

While McMahon – a stand-in proxy for the straight male audience watching at home – looked relatively non-plussed, Jimmy Hart congratulated his charge on his bravery. Seeing how Adonis, the heel, would be antagonised by good guys like Hogan and Piper in the months that followed is even more bizarre when viewed through a modern lens with the benefit of hindsight.

Adonis maintained a high profile throughout 1986 and was all over WWF television. When old friends Ventura and Piper temporarily left the Federation in the spring, McMahon toyed with the idea of a Gorilla Monsoon-fronted interview segment to replace 'Piper's Pit.' Instead, the honour went to Adonis, whose Flower Shop aired every week on *WWF Championship Wrestling* from 5 May to 30 August (the long-running show's last episode).

Segments on *Tuesday Night Titans* to force home the effeminate nature of the character included a fashion parade, a makeover, and flower arranging. Meanwhile, Adonis' verbal talents were put to use on his interview slot, as Adonis spent the summer as a set-up man for the rest of the roster. Despite a noticeable decline in the quality and clarity of his verbal delivery, Adonis' Flower Shop was the primary backdrop for the company's two biggest storylines – his own, with Roddy Piper, and Paul Orndorff's slow-building heel turn against his friend Hulk Hogan, with Adonis relentlessly needling Orndorff about living in Hogan's shadow.

Adonis enjoyed a victory over Uncle Elmer at *WrestleMania II*, possibly the only man on the roster at the time in worse shape than he was. He was also the heel fodder of choice for WWF Champion Hulk Hogan for a number of the major house shows, including February and March appearances at the Cow Palace as well as other major markets including Chicago, St Louis, and Minneapolis.

In New York and Pittsburgh Adonis formed a short-lived and unlikely tandem with Randy Savage to tussle with Tito Santana and Bruno Sammartino. The pair were victorious by count-out on June 14, 1986, at Madison Square Garden, which set up a rematch in a cage won by the babyfaces the following month. These occasions would be the final time Adonis headlined Madison Square Garden, the latter also Sammartino's last match at the storied venue. Still a great worker, Adonis relied on his ability to propel himself around the ring for comic effect to a greater degree than ever.

While many longed for his performances of earlier years, some appreciated the effort. Writing to the *Wrestling Observer* in May 1986 following a house show in Tacoma, Washington, wrestling historian J Michael Kenyon noted:

> *"I thoroughly enjoyed the performances of Terry Funk, George Steele, and Adrian Adonis. Adonis, at more than 300 pounds of blubbered rouge, is taking the art of preposterous to new heights."*

Adonis' most significant confrontation of 1986 did not happen inside the ring but backstage. In preparation for his big money house show run with Hogan, which started proper in May, Adonis was built up with a string of squash match victories over lower card talent such as George Wells, Scott McGhee and Lanny Poffo.

Confident that he was protected by virtue of his upcoming main event run, Adonis indulged himself by taking liberties with his opponents, much like he had with Terry Daniels, Matt Borne, and others lower than himself on the card – laying in extra hard shots, and generally delivering unnecessary roughness rather than looking after his opponents. With their relatively lowly status Adonis was aware the likes of Poffo and McGhee would not speak up. That was not the case when Adonis tried the same tactics with Danny Spivey.

A strapping, bleach blonde grappler who drew superficial comparisons to Hulk Hogan, Spivey had been brought in the year prior to replace Barry Windham in his team with Mike Rotundo. When Rotundo left, Spivey was given a minor singles push, with the nickname of "Golden Boy," of all things. Spivey was Adonis' opponent at a WWF TV taping on May 4, 1986, at Maple Leaf Gardens. Adonis employed his familiar bullying approach in the ring and visibly whispered to Spivey numerous times throughout the match, which aired two weeks later on *WWF Prime Time Wrestling*.

After the match, a furious Spivey was moved on by the British Bulldogs and McGhee before a real-life fight could break out. The next night they would not be so lucky. On May 5, at a house show in Flint, Michigan, the two were paired up again. This night, Spivey took exception to Adonis' perceived disrespect and aggression, and started legitimately pummelling Adonis before telling the referee that he had changed the planned finish. Spivey reached the dressing room first and Adonis joined him moments later, with both men equally furious. As Spivey told it, Adonis dived at him and Spivey knocked him out twice, causing Adonis to bleed profusely. Writing on Facebook in 2015, Spivey explained:

> *"It was chaotic, the boys separating us, Adrian bleeding, when Randy Savage came over and took me to his dressing room, to get me away from Adrian. My hands were so swollen from busting open Adrian, I had to ice them down before leaving and Adrian, he ended up with 200 stitches. The next day I had to call Vince, he told me to stop beating up his talent, which I replied, 'He's not very talented.'"*

The shoot fight between Adonis and Spivey has been much discussed by wrestlers and fans in the years which have followed, with many of those in the dressing room at the time discussing the topic from their perspective. Whether Jim Brunzell, Honky Tonk Man, Brian Blair, or another, everyone seems to agree – Adonis' reputation and behaviour was the cause, and Spivey 'won' without question.

Hogan recounted the fight in his 2002 autobiography, the only mention of Adonis in either of his tomes (*"He partied a lot and drank and raised hell and was generally a good-natured guy."*) Hogan's abiding memory was of the heat he personally received for being part of the group that broke up the fight in progress, something against the wrestler's code, as he recounted.

Laying on the dressing room floor dazed and bloodied in Flint, Michigan, did Adonis realise the irony of being floored by the man who now wore the name of "Golden Boy"? Or did he simply think back to the time when he was the man who struck fear into fans and workers alike with his shoot-fight challenge from the Amarillo days?

Those days were gone. While Keith Franke may have still considered himself a tough-as-nails street fighter, the reality by the summer of 1986 was quite different. Slow, bloated and battered, Adonis needed something special to rescue his reputation. That would come as Adonis entered the second half of the year, black eye and all, in the form of a reunion with his best friend. One which cemented both men into wrestling history.

Chapter 15: Love, rockets, and other distractions

"The man is clearly out of it."

-    *Love and Rockets, 1986*

A successful career in professional wrestling can bring with it all kinds of opportunities. While Hulk Hogan, the top star of the era, had to settle for a career as a b-movie actor and later reality star, the modern pro wrestler has a glut of other opportunities open to them.

Dwayne 'The Rock' Johnson, son of one half of the team Adonis and Murdoch defeated for the WWF tag titles, is arguably the most successful man in Hollywood. Erstwhile WWE colleagues John Cena and Dave Bautista have headed in a similar direction. Brock Lesnar translated pro wrestling fame into mainstream recognition via the UFC, while plenty have transitioned from the squared circle to the political arena – most famously, Adonis' old partner Jesse Ventura, and more recently Glen 'Kane' Jacobs. For a while now the savvy pro wrestler has been able to leverage fame inside the ring into fortune outside of it.

This has not always been the case. Vince McMahon Junior, armed with a marketing degree from East Carolina University and a desire to make as much money as possible from his dad's booming business, has been widely credited with exploiting professional wrestling's potential to licence itself across any form of media imaginable.

Wrestling merchandise existed before McMahon Junior took the helm of the WWF in 1982, largely in the form of magazines, programmes, cards, and t-shirts. No one could have quite predicted the commercial extravaganza that would take place when McMahon set forth his plans to take the company global, something set in motion immediately after purchasing the group from his father and the other stakeholders of Capitol Wrestling Corporation, the Federation's original parent company.

Saturday morning kid's cartoon *Hulk Hogan's Rock 'n' Wrestling* debuted on CBS in September 1985 with a cast drawn from the Federation's colourful roster at the time; Adonis was not one of them.

Six months earlier the company debuted in select areas on pay-per-view in the form of *WrestleMania*, the first time a professional wrestling event had aired in the fledging format in the United States. In the interim, the company debuted on network television as *Saturday Night's Main Event* took the coveted late-night timeslot NBC usually reserved for *Saturday Night Live*, thanks to a blossoming relationship between McMahon and television executive Dick Ebersole.

Each of these was a significant milestone, and one to which modern professional wrestling owes a significant debt. One less discussed but equally important landmark is the wave of action figures that the WWF introduced to the market in 1984. Titan Sports contracted toy manufacturer LJN to produce and distribute the line of figures, one which was soon joined on the shelves by a rival line produced by the AWA and Remco around the same time.

Though basic by modern toy standards and lacking the now-standard articulation, the LJN figures have become cult collectibles and are fondly remembered. LJN produced more than sixty figures between 1984 and 1989 under its 'Wrestling Superstars' banner, with "Adorable" Adrian Adonis featured as part of the fourth wave of figures in 1987.

After Japanese magazine tributes to Adonis and Murdoch, and a trading card in the 1982 "Wrestling All-Stars" series produced by Jim Melby and Norm Keitzer, Adonis' LJN figure was the only merchandise produced for Franke during his lifetime that was not a t-shirt, magazine or trading card.

Ironically released only a short while before Adonis' abrupt departure from the WWF in spring 1987, the 8-inch rubber figure displays an overweight, heavily made-up Adonis in garish pink tights, complete with limp hand gesture. It is unlikely that this first foray into the realm of children's Christmas toy fodder held much interest for the veteran grappler, being more used to pulverising opponents than having his likeness used to promote kid's toys. The figure featured prominently in at least one promotional poster. Amusingly, Adonis was also one of three WWF wrestlers portrayed by children, alongside Hogan and Randy Savage, in a 1987 TV advert from Canadian toy chain Grand Toys, in a short clip which resurfaced online years later.

A prototype of the Adonis figure wearing a multicoloured scarf, also featured in the same magazine advert, but was never released to the public. Other versions of the figure which did hit the shelves, albeit in limited quantities, including odd twin-packs bundling Adonis separately with Corporal Kirchner, his *The Wrestling Classic* first round opponent, and mild-mannered WWF announcer Vince McMahon, of all people.

Like many features of 80s wrestling paraphernalia, LJN figures now sell for handsome sums, including the Adonis doll when it occasionally turns up for sale. A reissue of the Adonis figure with a black card background has become particularly sought after due to its scarcity and was at times believed to be a myth since it was released as part of 1989's sixth series, well after Adonis had left the WWF and died.

Elsewhere, Adrian Adonis made his comic book debut in a story which was only noticed by a handful of fans at the time and has been largely forgotten today. Nevertheless, it holds a small but important place in comic book history, due to it being the work of one of the medium's most legendary creators.

The comic book in question was issue sixteen of the first volume of *Love and Rockets*, published by Fantagraphics in March 1986. The brief but absorbing tale, titled 'A True Story,' stretched to only four and a half pages in length, but demonstrated a fascinating overview of Keith Franke's career up to that point despite the modest page count. The story was written and drawn by Gilbert Hernandez, aka 'Beto.'

Comics-creator brothers, Gilbert, Mario and Jaime Hernandez gained recognition in the 1980s for their work on the *Love and Rockets* series, an early example of the wave of non-superhero, alternative comics that rose to prominence throughout the decade. Still published more than forty years later, *Love and Rockets* started in 1981 and quickly received critical acclaim, drawing its stories from a range of influences. Over the years these inspirations have included the brothers' Mexican American heritage, punk rock music, and, often, their childhood fascination with professional wrestling.

Youngest brother Jaime Hernandez is the member of the trio most strongly associated with wrestling and has written several comics over the years displaying his fascination with women's wrestling in particular. In 1986, a chance encounter with the latter-day Adonis prompted Hernandez to recall a memory of the man he used to be.

On December 11, 1985, just days before the increasingly effeminate Adonis would 'come out of the closet' on WWF television, Hernandez and his then-girlfriend (and now wife, Carol Hernandez) were among 9,000 fans who attended a house show at the Los Angeles Sports Arena. What he witnessed at the show, both in the ring and outside it, led Hernandez to spend the first few weeks of 1986 working on the story in question.

Hernandez and his brothers grew up in Oxnard, California, one of the regional strongholds of the NWA's Southern California territory for many years. The group promoted several Mexican stars to appeal to the local Hispanic demographic and was Hernandez's first exposure to wrestling. Hernandez explained why he and his brothers were drawn to professional wrestling at such an early age, taken in by the realism and violence of the action as many young children of his generation were. He said:

"As a kid we started watching wrestling in the mid 1960's. I thought it might be real as we would see violent stunts that promoted upcoming live shows. The most disturbing was a locker room interview where a handcuffed Killer Buddy Austin beat up Mark Lewin pretty bloody. Only on wrestling could you see such violence on TV.

"I was from an earlier time, so my heroes were Bobo Brazil, Luis Hernandez, The Destroyer, Pedro Morales and The Medics. Later it was El Santo in monster movies and then Piper and especially Ric Flair! Dusty Rhodes had the funniest mouth of all I have to say. Jaime features the women because he's always liked them more than anything else in rasslin'."

The autobiographical comic strip told a similar story, as the first panel recounted Beto watching wrestling at a friend's house ten years prior, circa 1977. Having not watched wrestling since his youth, Hernandez, now about twenty years old, had his attention drawn to one man in particular, *"flipping about putting on a show worthy of the grapplers of my youth."*

Hernandez recalled his younger brother, Jaime, attending one of the weekly shows in Oxnard, and reporting back as to the identity of the man in question (while copying his trademark 'bulldog' manoeuvre in the backyard). It was of course, "Gorgeous" Keith Franks, who spent a transformative six months of his early career fighting the likes of Roddy Piper and Tank Patton across California. His interest piqued, the writer as a young man attended a show for himself. "I myself brave the local matches and witness the man at work myself," the story continued. "I am not disappointed." He added:

"I only went to one show in Oxnard and I thought Franks was old school funny. Somebody from the audience asked him if he was going to a burger joint afterwards and he smoothly said, 'I only eat prime rib.' You had to be there. The show ended with a spectacular battle between Piper and TNT Tom Jones. They ran outside the building fighting and the crowd followed them. Piper and Jones had to continue the 'act' by smashing trash cans over each other and ending it with Piper running into a building and locking out Jones!"

As the story described, life went on and wrestling and all its colourful characters, Franks included, faded from the television screen, and mind, of Gilbert Hernandez, who proceeded to forge a highly successful career as a comics writer and illustrator. Readers saw a glimpse of Debbie Harry from Blondie alongside Andre the Giant on the cover of *The Ring's Wrestling* magazine from 1980, but the fad had passed, for all intents and purposes. That was until the blossoming relationship between the WWF and Cyndi Lauper.

Gilbert spotted his younger brother watching wrestling on television several years later, and noticed Lauper being interviewed by Piper. The ensuing media attention – coined the 'rock and wrestling connection' brought about another heyday not enjoyed by the industry since the 1950s.

Among the many colourful characters now on the scene that Gilbert noticed, such as Dusty Rhodes and King Kong Bundy, was his old favourite Keith Franks, albeit with a new persona: *"That's right! Gorgeous Keith Franks is back with a brand-new identity!"*

This time it was his then-girlfriend that attended a show with some friends, reporting back that Adrian Adonis, as he was then known, received significant abuse from the crowd. Hernandez decided to accompany his girlfriend to a show and see for himself the man who had entertained him all those years earlier.

At the LA show in December 1985, Hernandez and his girlfriend had no idea what they were in for, as the former Keith Franks put on a display of erratic behaviour for which he had become increasingly known within the industry. Before the show, Hernandez's girlfriend, a photographer, staked out the arena entrance to get some candid shots of the wrestlers making their way into the building. When they spotted Adonis making a call in a phonebooth, he saw them watching him and poked his tongue out at the pair, which they originally mistook for playful banter. When he finally emerged, Hernandez's girlfriend summoned the courage to request permission to take a picture.

Adonis, like many pro wrestlers of the era, stayed in character as a nasty, unapproachable heel and yelled at the young lady, before reluctantly allowing her to take a snap. As she walked away, he also threw some insults the way of her boyfriend for good measure. Hernandez wrote at the time: *"We decided to sit down and reflect upon what the hell had just happened."*

As they did so, they overheard a conversation between arena staff about a wrestler who had taken food from the concession stand without paying and insulting the ladies behind the till until they had to call security. The pair speculated this too was likely Adonis, who had meanwhile been mixing with fans and starting arguments before the show began. Things didn't improve when the bell rang. Hernandez recalled:

> *"That night he was acting up a little meaner than usual. He threatened the concession stand ladies for not giving him free hot dogs. C'mon, these were just older moms and they looked scared. He pretended to snort coke off the ropes which the promoters weren't too happy with."*

The 'rope snort' bit was definitely something Adonis knew would draw heat from the crowd, as it had done years earlier in the AWA when he first performed it. The

181

comic described the opening matches of the card, one of which featured "Iron" Mike Sharpe defeating S.D. Jones.

Hernandez had his doubts about whether Adonis would be allowed to perform in his condition, being clearly intoxicated. To his astonishment, Adonis made his way out for a match against an enhancement talent named Billy Anderson. Page four of the comic stated:

> "The man is clearly out of it. He's staggering and strutting all over the ring making lewd gestures to the audience. At women and children too!"

As was the case throughout his career, Adonis managed to put in an action-packed performance despite his outside of the ring distractions. From beating his opponent, a little too convincingly, to the point the referee looked concerned, Adonis proceeded to mimic snorting cocaine off the ropes, as Hernandez illustrated months later.

Once the match was over, Adonis grabbed the house mic and insulted the fans, throwing a chair at the ring announcer. Adonis was escorted away from ringside by security while starting a fight with a fan. He then turned his ire to a security guard, before being physically pulled behind the curtain by fellow wrestler-turned-agent Chief Jay Strongbow.

To Hernandez's amusement, when the ring announcer thanked fans at the end of the night and read some of the names who would be in town the following month at the same venue, fans saved the most rapturous reaction for Adonis. His antics, while worrying, had gone down a storm.

Adonis was indeed on the card the next time the WWF came to town, but it was a very different man who took to the ring on Valentine's Day of 1986 – an 'Adorable' one in fact. As Hernandez concluded in his comic, written around the same time:

> "Adonis has since then modified his act in that he's aping the late Gorgeous George's routine...the 'new' Adonis is getting popular with the fans now. Sigh, I guess you just never know, huh?"

The air of bemusement was topped off in the final panel as an impression of the 1986 Adonis, prancing and preening, with a flower atop his head, beside an approximation of the photo from his girlfriend a few months earlier. In between the two stood a bewildered self-portrait of the author, likely channelling the emotions of many wrestling fans and onlookers equally baffled by the transformation of "Gorgeous" Keith Franks that had taken place.

Hernandez in 2020 recalled the nasty demeanour Adonis displayed that night, and the added weight he carried, but also the talent and charisma the wrestler still displayed:

> *"He was a little dumpier in his later days but never lost the wise-guy humor. I don't remember if I ever saw the photo [we took],"* noted Hernandez. *"I don't know if he ever saw the comic."*

Alluding to the chaotic aura which seemed to follow Adonis around, Hernandez added: *"When I heard he died in a car wreck hitting a moose, I wasn't surprised."*

Perhaps an updated edition of the modest, five-page "True Story" comic is overdue.

Love and Rockets Issue 16 (February 1986) – "True Story"

Copyright Gilbert Hernandez and Fantagraphics. Reproduced with permission.

Chapter 16: WrestleMania III

"That could be something from a mad dream or nightmare that I have nightly."

- *Adrian Adonis, 1987*

The antidote to the black eye from Dan Spivey was soon at hand. As Adrian Adonis entered the summer of 1986, Franke continued to fully embrace the character which had shocked fans and was already erasing the work of the last twelve years in their minds. Adonis was about to launch into the feud which defined him and led to the one match of his that every wrestling fan is familiar with, thanks in part to the man who stood across the ring from him. It was, of course, "Rowdy" Roddy Piper. It could not have been anyone else.

The careers of Piper and Adonis intertwined early, and they developed a firm friendship – and tag team – in California, in the embryonic stages of their careers. By the time they met again in the ring in Portland, both had grown significantly as wrestlers. When they jumped to the WWF at the start of 1984, not only were they together once more but their divergent paths had seen them grow into two of the most engaging wrestlers of their generation, Piper especially. For each other, they represented humble beginnings, a shared respect, and how far both had come. Most importantly, they represented friendship in an industry which often made such a thing hard to find.

Born within a few months of each other, Roderick Toombs and Keith Franke shared more than just a career path. Each man had overcome a degree of upheaval in his early life. The future 'Hot Rod' was kicked out of high school and the subsequent falling out with his father prompted him to leave home at just fourteen.

Franke meanwhile was adopted at a week old, given up by a mother who did not feel she could cope. Piper theorised in later life that each man harboured a fraternal gap in their lives that was filled by the other. Finding themselves in each other's orbit during their wrestling careers was far from a coincidence.

Piper appeared as a guest on the *Steve Austin Show* podcast in January 2014. Austin, whose own wrestling career began only after Adonis had passed away, has made his admiration for the "Adorable One" no secret, and professed his love for Adonis' work as a heel on the show, dubbing him *"one of my favourites of all time."* Piper opened up about his own love for Adonis:

> *"He thought I was his brother. When we were in LA, when we 22 years old, we were called the Twenty-Twos, I had to pull him off Mil Mascaras, he was stretching everybody. And he was an orphan. And he looked*

horrible, big boy, and God bless him, he'd be in the gym, 'How do I look Pipes, how do I look;' 'You look great Adey. Eat more tuna fish, do whatever you want!'

"He came from a little bit of a mobbish background, and he loved me, he saved me, a couple of times. But the one big time we were in Poughkeepsie, and I was having issues, and he says 'come here, come here'. He says, 'you know what's wrong with you – you need to buy a house. Put your kids in it.' I'd never had a house, I didn't understand...I'd never had a home. I don't have a place I grew up. So, I bought a home and that's thanks to Adrian.

"He was the last funeral I went to. I did the eulogy at his funeral. And his wife was there, and I always used to tell Adrian – I still do – 'I love ya.' And I meant it, and he'd say it back to me. And she'd say, 'What's wrong with you guys.' I remember Adrian and I were talking one time, and he said, 'Pipes when I die, I want them to throw a party.' I was doing the eulogy and it comes to my mind and I said it and the casket was closed. And from the lady came a sound of pain I can't mimic. And then she came over to me and she said, 'Now I know why you guys said that.'"

It is tempting to think that fond recollections of his late friend were a trait only in Piper's later life. It is true that Piper, increasingly sentimental in the years before his own passing, mentioned Adonis more the older he got, but his friend was always closed to his heart.

The *WrestleMania III* match was cited by Piper in a 1995 issue of *WWF Magazine* as the one which he felt best summed up his illustrious career. While this was a kayfabe publication aimed at an adolescent audience, it is notable for the mere mention, and photograph, of Adonis, as part of the article. Adonis had barely been mentioned in any official WWF channels since his departure.

The pair had a bond outside of the ring like few others. Inside the ring, they shared something just as valuable: chemistry. When Piper returned from his post-*WrestleMania II* acting hiatus, he needed a reliable and compatible opponent to re-establish himself as a fixture in the top tier of the World Wrestling Federation. There was only one man for the job.

The Piper-Adonis feud of 1986-87 is a perfect example of the long-term storyline and planning that many sceptics believe is missing from the modern wrestling product. Much has been written within wrestling that modern feuds are started and stopped with little opportunity for fans to get invested in what is happening, making it far less likely that they will feel able to get behind the protagonist.

That was not the case for Adonis and Piper, with the seeds of their on-screen entanglement planted as far back as May 1986, nearly a year out. Few guessed it at the time, but when Adonis took up residence as the host of the Flower Shop interview segment, he was unwittingly building the ire of the man he had usurped.

Piper's Pit had been a mainstay on WWF television programmes for more than two years by 1986, as Piper used his quick wit to throw the spotlight on other, less verbal wrestlers, often belittling them or raising their tempers. It led to plenty of memorable moments. When Piper left for Hollywood after his April 1986 boxing match with Mr T, Piper's Pit went with him. In his place, the despicable Adonis set up shop, literally, and put his own spin on the wrestler-hosted interview segment, still very much in its infancy as a concept.

Adonis could hold his own with most on the mic, though substance abuse had slowed his reactions. The Flower Shop was ever-present on WWF programming throughout the summer of 1986. In storyline, Piper returned to find he had been replaced and was not amused by what he found. To be supplanted was bad enough. For it to be at the hands of someone, something – like Adonis – was totally unacceptable.

Piper made his feelings known on the August 16, 1986, episode of *WWF Championship Wrestling*. Making his first televised appearance since *WrestleMania II* (he emerged briefly for a first-round *King of the Ring* loss to Don Muraco at a house show in June), Piper abruptly appeared in place of Muraco, Adonis' scheduled guest for that episode's edition of the Flower Shop. Piper's simmering anger was further amplified when it became clear that Adonis was also being seconded by "Cowboy" Bob Orton.

Orton had previously served as Piper's on-screen bodyguard in the WWF, a role which earned him the additional nickname of "Ace" Orton from the "Rowdy Scot." A week prior, Adonis unveiled Orton as his new bodyguard – pink hat and all – planting the seeds for what was to come.

> *"I would like to say that you have been doing a tremendous job in my absence and I would like to thank you for taking it over, but I am here to take my show back. And the first thing that has to go is these damn flowers,"* Piper admonished Adonis, after an initially friendly greeting.

When Adonis declined to move aside for the returning 'Scotsman,' things became tense. *"Wait, wait a second. You don't seem to understand something. I invented this!"* Piper was equally unimpressed when his former charge appeared at the side of Adonis. *"Acey, did I get that right? They call you Acey now? What are you doing man?"* Piper pleaded with Orton. *"Tell me something, man. How much money did he pay you to wear pink?"*

Orton ignored Piper's insinuations and made it clear that his arrangement with Adonis was strictly business, with his new 'employer' paying him more than the 'peanuts' he got from Piper.

187

The following week, Piper once again interrupted an edition of the Flower Shop, this time with Adonis preparing to interview the team of Nicolai Volkoff and the Iron Sheik, with their managers Freddie Blassie and Slick present. Fresh off a squash win over AJ Petrucci, Piper proceeded to admonish Adonis once more – throwing in some horrendously racist slurs in Slick's direction.

Astonishing by modern standards though it may be, in a few short segments, Piper, a heel in the spring, had established himself as one of the hottest babyfaces in the company. The fans, many of them just as misogynistic as the character Piper was portraying, were rabidly behind him and were already salivating at the prospect of Adonis getting his due.

The final ever episode of the syndicated *WWF Championship Wrestling* continued the story, with Adonis discovering that WWF higher-ups had granted Piper permission to appear as an 'official guest' on an upcoming instalment of the Flower Shop, overriding Adonis' wishes in the process. Protesting to commentators Vince McMahon and Bruno Sammartino, Adonis ranted as the show went off the air:

> *"Hold the phone and cut the garbage. Let me tell you something, Vince McMahon and Mister Bruno. Nobody dictates to the Adrian Adonis. They're trying to say that the WWF has overruled me and that Mr Piper or anybody else can go on my show at any given time. I made the Flower Shop, that is my show, I am the man of the hour. Who does Roddy Piper think he is - Judge Wapner?"*

Adonis could not resist the urge to shoehorn in a reference to the television personality and host of *The People's Court*, while getting his point across.

Adonis' fears were confirmed the following week on the inaugural episode of the rebranded *WWF Superstars of Wrestling*. A smug Piper informed Adonis that Piper's Pit was officially returning in place of the Flower Shop, to the delight of the fans. Upon hearing the news, Adonis duly went berserk, flying into a rage and destroying the set of his own show before being calmed by Orton.

On September 13, 1986, episode of *Superstars*, the shoe was on the other foot. With announcer Ken Resnick preparing to appear as the first guest of the new Piper's Pit, now it was the turn of Adonis, Orton and Jimmy Hart to do the interrupting. Adonis announced a challenge - a showdown. In two weeks, it would be the battle of the wrestler-hosted interview segments. The Flower Shop against the Piper's Pit. Adonis delivered the news in his trademark style – fascinating, rambling, and littered with references to what he had been watching on television recently:

> *"Punky Brewster? Let me tell you something Mr Brigadoon, you backstabber, you low-life, you lice-ball, you Judas, you egotistical*

hambone. You're old news Piper, you're old news. It's like I'm watching M.A.S.H. three times on one night. I'm gonna tell you something right now, Piper. The Flower Shop has class. You're so egotistical, I thought you were a man. I'm a real man. Let's put it this way, I'm 1995. You're old hat, you're stale.

"The Flower Shop is today, I made history on national TV. And I'm gonna tell you something Mr Piper. You had to go behind my back to the WWF higher echelon you sneaky lowlife...You ever heard of the Battle of the Bands? You ever heard of the World Series? Well, I'm gonna make a challenge right now. Two weeks, two weeks from today. I am gonna have a debate with you. What do people really want, the Flower Shop or Piper's Pit."

While WWF Champion Hulk Hogan continued his red-hot feud with Paul Orndorff and newer characters like Jake Roberts and the Honky Tonk Man were bedded in, the Piper-Adonis feud had quickly built to the most engrossing and consistent programme on WWF television in the summer and early autumn of 1986. Fans were with Piper every step of the way as he campaigned to remove Adonis from the talk show he had commandeered from its 'rightful' owner. The programme was built up diligently each week on television, with logical progress from episode to episode.

The September 20, 1986, edition of *WWF Superstars of Wrestling* advanced the slow-burn storyline a little more, with both parties shown preparing for the upcoming showdown of the talk shows in their own ways. Adonis and Jimmy Hart were seen busily tidying the set, with the former showing his anxiety over some "prize tulips" that Piper had supposedly knocked out of place earlier. Separate footage showed a broom-wielding Piper maniacally sweeping and swiping at a pile of rubbish on the floor which appeared to be the remains of a since-destroyed Flower Shop set.

The 'debate' took place a week later, as the week-to-week build for Adonis and Piper continued. The lengthy, ten-minute segment featured both sets placed next to each other for the duration and commenced with Piper preparing to open proceedings before being rudely interrupted by Hart and Adonis. Adonis duly introduced his special guest for the week, "Acey" Cowboy Bob Orton – mispronouncing his name and calling him 'Horton' on more than one occasion. He proclaimed:

"The super bodyguard of 1995, howdy doody; well, my reasoning for this week's Flower Shop to have you out here is to have your biased opinion on who is the best television wrestling talk show hostess and who has the best show on television today. Please give me the answer from the bottom of your heart."

189

Adonis became fond of his '1995' reference, a phrase he began using with increasing regularity during this period, to presumably signal himself as the future, though there was little evidence to back up this claim. Orton duly obliged with an insulting tirade towards Piper, before both were interrupted by vintage Piper. "*You sure are an ugly son of an unnamed goat, aren't you,*" Piper goaded Adonis. A raucous crowd cheered gleefully as Piper started to get the upper hand of the verbal dual: "*Listen, you old cow,*" Piper chided a flustered Adonis.

As the heels fumed, the camera followed Piper to his side of the set, and focus switched to Piper's Pit. The host finally announced his issue with Adonis:

> "*I am not trying to be the nicest guy in the world. What I think this guy is doing to wrestling is downright [wrong]. I think that for you looking like that and making a complete idiot of yourself I think that for my sport I think that it's absolutely silly.*"

Piper did not explicitly say he disliked Adonis for being gay, or for dressing and acting effeminately. He did not need to: "*That's okay sweetheart, we don't want you tripping on your pantyhose.*" Piper then unveiled his own guest, the Magnificent Muraco, who he also intended to antagonise for trying to fill his shows during his absence.

When an enraged Muraco admonished Piper for paying more attention to Adonis, Piper ranted that he was trying to stop the 'cartoon' show that Adonis is created. Muraco, playing the heel – although it is hard to tell by modern standards – then gave an impassioned plea in defence of Adonis, who very much looked like the victim of bullying at this stage.

"*This is America,*" shouted Muraco, "*we're allowed to dress as we like, come as we want, go as we want, do exactly what we please.*" Piper, finally, stooped even lower, casting homosexuality as a bad influence on children. "*I have children,*" yelled Piper. "*I have children and I don't want them watching this idiot.*"

All of this was a precursor for an attack by the heels. Muraco, Orton and Adonis easily jumped Piper and destroyed the set of Piper's Pit, leaving the 'hero' laying. Piper got a measure of revenge a week later, arriving on crutches and demolishing the vacant Flower Shop set with a baseball bat – the final on-screen appearance of Adonis' segment. Two weeks later, a recuperated Piper returned to host Piper's Pit, with Jimmy Hart as his guest. Piper appropriately tortured the weasely on-screen manager to the fans' delight. Curiously, Adonis was not present. He was not even mentioned.

It was not a coincidence. Shortly after facing Hogan in the main event of an Albany, New York house show on September 15, Adonis' bad habits caught up with him. Whether it was his weight, substance issues, hygiene, or general lack of effort, has never been completely apparent. What is clear is that it must have taken something significant for Vince McMahon to feel action was needed, as the decision came at the exact time that the pre-taped angle of Adonis and friends' attack on Piper aired in front of millions of fans.

To dismiss one half of a major angle, which the company had been building for weeks and had high hopes for into the spring, was not a decision taken lightly. The October 6, 1986, edition of the *Wrestling Observer* newsletter carried the news but could not discern exact details. Adonis, it was claimed, had either been fired for "irresponsible" behaviour, or otherwise had been suspended for "a month or two." Whatever the case, the Piper feud – and what would have been a huge blow off match – was off.

Immediately, the WWF pivoted to the next best option, placing Piper in a makeshift programme with Orton and Muraco, in Adonis' place. Things became a little clearer in the following week's *Observer*:

> *"After watching Saturday Night's Main Event, my first impression is that all this talk of Adonis getting fired is simply a cover story, despite the fact that it's the number one story in the business."*

The show, taped on September 13 but with commentary added shortly before airing on October 4, made it clear that Piper's issue was now with Muraco and Orton. During the second fall of the card's tag-team main event, commentator Jesse Ventura announced Adonis sustained a (kayfabe) shattered elbow as a result of Piper's attack, to explain his absence.

This was enough of a hint for Meltzer to suggest, rightly, that the firing was in fact a short-term suspension, and Adonis would return around Thanksgiving to "heat up" the original Piper feud. Rumours that LJN had not cancelled plans for the Adonis action figure in the works compounded the theory.

More conjecture featured in the newsletters in the month that followed: Adonis was definitely through with the WWF and would instead work part-time in Japan; Adonis was fired for trying to hold McMahon up for more money; Adonis was short on alternative offers and was keen to get back in the WWF's good books; Adonis would be back in the spring after cleaning up his act. Each had an element of the truth but in isolation was far from the full picture.

Fans did not have to wait long for their answer when Adonis returned at a pair of shows in mid-November 1986. He marked his return to television at the November 19 tapings for *WWF Superstars* and *WWF Prime Time Wrestling*, taping two squash match wins over Mario Mancini and Paul Roma, with Jimmy Hart back at his side.

At the same taping, Adonis wasted no time in taping footage for the resumption of the Piper feud. As Piper prepared to interview George Steele, Hart returned to seek revenge for his humiliation weeks earlier. The distracted Piper did not notice the returning Adrian Adonis who used a prop crutch to attack his foe, before locking in his famed sleeper hold. He did not sell his 'shattered elbow,' but it was acknowledged by Ventura on commentary when it aired on television on November 29.

Newsletters speculated at the time that Adonis had been a short-term fix called to fill in on house shows, while McMahon had little faith in Piper against Muraco and Orton as a major feud going forward. Just like that, Adonis was back on television, back in his role as a top heel in the company, and the WWF's hottest feud of the year could continue its build to *WrestleMania*.

Piper and Adonis traded barbs over the following four months as the eventual climax of their feud moved into view. By December 1986, newsletter gossip had rumblings of a celebrity-focused tag match for *WrestleMania III*, which might see former foes Piper and Mr T, now both on the side of good, take on Adonis and Orton.

Elsewhere, it was speculated that the WWF office did not think Piper was getting over effectively as a babyface and intended to turn him heel once the series with Adonis was done. The crowd reaction as Piper made his way through the curtain at the Pontiac Silverdome shows they could not have been more wrong.

In the ring, Adonis and Piper worked a number of house show matches to prepare for their climactic match in Detroit, including one meeting officiated by guest referee Andre the Giant at Nassau Coliseum, a month before *WrestleMania*.

Around the same time, Adonis participated in a series of six-man tag elimination matches throughout March and April of 1987. This was the test run for what became the hugely popular 'Survivor Series' matches that would feature on the pay-per-view of the same name. Adonis was gone from the company by the time of the first such show but did play his part in one particularly watchable match of this kind.

Adonis made his final appearance at Madison Square Garden, a venue he had frequented off and on for five years, on February 23, 1987. He teamed with Randy Savage and former NWA Champion Harley Race against their respective 'Mania opponents: Piper, Ricky Steamboat and the Junkyard Dog. The match was awarded a very respectable four stars by the *Wrestling Observer*'s fledging rating system, the highest any Adonis match ever received.

Prior to the showdown with Piper, a seed was also planted elsewhere which would play into one of *WrestleMania's* most historic moments. On the February 28, 1987, *Superstars of Wrestling*, Adonis teamed with the Dream Team of Brutus Beefcake and Greg Valentine against the Can-Am Connection (Tom Zenk and

Rick Martel) and Lanny Poffo in what was, for all intents and purposes, a routine six-man tag.

As Beefcake pummelled Martel in the corner, Adonis called on Jimmy Hart to supply an implement hidden on his person – scissors. Adonis then began snipping at the hair of the man stuck in the corner. To his dismay, Adonis – who had his eyes wide open and was not convincing in his role at all – 'accidentally' cut Beefcake's hair, not realising his mistake until it was too late. A furious Beefcake then lost the fall and the pair had to be separated. The 'error' was a set up for Adonis to feud with Beefcake on the other side of *WrestleMania*, by which point Beefcake would be a babyface. It never came to pass.

While the appearance of the scissors was somewhat random to television fans, relevance was attached shortly. Piper announced that the upcoming match with Adonis would be his retirement match from the World Wrestling Federation, win or lose, as he had plans to shoot further feature films.

Adonis added a detail of his own. Recalling their furious battles in their early days in California (although this was not acknowledged on WWF television shows of the time), Adonis declared their *WrestleMania* confrontation would be a 'hair vs hair' match – hence the new-found preoccupation with clipping other's locks. Adonis made his point by taunting Piper at ringside throughout March with scissors on more than one occasion, once during an edition of Piper's Pit at the Philadelphia Spectrum.

The match has gone down in wrestling history but very nearly didn't happen. Less than two weeks before *WrestleMania*, Piper was involved in an incident that almost cost him dearly. Piper worked the main event of an eight-man elimination tag match at the Los Angeles Sports Arena on March 16, 1987, designed as his farewell to the LA crowd he knew so well. As Piper wrote in his 2002 autobiography:

> *"The way the dressing rooms were set up, you got changed in one room and then went to another room to shower and then you came back to dry off and get dressed. Also, in this dressing room, they had many makeup mirrors, which had the big lightbulb lights around them, just like you see actors and actresses use in the movies. Well, as I was talking to the guys, I put my towel on top of my Halliburton, which was sitting on the top shelf near one of these lights. I stripped down into my birthday suit, and went to the other room to shower, forgetting to take my towel with me.*

> *"When I was done showering, I went back into the dressing room soaking wet, in search of my towel. Leaving a pool of water beneath me, I reached for my towel next to my case and I began talking to Harley. The next thing I knew, I slipped on the water that was dripping off my wet, naked*

body and fell toward the mirror. In the process of slipping on the drenched floor, my left index finger accidentally went into one of the empty bulb sockets, causing me to get electrocuted."

According to Piper, he successfully sued the arena management for compensation. Despite this impediment, *WrestleMania III* is rightly regarded as an extraordinary achievement in wrestling history. 'Mania was already established as the WWF's primary show of the year. Building on the celebrity-laden first edition of 1985 and the failed experiment of the following year, few could have imagined the heights the third instalment of the WWF's premier show could reach.

More than 93,000 fans (or 78,000, depending on who you believe), packed into the now-demolished Pontiac Silverdome for a card headlined by WWF Champion Hulk Hogan defending against his former friend, Andre the Giant. Images of the match, and the Intercontinental title fight between Savage and Steamboat, have passed into wrestling lore and shaped many a young wrestling fan's childhood. In a nostalgia-fuelled industry built around manufacturing '*WrestleMania* moments', this show had plenty. Adonis and Piper played their roles perfectly.

The match itself was just six minutes long, largely due to Adonis' limitations. But the drama the two built over the preceding six months had done its job. Fans bought into the animosity between the real-life friends and the heat was palpable. The time had come for Adonis to get his comeuppance, and Piper was just the man to do it. Piper remembered years later the once-in-a-lifetime feeling he had in front of so many raucous fans and recalled taking the rare step of gazing out into the crowd. He told the *Metro-West Herald News* in 2015:

> *"That was the first time in my career I was taken aback so much. I looked you [the fans] in the eyes. The moment the fans gave to me, it was very gracious. We looked at each other for the first time and said hello. It was 30 seconds and then it was back to work."*

And what work it was. Piper commented many times in the years that followed that the success of the match was all Adonis' doing. This might sound like mere generosity from a friend, it is hard to dispute when watching the match. The red-hot crowd did its part as Adonis bumped all over the ring for his buddy, determined to be the perfect bad guy. He succeeded.

Despite his ample frame, Adonis flew across, over and through the ropes, to give a convincing impression of Piper's invincibility, in the last great performance of his life. As a short but engrossing encounter, the match has stood the test of time as a lesson for any wrestler on how to get someone else over. Piper knew it too and was not shy to acknowledge the work Adonis put in to make him look great. He recalled the experience in a 2015 shoot interview:

"I was honoured to be with Adrian and Jimmy Hart. It turned out real interesting. They had a cart that looked like a ring that brought you down to the ring. Well, when my match was up the cart came back behind the curtain and something was wrong, a technical thing, I don't know what it was. And I just said, 'I'm going.' And I ran to the ring.

This led to a low-key iconic moment of Piper striding towards the ring on foot, the focal point among tens of thousands of wrestling fans who erupted at his entrance.

"And then Adrian being the great professional he was, it was his idea to have a hair match, just because he was that good a guy. And then we go on with the mirror and the hedge [clippers]. And if you've ever tried to cut somebody's hair when it's wet – it doesn't work. So, I wasn't being that nice and I said – Beefcake, you shave it!"

An opening exchange of blows quickly descended into chaos, as Piper whipped Adonis with a belt, before the 'Adorable One' returned the favour. A reversal of an Irish whip led to that old Adonis favourite, the flip bump head over heels into the corner all the way out of the ring. Adonis and Hart were yanked back into the ring, only for both to again be unceremoniously dumped outside to the concrete. For each bump, the crowd grew louder still.

With the help of Hart from the outset, Adonis took control at the two-minute mark and the action slowed right down, which was essential given the breathless start. After more interference, the stage was set for Adonis to lock in 'Goodnight Irene,' and tease that Piper might be done for.

A seemingly lifeless Piper was revived by Beefcake and promptly cleaned house. With one more comedy bump left in him, Adonis swung with the shears for Piper's head but missed, bouncing them off the ring ropes and back into his own face. All that was needed was for Piper to lock on a sleeper hold of his own, and for referee Dave Hebner to call for the bell. Cue jubilant scenes among the crowd.

Piper's victory was assured, but the mayhem was not over. A fan jumped into the ring and was unceremoniously dumped out. Adonis punched a mirror amid Piper's hazing. Newly turned babyface Brutus Beefcake was charged with the task of actually cutting Adonis' hair.

Initially using the garden shears with which he would become synonymous, Beefcake quickly turned to more traditional clippers, also proving difficult on the wet, sweaty hair of Adonis who can be vaguely heard getting annoyed with Beefcake. Three months earlier at the NWA's *Starrcade* pay-per-view Jimmy Valiant used a battery powered hair shaver on Paul Jones which avoided the problem. Just like that, Brutus "The Barber" Beefcake was born. Another component of WWF history to partially thank Adrian Adonis for.

It was not just fans who were entertained. The match earned a commendable three-and-a-half stars from the *Wrestling Observer*. Dave Meltzer wrote in 1987:

> *"While short, this was very entertaining. Piper deserves a lot of credit for putting on a good show as less than two weeks before match time he electrocuted himself while touring – I believe he touched a live wire in a hotel room while coming out of a shower. If Adonis isn't the grossing looking wrestler in history he's surely in the top four or five, but he can still perform."*

The *Observer* further noted a rumour that Adonis was to reappear in April with a 'Brian Bosworth-style' haircut. This was a reference to the NFL player-turned-actor who achieved stardom in the late 1980s, and sported a striking blonde mohawk-mullet hairstyle.

The sad but perhaps inevitable postscript to Adonis' WWF feud with Piper, and the pitch-perfect crescendo it reached is that it was essentially his last action in the company. After a three-week break and with head shaved completely bald, Adonis returned to wrestle at the April 23, 1987, television tapings in Worcester, Massachusetts. Adonis shot a promo with Gene Okerlund for a Duluth house show, as well as footage for Missy's Manor, a talk show segment hosted by WWF newcomer Missy Hyatt.

In both, he swore revenge on Beefcake before storming off. When Hyatt was canned, the talk show was dropped and none of her interview segments ever aired. He also wrestled his final ever television match (aired on May 2), defeating ex AWA jobber Jake Milliman in just over a minute with a sleeper, with Jimmy Hart once more by his side.

In both appearances, Adonis gave off a meaner, more serious air and no longer seemed to be doing the gay gimmick. While still nicknamed "Adorable," there was no make-up, no bows, no flowers. Perhaps the old attitude was to remerge.

Three house show matches followed, the last on April 27, each against Beefcake. Tellingly, of the three matches contested, each man won one each while one was a draw. This points towards Adonis' reluctance to be the heel fall guy again so soon after doing the same for Piper.

Much has been speculated about Adonis' final departure from the WWF and often it is said Adonis was unwilling to work a programme with Beefcake – or to have Beefcake come out on top. Beefcake has admitted as much in interviews and has suggested Adonis may have been encouraged in his attitude him by a former tag partner. He said in 2019:

> *"He was just obnoxious, his hygiene was horrible he dressed like a pig, he ate like a pig, he acted like a pig. Sometimes he was good guy, fun, but*

he also liked to screw with people. He was teamed up with Dick Murdoch, southern guy, super old school, thought us 'long hairs' didn't belong in the business.

"He was in Adrian's ear a lot and Adrian and I were supposed to work after WrestleMania. He completely poisoned Adrian, so Adrian quit, right after WrestleMania III, just walked out. He was supposed to work with me, but there was no way he was going to work with me. Murdoch had totally screwed his head up."

Despite Beefcake's claims, others have contended that Adonis was promised much after *WrestleMania*, and his exit was the result of promises unfulfilled. It is conceivable that McMahon pledged Adonis more money to see out the Piper feud, or a serious push as a top heel, without the gay gimmick, if Adonis agreed on the head shaving gimmick.

Daughter Angela Perides believed that to be the case, and that her father went through with the Piper match on the basis of reward to come afterwards. When that did not transpire, he was left bitter and disappointed with McMahon and the WWF as a whole. She said:

"Well with WrestleMania III, Vince had said, dad was supposed to take that, that was supposed to be his, Vince came to him and told him – this is from my grandmother – Vince came to him and asked him, 'Hey, Roddy's retiring, so we'll give this one to him, we'll give you WrestleMania IV and we'll give you a ten-thousand-dollar bonus for cutting your hair.'

"He said 'Yeah sure, that's fine,' because him and Roddy were friends outside - my grandparents had a ranch out in Bakersfield, California, they had Roddy Piper visit my aunt a couple times and they were really good friends.

"Roddy he was right with it but then when it came time to negotiate because it was all verbal, Vince said 'No, we're not gonna do that,' so my dad said, 'Well, I quit.' [McMahon] said, 'Well, you can't work anywhere you're under contract for six months, if you work anywhere I'm going to sue you.' So, my dad didn't work for six months."

Joey Gaynor likewise recounted knowledge of his friend being unhappy with his treatment post-*WrestleMania III* and pointed to it as the reason for Adonis' departure. He recalled:

"After WrestleMania III, money wasn't paid, he wasn't happy, he wasn't paid a bonus. He said 'I'm leaving the WWF to go to Japan.'"

Despite having a house show run with Beefcake advertised in towns until at least May 17, Adonis did not work again for the WWF after April 27, 1987. Posters were printed for a cage match between the two at the Rochester War Memorial – the site of one of Adonis' first ever matches for the WWWF twelve years prior– but it never happened.

Wrestling magazines such as PWI reported at the time that Adonis was fired by McMahon due to "dress code violations," an opaque reference no doubt to Adonis' apparent inability to take care of his physique, hygiene, or general reliability.

He would not be the only person given that curious reason by the WWF office in 1987, as Tom Zenk years later in a shoot interview cited the exact same phrase given by Pat Patterson and Terry Garvin when he was admonished for a perceived indiscretion.

At a time when McMahon was reloading the WWF with incoming stars such as the Ultimate Warrior, Ted DiBiase, Curt Hennig and Rick Rude, it is not hard to see why the cantankerous, curmudgeonly Adrian Adonis appeared like one headache too many. With the Piper feud and match done, it was easy to dispense of him. So that is what the WWF did.

Chapter 17: Adonis as gay stereotype

"Hey Adie, which way is the wind blowing today, brother?"

- *Hulk Hogan, 1986*

Jerry Graham's overweight, aloof style, and resplendent golden locks may have set Vince McMahon's creative juices flowing in 1985 but there are other obvious ancestors of the "Adorable" persona that Adrian Adonis eventually assumed.

In the 1930s, George Wagner was considered good but otherwise unremarkable during his first few years as a professional wrestler. That changed when he noticed a *Vanity Fair* article on fellow grappler "Lord" Patrick Lansdowne, the monocled 'nobleman' who wore glossy robes and walked to the ring accompanied by a pair of valets every night.

This inspired Wagner to reinvent himself in 1941 as Gorgeous George, a flamboyant grappler with a hitherto unseen glamourous image. Wagner antagonised the crowds with his foppish behaviour and became known as the 'Human Orchid,' his platinum blonde hair held in place with colourful pins. The most famous wrestler of his era, Wagner perfected the template of the arrogant bleached-blonde heel which would be carried down through wrestling generations like a precious family heirloom by the likes of Buddy Rogers, Ric Flair, and many others.

The key was not only in looks but also mannerisms. Gorgeous George showed how effective the effeminate persona could be at riling up a crowd to a wrestler's advantage. This baton was picked up with equal enthusiasm by the likes of "Pretty Boy" Pat Patterson (legitimately gay and Vince McMahon's right-hand man in 1985), Terry Garvin (who worked as Patterson's deputy), and more.

In many ways, Wagner and his followers simply echoed the Mexican wrestling tradition of 'exoticos' within Lucha Libre. Since at least the 1940s, the country has hosted male wrestlers incorporating feminine elements to their physical approach or costumes, challenging the typical masculinity displayed in pro wrestling. At first, these characters were overwhelmingly villainous, and fodder for the abuse of crowds of men desperate to prove their manliness while watching partially clothed guys struggle with each other.

Wagner was influential in other ways, inspiring fans far and wide through the emerging platform of television in the 1950s. Many such onlookers grew up to become stars in their own right and interpolated Gorgeous George's sense of pizzazz and excitement when they performed. James Brown, Bob Dylan, and

Muhammad Ali are just some of the mega stars who have cited Wagner as an influence on their showmanship.

The number of wrestlers who did the same could hardly be counted but would certainly include the likes of "Superstar" Billy Graham, Dusty Rhodes, Ric Flair and more. Ali, famed for his 'trash talking' patter, credited Gorgeous George as the inspiration for his seemingly arrogant public persona. Ali was taken in by Wagner's manipulation of the crowd when he witnessed a match in person in Las Vegas in 1961. He told a reporter years later:

> *"Oh, everybody just booed him. I looked around and I saw everybody was mad. I was mad! I saw 15,000 people coming to see this man get beat, and his talking did it. And I said, 'This is a good idea!'"*

The pair supposedly met backstage after the match, and George educated Ali – already an Olympic gold medal winner – on the importance of showmanship for selling tickets. If you can create a persona which people want to see lose, you have done well. If they will spend money to see it, even better. This has been the essential formula for professional wrestling for as long as the pursuit has existed; to create enough interest in seeing a performer defeated to encourage people to part with their money to see it. It's a business model wrestling promoters have sought to emulate over the years with varying levels of success.

A more immediate example of inspiration for Adrian Adonis in mid-1980s American wrestling was "Exotic" Adrian Street. The Welsh son of a coalminer, Street was a skilled wrestler with a muscled physique who prided himself on being a real-life tough guy. This straightforwardly masculine presentation was juxtaposed with stylings inspired by the British glam-rock scene of the 1970s.

Street, accompanied by real-life wife Linda as his valet, proudly exuded sex appeal and power in a confusing but intriguing mix. It is a cocktail that has inspired many imitators in wrestling, from Adonis to Goldust to Rico, but none that have done so while harnessing the delicate ring psychology so masterfully. In a 2019 interview, when asked about Adonis, Street noted:

> *"Mimicking or copying my mannerisms, like the limp hand and all that sort of stuff, that's easy to do. I've never ever seen any of them try to copy my wrestling skills because they can't do it."*

He later added:

> *"He was a good wrestler as Keith Franks, [but] totally pathetic as Adrian Adonis; he didn't have a clue."*

Street was well known in North America by the mid-1980s for his successful tenures in Calgary's Stampede Wrestling, Florida, and Mid Atlantic. But by the end of 1985, Adrian Street was 45 years old; too old, in Vince McMahon's eyes, to bring the "Exotic" character to his vibrant, colourful World Wrestling Federation.

McMahon had the next best thing – an Adrian of his own (although the shared first name, which Street was born with and Adonis picked up in 1978, was likely a coincidence). It must have sounded a fair proposition to Adonis. Having been the target for homophobic chants from the crowd since as far back as at least 1981 in both the WWF and AWA, perhaps he felt the time had come to give those same fans what they seemed to want – a gay man to yell slurs at. What he actually achieved was an abomination.

In the summer of 1984, a full eighteen months prior to the first appearance of "Adorable" Adrian, the WWF debuted a character which might be seen as a milder practice run for the eventual Adonis persona. Brutus Beefcake, portrayed by Hulk Hogan's real-life best friend Ed Leslie, debuted at a July 31 television taping, and was initially conceived as a male stripper.

With his name possibly inspired by the music video for Cyndi Lauper's "She Bop" single which premiered on MTV four weeks earlier, Beefcake's arrival was accompanied by a lengthy (and excruciating) vignette in which he danced awkwardly for a group of women in a bar, removing his top as he did so.

Just to make sure the crowd new exactly what they were getting, ring announcers declared the new arrival's place of origin as San Francisco, rather than Leslie's actual hometown of Tampa, Florida, given the California city's reputation as an unofficial 'gay capital' of the world. The mildly sexual element of Beefcake's persona, one which may have drawn the ire of male crowds, was largely written out within weeks of Beefcake's first match and he continued in the vein of a more anodyne heel.

It is a fleeting example of the long-held practice of queer coding within professional wrestling, when a character 'seems' gay, bisexual, or lesbian. While this depiction may never be explicitly confirmed within storyline, such characters will often display stereotypical traits or behaviours to distinguish them from 'normal' heterosexual characters. Examples occur in all media, with one example being various Disney animated movie villains, with flamboyant male characters surrounded by meek minions, from Scar in *The Lion King* to Captain Hook in *Peter Pan*.

Adonis was probably not subtle enough to reach this classification. Instead, it was an uncultured attempt to use the vehicle of a 'gay' man to elicit heat from the crowd. That intrigue, the WWF hoped, would lead those same fans to pay to see Adonis in person, or on pay-per-view, to get their points across. At best, it had a mixed effect.

Bill Apter, long time wrestling journalist and photographer, spent many years at ringside taking pictures of Adonis and his colleagues in action during the late 1970s and 1980s, as well as writing about his exploits in the fondly remembered 'Apter Mags,' including *Pro Wrestling Illustrated*. He was also responsible for the picture of Adonis and Ventura on the cover of the June 1982 edition of PWI, photographed at a studio Apter rented in Midtown Manhattan.

Wrestling magazines and newsletters had a field day with Adonis' new character, receiving plenty of feedback into their mailbags in response to articles such as the cover story on Adonis which featured in the September 1986 issue of *The Wrestler*.

Adorned in a cape with a flower in his mouth, Adonis was pictured under the headline: *"From leather to lace: Adrian Adonis' startling transformation."* While some fans were clearly dismayed, Apter recalled a mixed response:

> *"I don't know why he agreed [to the gimmick]. Sometimes when you work for a company you do what is asked of you. Vince McMahon and creative thought this would probably be outrageous enough to get him over in a huge way. [Readers had a mixed reaction] Some laughed, some hated it, some loved it."*

Perhaps for older fans, reared on Gorgeous George, the character was not completely unexpected. Homoeroticism and homophobia had always been part of professional wrestling. Adonis was certainly not the first blonde bombshell of 'questionable' intent to enter 'their' arena, in the eyes of some. Likewise, any onlookers with experience of Mexican wresting by 1986 were familiar with the practice of the flamboyant male high-flyers, something which evidently took a while longer to catch on in the States.

Gorgeous George is typically the starting point for discussions on displays of non-traditional masculinity in a wrestling ring. With a profile enlarged by the rise of television, Wagner became the inadvertent inspiration for many that followed.

Featured in magazines, television shows, and on film, Gorgeous George even had the honour of inspiring a lookalike on the small screen, in the form of "Ravishing Roger," a carbon copy who took to the ring in a 1951 Warner Brothers animation. Of course, the prancing Roger was made short work of by wrestling champ the Crusher – until Bugs Bunny intervened.

Wagner inspired two sides of the same coin: blonde bombshells like Jerry Graham and Pat Patterson, to name a few. And the golden-haired, muscle-bound posers – anything but gay, of course, – Billy Graham, Austin Idol, and a certain Hulk Hogan; homoerotic musclemen all, ever treading wrestling's thin heteronormative line.

On December 30, 1985, while commenting on Adonis as he made his entrance to face Lanny Poffo at Madison Square, commentator Gorilla Monsoon informed fans that the newly blonde heel had "shades of Gorgeous George." Monsoon was one of many in the WWF office at the time who may have crossed paths with Wagner but if he or any of his peers gave Adonis pointers on how to mimic the great man, he does not appear to have paid attention.

In many ways, Keith Franke was always playing a gay character, whether he knew it or not, years before mincing out with flowers in his hair in 1986 alongside Jimmy Hart. From the first time he took on the "Gorgeous" moniker and portrayed a young playboy, feuding with the likes of Roddy Piper and bloodying his handsome 'Roman' features, Franke hinted at a proud sexuality.

Naming himself 'Adrian Adonis' amplified a sense of sneering self-love, while echoing a name often mistaken for feminine (i.e., 'Adrienne' or 'Adrianne'), all with a playful alliterative pattern that echoed the Village People's catchy "Macho Man" – also famously employed by a pro wrestler. Next came the leather jackets, which made it look like he was auditioning to be a member of the aforementioned band.

Franke even admitted openly to *People* magazine in 1982 that people "think we're queer" in reference to himself and Ventura. Neither of the pair could have failed to hear the 'f-word' chants which followed them, and Adonis in particular, from the AWA to the WWF throughout the 1980s. All this before declaring himself 'adorable.'

When he did pick up the bows and ribbons and lean fully into the 'gay' gimmick for the WWF in 1986, Franke's portrayal of the character was horribly hackneyed and predictable. He may have intended to copy Adrian Street, but the Welshman's success came from his ability to convincingly transmit menace, despite all the distractions and trappings.

For Adonis, it was awkward segments on *WWF Tuesday Night Titans* which showed him arranging flowers with 'Bruce,' having a makeover from 'Jack Darling,' or taking part in a fashion parade. Fans cringed at the obvious innuendo that Adonis, McMahon and company exchanged with the actors, and each other. Franke's unsightly weight gain and general lack of passion for the job soured fans further on what they were seeing.

It was not just the fans who were turned off by the new-look Adonis. Ahead of a run of house show matches in 1986, WWF Champion (and real-life friend) Hulk Hogan made sure everyone knew exactly why Adonis was worth demeaning. Interviewed prior to a match at the Cow Palace, he declared in character:

> *"Well, you know, "Mean" Gene, "controversial" is not the word for this dude, man. I mean, hey Adey, which way is the wind blowing today,*

brother? Have you taken a walk on the wild side in a while? Well, all I've got to say to you, Adrian Adonis—Cow Palace, San Francisco! This is Hulk country, brother. And you're going to take a walk on the wild side.

"Not the kind of walk you like to take, because there ain't going to be any swishing around. You're going to walk right into the pit of the combat zone, brother. You're going to face the eye of the Hulkster, brother, and then you're going to go down. You know, "Mean" Gene, I just wonder what kind of entourage Adrian Adonis – Adorable Adrian – is going to have with him at the Cow Palace."

The January 26, 1987, edition of the *Wrestling Observer* newsletter carried its annual awards for the previous year. The honour of 'Best Gimmick,' went to Adrian Street. Clever, fierce, and popular with fans, the achievement was even more impressive considering he did not work for a national promotion. Nevertheless, Street won a close reader vote, edging out WWF star Jake Roberts.

Contrast this to Adonis, who won the double 'raspberry' of 'Most Embarrassing Wrestler' and 'Worst Gimmick Performer.' Overweight and shunned by fans and critics alike, it was quite a fall for the man ranked joint best in the world by the same publication less than five years earlier. Adonis again won 'Worst Gimmick' in 1987. For wrestling historian Karl Stern, it's not hard to see why. He said:

"I thought it was horrible. It was offensive to homosexuals, there was nothing flattering about it. It was just an excuse to make a fat, slobby, stereotyped effeminate character and it did a disservice to Adonis and the LGBT community as well.

"I believe Vince McMahon must have liked the Adrian Street character and this was his vision of what a WWF version would look like, but he missed every bit of the nuance and turned it into an embarrassing joke. I have no idea why Adonis agreed to it beyond that was his job and he was probably getting paid pretty well."

Since Adonis, the WWF/WWE has followed up over the years with a variety of 'gay panic' gimmicks, most famously Goldust in 1995. The son of Dusty Rhodes was painted up to look like a living golden Oscar statue, and McMahon again took pleasure in tuning fans' minds towards what they were seeing, with "bizarre" and "androgynous" the favoured phrases of the former chairman, echoing how he described Adonis in his first WWF run all those years ago.

Others have come and gone. The gyrating Rick Rude, "male model" Rick Martel, hairdresser Rico, gay couple Chuck & Billy who (almost) married on air (a storyline offered years earlier to Brian Christopher and Scott Taylor), party animal Adam Rose, and the preening Tyler Breeze, to name a few. Outside WWE it is a similar story, with Johnny B. Badd a cut-price Little Richard, the 'West

Hollywood Blondes' in WCW, and more. During his lifetime, Adonis inspired a couple of copycats too, notably John Foley in Canada for a time.

Other ideas have been considered and never made it off the drawing board – such as the plan to debut Mike Enos and Wayne Bloom in 1991 as the 'Bomber Brothers.' Supposedly they would portray a pair of brothers curiously over familiar with each other. Instead, the name was toned down to 'Beverly Brothers,' and the duo got away with only having to dye their hair platinum blonde (of course) and wear capes. They did gain a manager, the girlish 'Genius,' portrayed by Lanny Poffo.

Poffo worked with Adonis years earlier in the Carolinas and has claimed since that he could have done a much more nuanced and convincing take on the 'Adorable' character in 1986, only for Vince McMahon not to give him the chance. He remarked:

> *"Adrian Adonis announced on [Tuesday Night Titans] that he was gay, and I noticed that everybody said, 'oh good for him.' The thing is, he wasn't gay – he was far from gay, absolutely not gay. But he said he was and that was the rub.*

> *"Now I'm not gay either but as The Genius, I denied being gay and that caused everybody to call me gay more. You act defensive, and I would've listened to the reaction of the people, I would look gay, walk gay, talk gay, wrestle gay and...deny gay, you know so that was where the fun was."*

The 'Adonis' trend has been mimicked outside of wrestling over the years. In popular animated series *Futurama* (2000), hard-drinking robot Bender found success in one episode within the 'robot fighting league' with a 'Stone Cold' Steve Austin-style tough guy character known as 'Bender the Offender.' When Bender's fan power started to wane, a sleazy promoter type suggested a new, daring direction – the 'Gender Bender.' No longer a tough guy, instead Bender now wrestled in a pink tutu, under a girly wig – blonde of course. It is not hard to see where the inspiration for the episode came from.

WWE, and wrestling as a whole, has a chance in 2023 and beyond, to move beyond the gay moral panic approach that has been the touchstone in the past. Openly gay wrestlers work on the main roster of WWE and have done since Darren Young confirmed his sexuality publicly ten years ago. Gay, lesbian, and bi wrestlers are signed to major promotions in increasing numbers and promotions are making up for lost time in terms of operating as forward-thinking, progressive company. Employing and spotlighting the likes of Sonya Deville and Shayna Baszler is evidence of that, with no offensive sexuality or gender-based aspects to their on-screen personae – as it should be.

In many ways, the narrative arc of "Adorable" Adrian is extraordinary when viewed by modern eyes and the cliché that it would never happen nowadays is true. In storyline, Adonis – the bad guy, remember – decided to be true to himself and his inner feelings and decided to start dressing and acting how he wished. He even went so far as to confirm publicly that he was gay. While (heel) managers and commentators such as Jimmy Hart and Bobby Heenan encouraged and sympathised with Adonis, every other 'right thinking' person in the company was dismayed, sending the message to fans that they should be too.

When Adonis did 'come out,' McMahon, interviewing him, mustered only a roll of the eyes and a dismissive 'whatever.' The sentiment was summarised for all to see (and hear) that year at *WrestleMania II*. Adonis' opponent, the risible Uncle Elmer was a loveable hillbilly redneck character. Adonis was, as always, the villain, and the fans reminded him with loud, homophobic chants at every turn throughout their (admittedly awful) match. It would be a similar story too in the best remembered feud of his entire career – the final showdown with "Rowdy" Roddy Piper.

Chapter 18: A return to Verne

"A lot of things are strange. Tiny Tim was strange, Johnny Carson gets strange, everybody gets strange.

"Even once in a while I get strange too."

- *Adrian Adonis, 1988*

After departing the WWF for the second time in a little over six months, permanently this time, Franke returned home to Bakersfield to take stock of his career options and plot his next move.

Heavier than ever and bald as a coot, Franke found himself hampered by a gimmick and reputation that had lowered perceptions of him throughout the industry. To make matters worse, Franke was also on the outs with the number one employer in his field, one which was shrinking rapidly by 1987.

During two months at home, he was able to revel in some extended time with his young family, a rarity during the previous decade, with daughters Angela and Gena now aged seven and two. As Fumi Saito had noted during his visit two years earlier, the Frankes enjoyed a happy home, but one which Franke himself found difficult to be completely comfortable in.

Unable to truly relax and enjoy the fruits of his labour for too long, Franke knew that he would be back on the road before too long. As he had done so many times in the early days of his career, when he looped back to Vancouver, California, and Japan, Franke returned to an old territory to get back on his feet.

By the summer of 1987, the American Wrestling Association (AWA) was a shadow of its former self. Much like the career of Adrian Adonis himself, the AWA was once respected and revered for its focus on serious wrestling but had since seen the world of pro wrestling pass it by. Now too late to reverse its reliance on ageing stars, the AWA limped along for the second half of the 1980s.

Whereas the early part of the decade had been a three-horse race for supremacy between the AWA, the WWF in its pre-expansion phase, and the Jim Crockett Promotions arm of the NWA, the Minneapolis-based company failed to match its competitors as they moved into the pay-per-view era of the mid-1980s.

As Vince McMahon confounded his critics by expanding his company's success into children's cartoon shows, network television slots, a slick magazine, must-have action figures and more, the AWA could do little but look on longingly. The pill was an especially bitter one to swallow considering much of the New York company's success stemmed from one man, Hulk Hogan, who had spent years as a headliner for the AWA, with Gagne unable or unwilling to capitalise.

While the AWA did pack more than 20,000 people into the Hubert H. Humphrey Metrodome in Minneapolis for its *WrestleRock* show in the spring of 1986, the card was not well received. Viewed as a pale and belated imitation of the WWF's successful 'rock and wrestling' motif, fans were unimpressed, and it proved to be the company's final ever stadium show.

By comparison, the AWA's next major card the following spring, *SuperClash II*, welcomed fewer than 3,000 fans to San Francisco's Cow Palace. Despite featuring promising young talent such as The Midnight Rockers, Sherri Martel, Madusa Miceli and Curt Hennig – who defeated 51-year-old Nick Bockwinkel for the company's world title – the show did little to counter the impression that the Minnesota territory was now a dumping ground for the has-beens, the never-wases, and the occasional prospect who would move on to greener pastures before long.

Given the transformation to Adonis' physique, character and reputation, and the rapid changes to the wrestling landscape during the mid-1980s, his options were limited. Dave Meltzer explained:

> *"The Adorable gimmick would've really hurt him in other territories, like Jim Crockett Promotions, it would be tough to overcome it. And the flipside is, Verne [Gagne's territory] was dying by that point. There weren't a lot of alternatives, that was the sad part of 1980s wrestling. You've had your run and they're done with you. Memphis was no money. Everyone else was dying or bought. It was real tough even for a guy with years and years on national television."*

It must have been a chastening experience, nearly 15 years into a career which had spanned the globe. This was the setting for the return of Adrian Adonis to the AWA, bringing the "Adorable" nickname with him. Jake Milliman, Adonis' last televised opponent in the WWF, spent the bulk his career in the AWA, and gave his thoughts on Adonis' return to working for Gagne in a 2018 interview with writer Steve Johnson. He said:

> *"They had shaved Adrian Adonis' head, and that was the last TV match he did [for the WWF] before he got killed in the car wreck. Verne wouldn't take him back [in 1987] until he slimmed down. I didn't know any of that at the time.*
>
> *"After he left Verne, he just ballooned right back up again. He was light, he was really light. I've heard guys talk about him that was the best*

compliment you could get in this business; he was that good. He was a little reluctant to take bumps but that's all right."

Though fans would have certainly followed his travails in the WWF, given the Federation's heightened national television exposure, Adonis had not appeared for the AWA since a double count-out with Greg Gagne at a house show in St Paul in November 1982. Much had changed in the intervening five years for both performer and company. While the AWA still had a national television deal, with ESPN no less, it left a lot to be desired.

The Gagnes, along with ESPN network executives, had been keen to find a new location in which to shoot matches when the deal was signed in 1985. They chose the Showboat Sports Pavilion, a large unused space on the second floor of the Showboat Hotel & Casino on the Las Vegas strip, converted in the early 1980s to host roller-skating and boxing.

Adonis appeared first at a house show on June 30, 1987, defeating jobber Stoney Burke, followed by two more appearances in August, all in the Minneapolis area which remained the group's home turf. Each show struggled to get more than 1,000 fans into the arena, which only enhanced the impression of a business on the decline.

His second appearance, defeating Bobby Bold Eagle on August 1, aired four weeks later on AWA television, marking his on-screen return. A subsequent squash match that aired in mid-September was followed by a promo by heel manager Paul E Dangerously (Paul Heyman), making it clear that, in storyline, Adonis' return had been engineered by the leader of Dangerous Alliance.

Adonis first had the pleasure of the Showboat at a September 18 television taping where, along with two more squash victories, he interfered in the affairs of former NWA Champion Tommy Rich, setting up a mid-card feud. Despite all Adonis' faults and the many apparent reasons not to, it was clear that the AWA, limited as it was, would give things a try with Adonis. Presented as an important heel, squashing jobbers, placed in a notable feud, alongside an upstart manager, things could have been much worse.

The vastly overweight Adonis returned to television with the same gimmick that had carried him to the most profitable year of his career with the WWF. Once more, he was "Adorable." Verne Gagne, still in charge of the company and ever a traditionalist, expressed a preference that Adonis return with his early 1980s leather jacketed-biker look.

Adonis declined, believing it made sense to cash in on the national exposure the effeminate, preening WWF run had gained him. This may be evidence that he did not hate the 'gay' tag, nor that it was 'forced' on him by Vince McMahon. Perhaps by this point he felt he had no other choice. Either way, the Adonis that emerged in the AWA in summer 1987 picked up where he left off in the Federation.

Heyman and Adonis had good chemistry, and Adonis showed he still had the tools to be an effective bad guy, just about. The vast majority of his technical wrestling skill had vanished, but Adonis still had the ability to fly around the ring and bump, even if those bumps did look more laboured and telegraphed.

Heyman was just 21 years old and in his first year as an on-screen wrestling manager. His insight and expertise would see him go on to become one of the most notable careers in professional wrestling over the decades that followed, from performer to promoter, to executive producer and more.

He has spoken little over the years since about his time at Adonis' side in the AWA, brief as it was, but Heyman's year in the AWA did feature prominently in his popular 2014 WWE-produced DVD, '*Ladies and Gentlemen, My Name is Paul Heyman.*' Adonis featured in more than one segment. One comment Heyman has made followed Adonis' death and appeared in the March 1989 issue of *Pro Wrestling Illustrated.*

PWI bestowed a special 'Editor's Awards' to Adonis and Bruiser Brody, both killed within the a few days of each other the previous July. The pair's widows were pictured with plaques for their late husbands, and the accompanying article featured words from Heyman. Despite existing in what was a fully kayfabe publication, the comments gave a realistic approximation of what the future ECW supremo likely felt in reality. Heyman told PWI at the time:

> "*Adrian was a great wrestler and he wanted people to respect him for his ability, which was pretty impressive. But on the other hand, he had to make a living and when he was in the WWF things were very competitive. Let's not forget, however, that earlier in his career, Adonis was one of the toughest-looking men to ever step foot in the ring.*"

Adonis was not alone under Heyman's tutelage in 1987. Together with Randy Rose and Dennis Condrey, the Original Midnight Express, the quartet briefly formed the original version of the Dangerous Alliance. The Alliance would gain far greater acclaim when Heyman reformed the faction in WCW with the likes of "Stunning" Steve Austin and "Ravishing" Rick Rude.

The AWA iteration of the group was short-lived, with Adonis done with the promotion in the spring of 1988, while Rose and Condrey jumped to Jim Crockett Promotions, and Heyman departed for the independent scene before joining them.

Adonis went through the motions in his short feud with Rich, attacking him and smothering him with lipstick in one particularly heated encounter to build to a blow-off. Otherwise, it was a largely forgetful stint on in Minnesota, characterised by renewed alliances with old acquaintances, and sharing some of his experience with younger stars on the rise.

It was alongside Heyman during the Rich feud that Adonis made one of the more noteworthy pronouncements during this brief run. The pair taped an interview segment with Larry Nelson which was inserted into a November episode of the AWA's weekly television show, alongside matches from a Sports Pavilion taping that took place on October 30, 1987.

Among typically offbeat comments about Liberace and Rock Hudson (both gay icons, of course), as well as Seattle Zoo, Adonis spoke of rubbing shoulders with celebrities – namedropping Sam Kinison, Joey Gaynor, Sylvester Stallone and Cyndi Lauper, the latter of whom he presumably met whilst in the WWF in 1984. It was around this time that Gaynor helped his friend explore other opportunities within the showbusiness industry, as a fall back if his wrestling career continued to stall. He remembered:

> "I said before you go to Japan why don't you come and meet my agent. For four years I was telling him to meet my agent. He said 'No, no I've got a guy, he's in Minnesota.' I said, 'Yeah he's getting you a lot of movies!'

> "Finally, he comes in and meets Joe Kolkowitz from Sports Casting. I sit out in the lobby, he comes out and says, 'We [now] have the same agent.' Joe wanted him forever. He did a Sports Illustrated commercial, and one for Japan, and was then killed that July."

Kolkowitz is a character with an interesting connection to pro wrestling. A former tennis professional turned long-time Hollywood talent agent, Kolkowitz repped the likes of sports analyst Howie Long and college football coach Mike Leach. He was also known for his friendship with O.J. Simpson. Kolkowitz developed a knack in the 1980s for helping sports stars into acting careers, largely in generic 'tough guy' roles.

His wrestling clients included "Superstar" Billy Graham, Outback Jack, and Tiger Chung Lee, the latter of whom starred in a number of high-profile action movies including Eddie Murphy's The Golden Child. Kolkowitz recalled his brief but memorable business relationship with Franke in an interview years later. He said:

> "We only met in person a couple of times, we spoke on the phone fairly frequently because I would get him auditions and he did a couple of commercials for me before he passed and he was actually starting to get some traction because I think he had, as I recall, a couple of auditions for films, although he never booked anything.

"But his appearance and how he portrayed himself was nothing like what he was like in reality. The whole effeminate side and the dressing and all that stuff was nothing like he was. And he was very funny. That's how he related to Joey [Gaynor] because Joey was a stand-up comic. He loved comedy and he was quite amusing and he would tell stories and I couldn't repeat them because it was so many years ago."

Confirming that he was the one who secured the spot in the 1987 *Sports Illustrated* commercial, Kolkowitz described the qualities that made Franke appealing for the screen. He addedL

"He was way overweight, and he was kind of past his prime, and he changed personas a couple of time. He was kind of a stud-type guy and then he became sort of an overweight cartoon of himself, so to speak. But he was a character, just a real character, and he was very natural.

"Whenever he auditioned, he was very likeable, just a likeable guy. Whereas when you're a wrestler you're either really likeable or really hateable. But when he came off in an audition he was just likeable, kind of a sweetheart, just a nice guy, a nice person. He was also a family guy, not a selfish cat, he cared about his family, was protective of them, I do remember that."

Back in the AWA, one of those old faces Adonis worked with once more was "Cowboy" Bob Orton, himself fired from the WWF in November 1987 for causing a disturbance at an airport. Again, he was installed as Adonis' bodyguard and partner. Introducing Orton in a January 1988 promo, Adonis bragged to interviewer Bill Apter:

"Well, I don't think we're going to be kissing cousins to put it bluntly, but Bob Orton comes where the money is. And also, he's a very good friend of mine, and he's not a social butterfly, he's not a social climber. You might say Mr Orton's here for the money, he's here for the challenge, because they do say that the AWA is a place of wrestling.

"A lot of things are strange. Tiny Tim was strange, Johnny Carson gets strange, everybody gets strange. Even once in a while I get strange too."

With that, Adonis turned to show his backside to the camera. If fans had been in any doubt before that they were getting a half-hearted, reheated, lower budget version of Adonis and Orton from a year earlier, they weren't any longer.

Two young tag-teams that would go onto greater things were resident in the AWA at this point, with Adonis spending time with both inside and outside the ring. Adonis and Orton's match with the Midnight Rockers, Marty Jannetty and future Hall of Famer Shawn Michaels, aired on AWA television in February 1988. It was

Adonis' most memorable in-ring showing during this period, largely thanks to the athletic young men across the ring.

Also in the dressing room was the tag team of Jerry Sags and Brian Knobbs, who had started teaming as The Nasty Boys in the AWA in 1986. Recalling how the team's aesthetic developed in its early days, Jerry Sags mentioned the influence of Adonis in a 2012 interview:

> *"Adrian Adonis saw us wrestle and told us 'I thought you guys were The Nasty Boys.'"*

Specifically, Sags noted, Adonis encouraged the pair to emphasise the more 'disgusting' interpretation of their moniker. Not known for perfect hygiene himself, Adonis masterminded the 'pit stop' manoeuvre whereby the Nasties would shove their armpit into a helpless opponent's face. Just like his influence on the Hart Foundation years earlier, Adonis was still giving out suggestions after all his ups and downs.

Another old face was Greg Gagne, the only man to face Adonis in each of his three stints with the Minneapolis-based company. The pair faced off in the finals of a tournament to crown the inaugural holder of the oddly-named AWA International Television Title.

The match aired on AWA *Championship Wrestling* on December 27, 1987, taped at the Showboat, and ended in victory for Gagne, although his reign and the title in general were very much an irrelevance in the overall landscape of wrestling.

Still very large, and way above the 290 pounds professed in the on-screen graphic, Adonis had made at least some effort to shed weight. With his hair growing back to a more recognisable wavy length, in his natural light brown, some signs of a return to normality were starting to flicker into sight.

Led to the ring for the showdown with Gagne by the mobile phone-wielding Dangerously and representing the Dangerous Alliance, Adonis was still referred to as "Adorable" Adrian and included only a fraction of the mincing, prancing affectations during his performance.

Adonis displayed a degree of technical ability against Gagne, albeit at a much slower pace than before. The finish came via an Orton run-in, prompting the disqualification win for Gagne and the short-lived revival of the Orton and Adonis pact. The title was such an afterthought, the AWA had not even created a physical championship belt for Gagne to carry upon his victory.

Orton and Adonis only wound-up tagging on a handful of occasions during this run, with their partnership lasting less than two months. In addition to their well-received match against the Midnight Rockers, they also downed the jobber tag team of Jake Milliman and John Stewart with an awful-looking spike piledriver on AWA *Championship Wrestling*, one week after the TV title match. An out-of-breath Adonis gave a post-match promo, explaining the renewed union to Mick Karch, and once again referred to Orton as 'Horton.'

> *"I don't have eyes in back of my head, I have gorgeous hair. These [Orton] are my eyes. After terminating first Roddy Piper, and now Tommy Rich, and Wahoo McDaniel...Greg Gagne's a sneak. Other people like him such as Wahoo McDaniel are a sneak. So, I have eyes and the bodyguard and the man that has the eyes is Ace Cowboy Bob Orton*
>
> *"That's right Jack, a friend in need is a friend indeed and you people haven't seen anything yet, you 9-to-5 morons that think you know wrestling haven't seen the master of disaster with his eyes walking into the squared circle because I...I...the Adorable One..."*

Adonis tailed off, unable to finish his thought. In what was one of his final ever televised promos, Adonis showed how promo ability had suffered. The words displayed fiery intent, but the old spirit was gone. These two 1988 promos alongside Orton are Franke's final ever recorded words and stand as sad, meaningless odes to a once great talent behind the microphone.

Accounts from fans who attended AWA events during this era, few though they were, have told a similar tale. One online anecdote described witnessing a despondent, perhaps depressed, Adonis staring glumly as he went through the motions at some sparsely attended high school gym. Perhaps understandably for a man who had been in front of 90,000 at the Pontiac Silverdome months earlier, he now looked like he would rather be anywhere else.

Despite coming up short in his only significant singles match of his short third spell in the AWA, a win for Adonis would have made little difference. The AWA was a bleak place, unable to innovate or emulate in the face of superior competition.

The writing was very much on the wall at the end of 1987. The elder Gagne promoted AWA cards until as late as May 1991, although the promotion had been inactive for some time by then and filed for bankruptcy soon after.

Ideas like the International Television Title, teaming up with the Memphis territory, and the lamentable Team Challenge Series of 1989 were misguided attempts to inject some impetus into the ailing territory but did little but embolden the impression of a company in the grave. Bringing in washed up stars who could no longer find gainful employment in the WWF was another sign of Gagne's desperation, and Adonis fit firmly into this category.

Both Adonis and Orton made plans to supplement their income by returning to Japan, specifically New Japan Pro Wrestling. The country had been an enjoyable and profitable destination for the pair, who teamed regularly in Japan, alongside an assortment of other North American wrestlers throughout the early part of the decade.

Adonis had not wrestled in Japan since answering Vince McMahon's short notice call to return to the WWF three years earlier, and fans had little idea how different the man from the "Big Apple" now looked and moved. They were in for a shock.

Nevertheless, Adonis spoke to Antonio Inoki and was booked on a tour that spring. Both he and Orton were due to participate in the company's New Year Golden Series, alongside the likes of Steve Williams, Steve Blackman, Owen Hart, and Buzz Sawyer. Only one of the pair made it to Japan, however.

Adonis and Orton were pencilled in to appear as a surprise on New Japan's January 18, 1988, television show, facing headliners Antonio Inoki and Kengo Kimura. Three days earlier, before they were due to fly out, Adonis competed in his final set of matches for this spell in the AWA at a television taping in Minot, North Dakota.

Recordkeeping of AWA matches in its final years is sketchy, and matches were not shown on television in order during this era, but often were saved up for several weeks before airing. Adonis bouts likely recorded during this taping included the Midnight Rockers match (aired on February 28, his last US televised appearance); a final grudge match against Greg Gagne (aired on February 19); and what should have been a nondescript squash over enhancement talent Ricky Rice (aired on January 30).

Adonis suffered a badly broken ankle during the match with Rice, caused when Adonis was whipped into the buckle by Rice. On his way to the corner, Adonis took a heavy step on his right ankle, and broke it in one swift motion. The injury was barely perceptible to viewers, perhaps a testament to Adonis' professionalism, or otherwise that it was edited out of the version which the AWA aired on television.

Either way, it was the first significant injury of Adonis' career to cause him to miss considerable ring time – not a bad record after 14 years in the ring. Doctors immediately ruled Franke out of action for at least two months, though it proved to be closer to four in total.

The injury meant Adonis missed his valuable Japan tour, and worsened a financial situation already made precarious by the actions of Verne Gagne, who, according to the *Wrestling Observer* newsletter, had cut off Adonis' weekly guarantee at the end of December. To make matters worse, Adonis believed the ankle fracture was the result of a faulty AWA ring, and blamed running over a hidden bump in the mat for his woes. While Orton made his way to Gifu to face Tatsumi Fujinami a week later than planned, Adonis was left to stew at home over his bad luck.

After losing out on pay for what would have been a two-week tour of Japan, and not receiving any money during his injury layoff from the AWA, Adonis had few options open to him. According to the same newsletter, a request during February for financial assistance from Gagne was rebuffed, and led Adonis, understandably, to consider suing the company for its supposedly dodgy ring. It is not clear if such a case was ever filed, but one thing was clear.

Adonis became more adamant than ever that, once he returned, he would not do so for Gagne. Their relationship had been strained even back when the company was hot, when the East West Connection had to strive for screen time amongst the company's old guard. This time, it had been a marriage of convenience, heading to a permanent divorce.

When enquiries to return to the WWF were rebuffed, Keith Franke committed to the one person he could rely on – himself. Using the first and only lengthy downtime of his career to his advantage, Franke resolved to take his career seriously for the first time in years. Well overdue, Adrian Adonis was going to lose weight and roll back the years.

With his ankle on the mend, Franke got himself booked on the first night of New Japan's IWGP Champion Series 1988, due to fly out in mid-May. Determined to make a positive impression on the Japanese fans he had wowed years earlier, Franke spent the weeks beforehand training harder than he had for years. Finally, the time had come to lose weight, get in shape, and take himself seriously again. Adrian Adonis was back.

Chapter 19: A trip to Newfoundland

"'No, no,' he goes. 'We'll talk when I get back.' And he never got back."

- *Tom Touchstone, 2021*

Adonis' belated return to Japan finally took place on May 20, 1988, at Korakuen Hall, about three months behind schedule. The match was Adonis' first in Japan since jumping back to the WWF to replace Ken Patera three years earlier, and Adonis first match of any kind since suffering the injury to his ankle in January during what turned out to be his final appearance for the AWA.

On the first night of New Japan's IWGP Champion series, the returning Adonis wrestled veteran Kengo Kimura, co-holder of the company's tag titles, in a mid-card match, losing by disqualification in nine minutes. Adonis had spent much of his injury layoff diligently working out at Gold's Gym in Venice Beach. While his physique had improved, and his hair was back to its natural dusty brown colour, he was a long way from what Japanese fans remembered.

Dave Meltzer recounted in the June 13, 1988, edition of the *Wrestling Observer* newsletter:

> *"Adonis is using his old black jacket gimmick and was cheered heavily upon his arrival here since he was a major star years ago in Japan, but the fans were shocked when he removed his jacket and they saw his new physique. Even though Adonis has dropped considerable weight, he's still far heavier than he ever was in his glory days in Japan."*

Friend and fellow Bakersfield resident Tom Touchstone was Adonis' workout partner before he left for Japan. Touchstone, who was victorious in the 1985 California Championships and runner-up at national level the following year, was impressed with his friend's commitment to the cause.

Adonis' renewed dedication to working out was a step in the direction. Despondent after his exit from the WWF and dejected by the state of affairs in the AWA, Adonis told several friends of his intention to seize the initiative and get back into shape for the good of his career. He was determined to keep his promise, as recalled by Fumi Saito in a July 2019 interview with Jim Valley:

> *"He dyed his hair back to his normal dark brunette black, he was trying to go on a diet, he quit all the chemicals, and he was trying to have a very good attitude about wrestling again. Quit WWE, I'm going to start going*

back to smaller territory, I'm going to start going back to Japan, I'm going to lose 50 pounds and I'm going to have another run.

"And right when he had this great attitude, in the first territory he went to, summer territory in Newfoundland, right when he had a good attitude, God had to take him."

Saito had barely spoken to his friend since his fun-filled visit to Bakersfield in the summer of 1985, such were the rigours of life on the road full-time with the WWF for Adonis. Now back in Japan for the first time in years, Saito was determined to make up for lost time. He recalled:

"I wanted to speak to him, so right when he came back to New Japan, I went to Keio Plaza Hotel [in Tokyo] and called his room for lobby and asked for Keith. He said, 'Who the fuck are you? Who is it?' I was very careful, I said 'This is Fumi.' He said, 'Oh right, come on up.' So, I went up to his room. Being heel [he said] 'Who is that?' because nobody calls him Keith [in Japan]."

In a further interview, Saito described the conversation the pair had once in the room:

"I was sitting around with Adonis and a friend joined – Cowboy Bob Orton. He was not on tour, instead he was 'Billy Gaspar,' the pirate. We all sat around and just talked and talked. I learned so much because wrestlers, all they talk about is wrestling.

"They talked about business, not just gossip, but what gets you over, what works and what doesn't, who is talented, who is not. I believe Adrian and Cowboy Bob Orton were very close friends too. They were a tag team in Japan before Dick Murdoch. He said he'd start getting in shape, losing weight and working out every day. And he said I'm going to start going back to smaller territories. I asked him, 'What are you going to do?'

"He said, 'I'm going to a summer territory in Canada this summer.'"

Other foreigners on the tour included Murdoch, Orton, and the Calgary-based pair of Jason the Terrible (Karl Moffat) and Owen Hart. Orton and Moffat worked under masks as the short-lived tandem, the Gasper Brothers. Adonis, meanwhile, largely stuck to tag team and six-man action. Five days into the tour, fans even witnessed a short-lived revival of the North-South Connection as Adonis and Dick Murdoch teamed for the first time since Adonis' last Japan tour in 1985. Nostalgic fans were excited for Adonis' return, according to Saito:

"When they announced Adonis was coming back, people popped. It was such a fond memory. He was part of the inaugural IWGP era too, IWGP

in New Japan is kind of overlooked because it's just a heavyweight title in Japan now. But it was a big project started by Inoki in 1980."

Adonis, Murdoch, and New Japan were confident enough in the reunion that the pair were signed up by Inoki to feature in the company's annual December tag team tournament. The tournament never took place, mothballed until 1991. If it had, it would not have featured the Connection. Nevertheless, the team featured in a handful of notable appearances during its final five-week spell together in the late spring of 1988.

On June 19, 1988, Murdoch and Adonis faced the fearsome combination of Masa Saito and Big Van Vader, the company's new monster heel who had debuted six months earlier with a crushing defeat of Inoki. The match was the only time Vader and Adonis shared a ring and stands as one of those moments in time which does not feel like it could have happened; two distinct generations of wrestling crossing paths in the night.

The match itself was not particularly competitive, with Adonis and Murdoch clearly ordered to make Vader look strong and duly obliging. The comparative physiques of Adonis and Vader make for an interesting demonstration of how a large but agile heel like Vader should look in 1988; five years earlier, such a label had been attached to Adonis.

Adonis and Murdoch went to a double count-out with the Gaspers on the June 10 show, with the *Wrestling Observer* unimpressed. The July 4, 1988, issue again reviewed the action, with a snippet about Adonis in his return to combat:

> *"They didn't work well together and the match didn't have as much heat as it should have. Neither Gasper looked particularly good here. Adonis, who looks to weigh maybe 315 - still awfully heavy, but a good 50 to 60 pounds down from his AWA weight – did some good moves but overall couldn't sustain hot action for any length of time due to his weight. Murdoch, who juiced heavily, was good."*

The following week carried a similar review, this time of the match with Vader and Saito at Korakuen Hall. Meltzer wrote:

> *"The finale saw Adonis and Murdoch take on Saito and Vader. Although both Murdoch and Saito looked very good, the match was mainly Adonis against Vader with Adonis selling like crazy to make Vader looked good. Adonis weighs more than Vader, which tells you how his diet is going.*
>
> *"However, he sold all the size and power moves and took excellent bumps, especially when you consider he looked to be in the 325-pound range. The finish saw Vader simply beat-up Adonis and pin him after a powerslam which is a minor surprise."*

219

It was not the only story about Adonis in the issue.

The final paragraph of the July 11, 1988, *Wrestling Observer* newsletter carried a late-breaking newsflash. Dated a few days in advance of the date it was written to allow for postage time to subscribers, the newsletter carried news from several days before the cover date. Sometimes salacious titbits would come in at the last moment and needed to be tacked on.

Shortly before going to print on this occasion, Meltzer received word of a story of such magnitude, it had to be squeezed in on the back page in the form of an additional paragraph added at the eleventh hour.

Adrian Adonis was dead.

~~~

Keith Franke was determined to show people that he still had what it took. He was determined to show himself. After allowing himself to be laughed at for his final year in the WWF, he wanted no more laughing. Adrian Adonis was serious now.

As the Regan presidency entered its final stretch, the politics of selfishness was firmly entrenched in office, with Vince McMahon's vision of wrestling-based entertainment keenly mirroring the then-President's legacy. The bodybuilder aesthetic had well and truly consumed professional wrestling, swimming as it was in physique-enhancing steroids. Now more than ever, a wrestler had to think about himself. He had to look the part. Franke, belatedly, took the hint.

With his injury layoff giving him a rare chance to consider the state of his career, Franke knew he had to slim down if he was to salvage anything. Years earlier he had formed a close friendship with retired wrestling manager Bobby Davis, another Bakersfield resident.

Throughout the 1950s and 60s in the northeast territory which Franke grew up watching, Davis created the template for the on-screen wrestling mouthpiece which has been duplicated numerous times in the years since; Davis was even the reason Raymond Heenan, perhaps the greatest wrestling manager of all, was named 'Bobby.'

By the time Franke moved to California, Davis was largely out of the business, and instead had become an early and very successful franchisee of the Wendy's fast-food chain. Davis witnessed the dedication Franke showed in those final months of his life, as he told *Entertainment Tonight* in the weeks after his death:

> *"In the two months before he passed away, Adrian trained twice a day, two hours a day at Gold's Gym. Trained off 127 pounds. An unbelievable dedication."*

Tom Touchstone was present at Gold's Gym for Adonis final training session before he flew out, and made plans to meet up with his friend upon his return from Japan a few weeks later. He did not find out until later than Adonis had accepted a late booking for a small-time independent show in Canada.

Adonis had told those close to him that he was going to work his way back up from the bottom if he had to, taking bookings at smaller independent shows to hone his craft. There could have been fewer places more appropriate for getting back to basics than the shows he agreed. Touchstone, who accompanied Davis for the *Entertainment Tonight* interview that was recorded at Strongbow Stadium, remembered:

> *"The very last conversation I had with Adrian, we were training at Gold's Gym Venice, and I'll never forget it because we never spoke again after that. He was travelling to Japan, and after he was finished in Asia then after he got the gig to go to Canada.*
>
> *"We had finished working out and Adrian came out and just said, 'I hope when I get back, we're not going to do those stupid hundreds again!' I was doing some guest posing and he was going to Asia. I thought he was going to be back but then he picked up the gig in Canada.*
>
> *"It was interesting because I wasn't having probably one of my best days and I walked out of the gym and as I was getting in the car, I saw Adrian come out. I rolled the window down and I said, 'Hey, is there anything else?'*
>
> *"And he stopped and he said, 'No Tom, never mind, we'll talk when I get back.' My wife knows, that's something I've shared with her. I always left it on a note of maybe [we should have had] another conversation. 'No, no,' he goes. 'We'll talk when I get back.' And he never got back."*

Dave McKigney was a wrestler and small-time promoter better known as The Bearman, owing to his propensity for wrestling live bears on his shows. Truly embodying the circus sideshow element of professional wrestling's roots, McKigney booked cards in different parts of Canada under his Big Bear Promotions (also known as Big Time Wrestling) banner, a frequent summer territory·for wrestlers passing through. For one tour in July 1988, their number included Adrian Adonis.

The full story of the trip is retold in detail in the reprinted edition of Jim Freedman's *Drawing Heat*, first published in 1988. An updated version, issued in 2009 by Scott Teal's Crowbar Press, featured an in-depth account of the final days and tragic death of the Wildman, Adonis and tag-team wrestler Pat Kelly, titled "'The Final, Fateful Bearman Tour.'

The postscript, expertly written by wrestling journalist and historian Greg Oliver, included interviews with several wrestlers on the fateful tour: Phil Watson (son of former NWA Champion Whipper Watson), Ricky Johnson (brother of Rocky Johnson), and Sweet Daddy Siki, among others.

Watson was Adonis' opponent for some spots on the tour, including a match at Canso Arena in Nova Scotia booked for July 24, 1988. The match would not take place, but a poster was produced in advance to advertise the show and has lived on as a memento of a card that never happened. It has circulated on social media, shared by wrestling fans as a morbid curiosity of the final booking Adonis never made.

Adonis' last confirmed match was a couple of days prior to the accident against local wrestler Hartford Love, real name Wes Hutchings, and one half of the kayfabe 'Love Brothers' with Reginald Love. Adonis was the victor in Labrador West, as he had been ten years earlier in their previous meetings, when Love put over Adonis three times during his brief stay in Atlanta in 1978. The match, and the aftermath, would be Love's final one as well. He told Greg Oliver in 2011:

> *"That was the end of my wrestling career. I couldn't wrestle any more. I was getting at that age anyway. They were all good buddies of mine, and I just couldn't do it anymore."*

Also on the card was veteran Vic Rossitani, Adonis' old friend from years earlier in the Carolinas, now back in his Ontario hometown. Making full use of the tour's only act to have achieved high-profile success in the WWF, the poster featured Adonis as the top-billed star, proclaiming him a "former WWF superstar" from "Hollywood, California," oddly. Even more far-fetched perhaps was the poster's claim of Adonis' weight as 265 pounds. Speaking to Oliver years later, Watson recalled:

> *"[He was a] really, really nice guy. I'd only known him from just that tour. [He was] so used to being with Vince where money was no objective. I remember him coming in, and at one point where they missed the plane, or he'd missed a connection – he'd apparently come right over from Japan, right to the States, from the States right up. He hadn't even stopped in at home from the Japan tour.*
>
> *"In order to catch this show in Labrador City, he had to hire a small plane because he missed a connection somewhere along the line. I remember him coming in and handing Dave the paper out of his pocket. For the life of me, I can't remember; it was two ridiculous numbers – either $3,500 or $7,500 for the plane flight. 'Here, you'll need to pick this up too. I carried this.' He handed it to me, and I said, 'I'm not the guy to do this. Here, give it to Dave.' I just laughed."*

While their stories shared with Oliver for the republished *Drawing Heat* did not always align, one thing agreed on was that there was no reason for the four wrestlers who travelled together to be in the van that day – it was a day off. After four successful shows in the remote mainland towns of Labrador City and Goose Bay, the crew had split into two groups – faces and heels – and booked into two hotels. Adonis' group were staying at the Holiday Inn in Gander. Watson remembered to Oliver:

> *"I remember having breakfast with Adrian Adonis, about seven o'clock in the morning – he actually bought my breakfast for me. We were looking out at the icebergs. I said, 'Geez, we hit one of those, we'd be like the Titanic, eh?' He said, 'Yeah, my wife would be rich.'"*

The next show was set for Lewisporte Arena on July 5 – the day after the crash. Watson noted to Oliver that the group were probably heading into the town the night beforehand to have a few beers and set tongues wagging about the wrestlers who would be performing the next night, a tried and trusted form of free promotion in the era.

Ricky Johnson noted that Adonis was a proponent of a night on the town and had fit right in with the group of misfits, regaling the crew with stories of his years in wrestling's biggest companies, and his hard drinking. Rocky Della Serra, also on the tour, concurred, as he told Oliver:

> *"I can remember Keith Franke, one of the nights before we took the ferry, he was in the bar there. Most people would go buy one beer; he came back out of there with a six-pack for himself. I'm a pretty fast drinker, but I remember standing at the bar with him and for every beer I had, he must have had two or three beers down.*
>
> *"I don't know what he was going through at that point. I know he'd been finished up with WWF there for a while. Independent promoters were still using him because he was still fresh off the TV and was a drawing card. He was a really nice guy. I spent that week there and talked to him quite a few times. Thought he was a great guy."*

The reissued book contains a number of photos from the tour, including the final photos ever taken of Keith Franke. He is pictured on the ferry from Labrador with the rest of the crew of wrestlers, drinking beer (of course), and looking content with life. The photos feature Adonis with fellow wrestler Steve Irwin, who wrestled in the States as Steve E. Ocean, and later in the UK as Steve Adonis.

On the evening of Monday, July 4, 1988, while friends and family back in Bakersfield were celebrating the fourth of July holiday, Adonis boarded a rental van with three other wrestlers as they travelled to their next shows on the Bearman's tour of the East coast of Canada. The tour had taken the group to the province of Newfoundland, where the troupe had performed in Labrador City on the mainland, near the Quebec border. They had made their way to the neighbouring island of Newfoundland to perform at shows in local ice hockey arenas in Marystown and Lewisporte on the island.

Adonis travelled with McKigney and twin brothers Victor and Bill Arko (who performed as Pat and Mike Kelly) in a rented red Ford mini-van driven by Bill Arko. The van was making its way towards Notre Dame Provincial Park and the Notre Dame junction, from which point the troupe were to take the highway running north into Lewisporte.

As the crew travelled in convoy on the Trans-Canada Highway to the north-eastern town, Kelly suddenly lost control of the van around 40 kilometres west of the small town of Gander. As they drove over Indian Arm Bridge, a straight stretch of highway surrounded by lakes on both sides, the van and its occupants crashed into a body of water, a tributary of the surrounding Indian Arm Lake.

The precise location was highlighted the following day by helicopter footage included in a report by local new channel CKY.

The tragedy took place at about 9.30pm local time, with the sun still shining on account of the double daylight-savings time in the area. Records show the sun set at 9pm in Newfoundland on the day in question, making it one of the longest days of the year, and police speculated that low-lying sun blinding the driver may have been a factor in the crash.

The most commonly referenced reason for the otherwise unexplainable accident is that Kelly swerved to avoid a moose which ran in the road from the neighbouring wooded area. Moose-related vehicle accidents were common in the area, with Newfoundland densely populated with the animals. A 1991 study showed that between 1987 and 1988 there were 661 motor-vehicle accidents involving moose in the region; 133 people were injured and three died; Pat Kelly, Dave McKigney, and Keith Franke.

Though sparsely inhabited, the few residents who did live in the vicinity rushed to the site of the crash as Royal Canadian Mounted Police (RCMP) officers made their way to the scene. All four, not wearing seatbelts, were thrown clear from the van. Victor Arko, 40, of Hamilton, Ontario, and Dave McKigney, 56, of Aurora, Ontario, were killed instantly.

Victor's identical twin brother Bill was rushed to hospital in St John's, Newfoundland's capital city. Arko survived and was operated on the following day to repair a badly broken leg, crushed in the smash. Franke was alive too, but barely. Ejected from the back seat of the van along with the others, his body was thrown through the windscreen and into a shallow body of water and suffered

224

catastrophic injuries, including to his skull and back. Ricky Johnson, speaking to Greg Oliver in 2009's re-release of *Drawing Heat*, claimed:

> *"Dave was about 30, 40 feet from the van on some rocks. He got thrown right through the windshield. Adrian was still alive; he was in the water and he was saying, 'Help me, help me, help me.'"*

RCMP Sgt John MacKinnon was quoted by local newspaper reporters the following day and gave life to the moose-related speculation which has attached itself to the incident ever since. He told reporters:

> *"We don't know what caused them to go off the road -- whether they encountered a moose or for some other reason. It's not uncommon for a moose to walk out onto the highway here, but we won't be able to speak with the survivor until Friday to find out what happened."*

An unnamed ambulance attendant also present at the scene and interviewed by local newspaper reporters, added simply: *"It was gruesome. It was a real mess."*

Police speculated that Arko's attempts to steer around some errant animal may have caused the van to crash into the rocky embankment of a nearby body of water "15 feet wide and one foot deep."

The disparate nature of the surroundings and the lack of first-hand accounts has led to plenty of speculation over the years, and much misreporting in the years that have followed; they were thrown into a lake; they drowned; one or more were decapitated. While the latter never happened, it is generally accepted that whatever the cause, the van eventually ended up in a shallow brook or creek.

A separate car full of wrestlers on the same tour was following shortly behind and saw the immediate aftermath of the crash, helpless to intervene. They may not have seen exactly what caused Arko to swerve, but they did see the fallout. One passenger in the next vehicle was McKigney's son, Davey Jr., just eight years old.

Wrestler Bobby Funk (no relation to the Amarillo Funks) was driving the car and told reporters the rest of the tour had been immediately cancelled. Fellow preliminary wrestler Rambo Sam, a passenger in Funk's car, told local journalists:

> *"We just saw smoke and we slowed down, and we said, 'That's the van.'"*

By Tuesday 5 July, Arko was described as being in a "serious but stable" condition. After undergoing surgery to repair his fractured leg the following day, hospital director of patient services Gladys Peachey noted to media that Arko was "doing really well." The same could not be said for Franke. Despite fighting bravely, and the best efforts of paramedics, he could not be saved. Keith Franke died in a Gander hospital on the day of the crash.

He was 34 years old.

Chapter 20: The Afterlife of Adrian Adonis

"These moments are to be celebrated."

– Roddy Piper, 2009

In the immediate aftermath of the accident, word filtered back to the other wrestlers on the tour and an understandable sense of shock seeped in. As described in detail in the updated version of Jim Freedman's *Drawing Heat*, those who just hours earlier had been eating and chatting with the men involved struggled to come to terms with what had happened.

Speaking to Greg Oliver in 2009 for an in-depth interview released as part of the reissued book on the life of the 'Bearman,' Ricky Johnson recalled taking on the duty of breaking the news to Keith's family. Johnson shouldered the responsibility as the only one present who had ever met Bea Franke, backstage at a WWF show in Bakersfield years earlier. He said:

> *"I called her. 'Hi Bea. It's Ricky. Blah, blah, blah.' I could tell by her voice that she knew; why would I be calling her? She said, 'Ricky, what's wrong? I said, 'Bea, I'm sorry. I have some bad news for you.' That's when I told her there was a bad accident and Adrian was gone."*

Back in Bakersfield, a few hours behind and with the light fading, eight-year-old Angela Perides saw her mother walk away from the family gathering and into the house to answer the call. She heard a shriek that remains with her. She recalled:

> *"It was really strange because [it was] the Fourth of July we were all doing that and then my mom came out and screamed and cried and I'm like, what on Earth?"*

The tour was cancelled, and the wrestlers made their way home in varying states of disbelief, many relieved they had not chosen to share the same van for that fateful journey. Sadly, the drama did not end there.

Days after the crash, a ring-hand on the tour was arrested by the RCMP as he stepped off a ferry in Sydney, Nova Scotia. On Tuesday, July 12, 1988, Robert Leslie "Robbie" James, 30, from St Catharines, Ontario, faced charges at the provincial court in Gander of theft over $1,000 and public mischief, in relation to the alleged stealing of a safety deposit box from one of the deceased wrestlers – Adonis.

Scant details of the case have survived in news clippings but what does exist shows that James apparently pleaded not guilty and opted for trial by jury. He was released on $1,000 bail to return to the same court for a preliminary hearing four months later. Sadly, no outcome of the case was reported in the local press, although it was specified that money was stolen from the box which had been stored at the Holiday Inn in Gander, where Adonis had been staying.

According to those on the tour, James and another ring hand, 'Rambo Sam' – quoted by journalists at the scene immediately after the accident – came upon the wreckage shortly after it happened and pilfered money and valuables from the injured and deceased. This included the safety deposit box key that Adonis had used to store his substantial payday from the Japan tour.

According to future ECW star Sabu, in the process of joining the tour with his legendary uncle The Sheik, the alarm was raised after Bea enquired about the safe return of a diamond ring Franke apparently never removed. When it could not be located, questions were asked. Sabu told the *Title Match Wrestling* podcast:

> *"We weren't on the road together. They were already up there in Newfoundland, and me and my uncle were coming up to meet them later on. And before we left, they crashed.*
>
> *"From what I heard, they were driving, and the ring truck was behind them with the bear. They were drunk as hell and go into a pond or a creek. The ring truck follows them, goes down after them, picks their pockets, and then asks for help."*

When authorities saw the ring was not on Franke's person, they investigated and located it in the possession of one of the ring crew. Sabu further claimed that wallets, jewellery, and McKigney's cash box with the takings from the tour were also taken. McKigney's son, Dave Stevenson, has made the same claim, and the account correlates with what Adonis' eldest daughter has been told. She said:

> *"They went back to the hotel and the guy saw the hotel manager [who had] seen him with the wrestlers and let him in, he stole all their stuff and took off. So, I found out recently who that was from Dave [Stevenson]. He said it was the guy who used to put up the ring and stuff, there was two of them, and he remembers that very well because he was with one of the Kelly Twins' girlfriends in the motel room.*
>
> *"I remember my mother had told us that, she asked us, 'What do you think, shall we bury him in New York or back here?' I remember saying here so we can go and give flowers, so she said 'ok,' then she said, 'Well that guy, they caught him.' And I didn't know what she really meant either the authorities or other wrestlers."*

228

Per the limited local media coverage, James denied this allegation in court. While the possibility of the occupants and driver of the car being intoxicated cannot be ruled out, the *Wrestling Observer* noted in the weeks that followed that the blood alcohol level in the body of the driver was .06, under the legal limit of .08 considered as driving under the influence in Canada at the time.

Interestingly, in Bea Franke's own recollection of the crash, retold via her daughter Gena, the robbery story did not occur in the manner described, at least as it pertained to her late husband. Gena noted:

> "He had flown from LA to Japan, my mom met him, and he gave her the money and then flew to Canada, she had the money."

Friends and co-workers descended on Bakersfield in the days that followed as Bea arranged for the burial to take place near the family home as she had promised her young daughters. Attendees at the funeral included some of Franke's closest friends from the world of wrestling, and beyond, chief among them Roddy Piper, who gave a stirring eulogy.

Muraco, Orton, and the Hart Foundation were present, as was former partner Ron Starr, workout buddy Tom Touchstone, and Bakersfield neighbour Bobby Davis. Bea and her daughters were supported by Keith's family from New York, his parents and sister, as well as her own extended family. Touchstone, an honorary casket bearer for the solemn occasion, recalled:

> "A couple of days before I was in LA and I took a plane home, and I didn't realise it but Roddy [Piper] and I were on the same plane and Roddy came to see Bea. I was coming back into town, and I was walking on the tarmac in Bakersfield and we just noticed each other and we said, 'Hey, this sucks.'

> "We would always see each other in Gold's Gym but not usually in Bakersfield. The next day would be at Keith's funeral."

Piper, Muraco, Orton, Mando Guerrero, Bobby Davis and Red Bastien were casket bearers. Touchstone, Gaynor, Bret Hart, Jim Neidhart, Chavo Guerrero, and Dr Bob Paunovich were noted in the order of service as 'honorary' casket bearers – with Neidhart listed as 'Jim Anvil.'

Paunovich is a minor footnote in wrestling history. A Colorado-based doctor referenced in the 1994 steroid trial of Vince McMahon, he was name-checked as having supplied prescription steroids to Hulk Hogan at one time. He also made appearances on WWF television in 1986, likely when he met Franke.

WWF talents Hart, Neidhart and Muraco were given brief leave from their duties to attend the funeral and were back working the house show circuit immediately afterwards. There was no other representation from the WWF at the service. Muraco was one of the many friends of Adonis who found his death incredibly hard to take. He noted:

> *"We were extremely young at the time, we weren't kids, but we were in our 30s. It was shocking, it was depressing. He was that good a friend and he then he passed. And it was kind of needless.*

> *"And you blame substance abuse and everything else, he could have still been with us and doing well you know they ran into a moose in the middle of the night in that desolate [area], kind of a sad, lonely, tragic type of death."*

It was a similar feeling of shock for Fumi Saito, who had been assured by Adonis just weeks earlier that he would see him back in Japan before the end of the year. He remembered:

> *"I heard the very next day. I couldn't believe it because I saw him not even a month before. He told me he was coming back [to Japan] in fall. He had no desire to go back to WWE."*

Keith Franke was laid to rest a week after the fatal car accident on July 11, 1988, with a slight delay as his body was transferred back to the US. The service took place at Greenlawn Memorial Chapel in Bakersfield, with burial at the adjacent cemetery. Piper, connected to Franke through thick and thin, took the news particularly hard.

The habit of saying goodbye to departed friends became an unavoidable part of the wrestling business for Piper, as it did for many others. He later claimed that Adonis' funeral was the last one he attended, unable as he was to deal with the emotional toll such occasions took. He later wrote:

> *"Adrian had told me that if he ever died, he didn't want people mourning over him; he wanted them to have a party and celebrate his life. So, when I was giving his eulogy, I said this, and his wife let out a moan that would just sink your heart. A moan of sorrow and sadness that will live with me forever. When I looked into his kids' eyes, what was I supposed to tell them?"*

Years later Piper revealed a pastor travelling in the ambulance that arrived at the scene of the crash wrote him a detailed letter explaining the accident. A similar letter also made its way to Franke's widow, although whether from the same source, or the veracity of either, is not completely clear.

What is true is that Piper felt so deeply about losing perhaps his closest friend in a business built on brotherhood that he had to see where it happened for himself.

Within a year, he travelled to Newfoundland to visit the spot where the crash took place.

Other tributes from the wrestling fraternity were forthcoming, if somewhat brief. Undoubtedly Franke's death was overshadowed by the murder of fellow wrestler Frank "Bruiser Brody" Goodish just thirteen days later in a Puerto Rico dressing room.

The AWA, his most recent employer in the States, carried an acknowledgement of Adonis' death on it July 23, 1988, episode of *AWA All-Star Wrestling,* and a lengthy feature a few weeks later.

Six months later, Greg Gagne made a longer tribute while cutting an otherwise routine promo for an upcoming match with Jerry Lawler in Manitoba; the proximity to where Adonis died perhaps being the reason for the somewhat random insertion. In between promoting the Lawler bout, he told interviewer Larry Nelson, in character:

> *"Adrian Adonis definitely was a tough guy and people here in Winnipeg remember he teamed up with Jesse "The Body" Ventura. They held the tag team championships of the world and all of us wrestlers know that it was Adonis that carried the load in that team.*
>
> *"He was the man in the ring, he was the wrestler, Ventura had the big mouth, and he had the strength, but it was Adonis that was the wrestler. Over the years he put on a lot of weight, but he was still a tough competitor, and he had a lot of endurance in there no matter what he looked like, and my hats go off to him he was a great competitor and a great wrestler."*

New Japan held a moment of silence for both Adonis and Brody on its July 29 television show, while popular independent highlight shows *Saturday Night at Ringside* with Mick Karch and Joe Pedicino's *Pro Wrestling This Week* gave their own dedications to the pair in July and August.

The companies that did acknowledge the death of Adonis tended to feel compelled to do so alongside that of Brody, given the close proximity of when each passed and the stunning nature of both. While this may not seem ideal when considering each man independently, it was more than some managed.

Writing in the August 1, 1988, edition of the *Wrestling Observer*, Dave Meltzer noted without much surprise the lack of any response from the two major American wrestling companies.

> *"Being that it is professional wrestling, the public reaction from the wrestling community was predictable. Neither the NWA nor the WWF*

acknowledged anything. It wasn't surprising, since the WWF never even acknowledged the passing of Adrian Adonis either, who was a major star for them, while Brody had never even worked for the group in the 'new era.'

"Both the major groups have a policy of being oblivious to anything that happens outside of their promotion. In the case of the NWA, they should have broken that rule since the TBS Saturday show is the most up-to-date national show on television."

He elaborated years later:

"I wasn't shocked, that's what they did in those days. They should have, but it was a different era. And that's just not what they did. If it was now, it'd be a 20 times bigger story. I remember an Entertainment Tonight segment, but I don't remember any mainstream stuff whereas now it would be everywhere. Back then, WWE didn't mention it. People didn't cover wrestling in the mainstream very much."

Despite Adonis working for the company only a year earlier, and for nearly three and a half years since returning alongside Murdoch in 1983, the World Wrestling Federation did not acknowledge his death.

No tribute to Adonis was ever made, and his family was not contacted in the aftermath. Wrestling in the 1980s was quite different to the nostalgia-fest fans experience, and encourage, today. In 2023, the death of even the most minor wrestling star produces international news headlines as a glut of websites clamour for content.

This was not the case in the late 1980s but was not unheard of. When undercard talent Rick McGraw died of a drug overdose in 1985, he was remembered in an issue of *WWF Magazine* weeks later with a full-page tribute. Twice in the space of a few months in 1984, the company held salutes or silences for the passings of Vince McMahon Senior, understandably, and David von Erich, somewhat less obviously considering he worked one minor match for the company in his life.

Younger daughter Gena noted:

"Nothing, not even a card, nothing [from the WWF]. People try to make excuses for them, 'Oh, the internet wasn't around back then, maybe they didn't know.' The whole wrestling world knew that he was killed, and you couldn't send a card. The people that did go – Bret Hart came in from Canada, he was a pallbearer, Roddy Piper, the Guerrero brothers were there, basically the true friends of Adrian Adonis were there."

The WWF did run three of shows in Newfoundland within days of Franke's death, likely a coincidence. Between July 29 and 31, 1988, the Federation played to small crowds in St Johns, Grand Falls and Cornerbrook. The small crew included The Rockers, Junkyard Dog, and Don Muraco. Muraco found the trip hard to take so soon after his friend's passing. He said:

> *"As kind of a thing to keep the territory running, I guess, they put us up there for three days running their major towns up there which was, I don't think we had a six-grand house. That was right after he'd passed, and I was really upset. It really bothered me, even just being there on those roads.*

> *"You know, they talk bad about Shawn Michaels and Marty Jannetty, but those guys took care of me and did all the driving, we had a van and they did all the driving, they did everything, and I kind of just stayed sedated in the back, I just didn't want to be there because, you know, losing him was, it was...Well he was like the first one, you know."*

One entity that did get in touch with the Franke family was the national news programme *Entertainment Tonight*. Bea spoke to the show from the family's Bakersfield home, while Meltzer and Bobby Davis also gave their thoughts for the brief segment which aired a month after Adonis' death, in early August 1988.

The WWF declined a request to participate or allow WWF footage to be used. Interspersed with footage of Adonis in action in the AWA in his 1987 run, the clip has been widely shared online between modern wrestling fans as a curiosity of yesteryear.

As a voiceover described the "bizarre end" which befell Adonis and the others in the van, b-roll footage of a lonely stretch of Newfoundland road was shown. A lake. A moose sign on the roadside. Even shots of the wrecked van, in a nearby garage. The ET item was a mostly straightforward news item which deviated towards tabloid sensationalism when it claimed the van "veered off a cliff."

An emotional Bea described her husband's love for the wrestling business while surrounded by their two daughters. She said:

> *"He loved it, I mean that was his life he trained for it he worked hard he wanted to be on top, he was on top. He went through hell to get there but he made it. I know he's gone now, and we all go but he was just...it's unbelievable, still."*

Bea gave an additional interview to a local newspaper two days after Franke's death, in which she shed some further light on her husband's plans for a career after wrestling. She said:

"He was in the limelight and had auditioned for parts in movies. I think he would have liked to get out of wrestling. But when you're in sports, it's hard to get out and sit behind a desk."

The WWF's lack of acknowledgement was voted the third most disgusting promotional tactic by a wrestling company in the *Wrestling Observer* newsletter awards for 1988. The fatal accident was considered the second most shocking moment of the year, behind Brody's death, naturally.

Pro Wrestling Illustrated awarded Adonis a special 'Editor's Award' in its year-end awards – again, shared with Brody. It was the only PWI award Adonis ever won, and Bea travelled to the magazine's offices in the northeast to collect the honour in person. Bea's picture appeared alongside an accompanying article in the March 1989 edition of PWI and Brody's widow Barbara Goodish did the same.

The wrestling community supported the Franke family through their grief. Piper, Muraco, Hart, Ventura, Verne Gagne, George Steele, or their wives, kept in touch with Bea in the months that followed. On one trip to visit Keith's parents in New York, Bea met for dinner with Bill Arko, the sole survivor of the van crash. Arko was forced to retire from the ring as a result of the accident with severe leg injuries but lived for several more years.

If he had survived the Bearman's tour, Adonis would have next worked for Walter "Killer" Kowalski. After the accident, Kowalski sent the payoff Franke would have received for the three shows he was due to headline in the towns surrounding the legendary heel's base in Reading, Massachusetts, to his widow.

Adonis had spent time in the spring and early summer of 1988 considering his options. He had lost weight – not enough, but a good start – and was still young enough at 34 for one more run with a major promotion. Just as importantly, he had shown himself he still possessed the ability to give his career and his body the focus it deserved. The next job would have been to convince promoters and fans. Overseas, there would be tours of Japan several times a year. Stateside was a different story.

Newsletters from the time noted that Adonis' first choice was to return to the WWF, the most lucrative employer in the wrestling business in the United States by far. Vince McMahon would not entertain the idea, with the memory of the tumultuous period spent dealing with Adonis still fresh in his mind.

Rumours have circulated that he had a verbal agreement to join Jim Crockett Promotions in the autumn of 1988 with both promoter Crockett and booker Dusty Rhodes fans of Adonis. If this was the case, it is likely that Adonis would have found himself back in the leather jacket 'tough guy' role from early in his career, working for the main branch of the NWA in between Japan tours. Joey Gaynor believed this to be the case. He said:

"He called me a month before he got killed and said I'm going to be going to work for Ted Turner, I want you to come in as my manager, his younger brother Caligula Adonis. I said I'll put on the toga and do the horse dance just like [Malcolm] McDowell [in the 1979 movie, 'Caligula,'] we were planning the whole thing, but he was killed."

Turner did not buy into the wrestling business until a few months after Adonis' death, but it is certainly conceivable, as other fading stars around this time found similar refuge with the company that would shortly become World Championship Wrestling when they were no longer coveted by the WWF.

Adonis' *The Big Event* opponent the Junkyard Dog made a surprise debut at December's *Starrcade* card in 1988, while former partner Murdoch started up with the group a few months earlier on July 3, 1988, as part of the *Great American Bash* tour – the day before Adonis died. Likewise, his recent AWA stablemates Heyman, Condrey and Rose also debuted with the group around this time.

If that had been the case, and Adonis had survived to make it to WCW, it is possible his poor luck from earlier in the year might have continued to undermine his efforts. With Turner purchasing Jim Crockett Promotions, Rhodes quickly became frustrated by the diktats laid down by Turner network executives' views on what was acceptable for television viewers and was gone soon after.

How Adrian Adonis would have fared under the Jim Herd of 1989 onwards, when the company pursued a policy of child-friendly cartoon gimmicks, is an entertaining thought. Perhaps the WCW era of Big Josh the lumberjack and Norman the Lunatic would have left Franke pining for the days of Titan Sports.

Fans never got the chance to witness anything of this nature. No short-lived return as a heel commentator on early 1990's episodes of *WWF Superstars*, and no late-career renaissance as a t-shirt and jeans-clad hardcore icon in the Heyman-led mid-90's phenomenon of Extreme Championship Wrestling.

A brief nod is owed to Herb Abrams. The controversial and colourful wannabe impresario raised eyebrows when he launched his Universal Wrestling Federation with a press conference at a fan convention. The ambitious Abrams told fans that both Adonis and Brody would feature for his new company. This despite the notable handicap of both having been dead for more than two years. It was not the last time Abrams exhibited bizarre behaviour.

For all his faults, at least Abrams mentioned Adonis' name. This was more than the WWF could muster. WWF's PR spokesman Mike Weber did give brief comment to at least one reporter in the immediate aftermath of Adonis' death, quoted providing some generic background to Adonis' career in the July 6, 1988, *Montreal Gazette* – but no company tribute.

No reference was made to Adonis' death by the WWF at the time, and he seems to remain unofficially blackballed by the modern WWE, with no Hall of Fame induction imminent. This fate has befallen many over the years. From Dave Shultz to Demolition, little coverage is given to a variety of characters deemed unworthy of WWE 'Legend' status.

Some are ostracised for legal reasons, others for publicly badmouthing the company. Adonis did none of these things– at least not publicly. It remains unclear why the company is so ambivalent towards the idea of Adonis. Perhaps that leaves scope for change. The most obvious answer is that WWE simply wishes to forget Adonis ever existed – or at least the troubling 1986 iteration of him. If it were not for his relationship with Roddy Piper, or more accurately, their match at *WrestleMania III*, it is doubtful WWE would ever mention him at all.

One man who always remembered Adonis was Bret Hart. His autobiography mentioned Adonis several times, including one particularly touching anecdote about a special cartoon he drew for Andre the Giant, presented to him in the locker room prior to *WrestleMania VI*. Hart recalled:

> *"Suddenly I realized that Andre was fighting back tears and frantically looking for an escape. He had way too much pride to break down in front of the boys. I quickly pointed out to him, and everyone else who was staring, my caricature of Adrian Adonis with angel's wings atop a cloud plucking a harp. Andre gave me a big smile and said, 'Thank you, boss.'"*

An updated montage of WWF superstars was included in the July 1994 issue of *WWF Magazine* and also included a heavenly Adonis.

Adonis' death hit Piper harder than almost anyone in the wrestling industry. Whether a reminder of his own mortality or simply a sign of the emotional turmoil which came from losing a close friend, Piper discussed Adonis at any opportunity, more so in his later years. Keen to keep his memory alive in any way he could, Piper shoehorned Adonis into his promos, which became ever more erratic as the years passed.

Piper returned to the WWF in 1996 and took up a feud with Goldust. The character portrayed by Dustin Rhodes drew comparisons to "Adorable" Adrian, as the WWF once more looked to exploit homophobic prejudice amongst his audience. Piper warned Goldust on the March 11, 1996, episode of *Monday Night Raw* that he had "already dealt with" Adonis, an allusion to the shared effeminate tendencies of both men.

On the December 20, 1999, episode of *Monday Nitro*, the company became increasingly desperate to inject a sense of realism into proceedings to compete with the huge success of the WWF. After smashing a cheaply constructed set used as the backstage office of heel authority figure Vince Russo, Piper rambled incoherently about frauds, dead friends, and respect for the business:

> *"Phony! How about my friends that are on the road that are dead now? Bret Hart, eh tu Bruti? How about Adrian Adonis, who died, he was no phony. How about Gorilla Monsoon, he was no phony. How about Owen Hart? I loved you, Owen. How about the fans?"*

Three years later, Adonis' name made an even more unlikely appearance, this time on the December 4, 2002, weekly pay-per-view for NWA: Total Nonstop Action, the company now known as Impact Wrestling. Once again feuding with Russo, Piper wore a shirt bearing the names of many of his wrestling friends who had passed away - Hart, Art Barr, Rick Rude, Brian Pillman, and of course, Adrian Adonis. The *Wrestling Observer* regarded the stunt as *"not only tasteless, but stupid beyond words."*

A much better-received latter-day utterance of Adonis' name by Piper took place on WWE *Monday Night Raw*. Building towards an encounter with Chris Jericho, Piper picked up the familiar theme of young upstarts failing to appreciate the sacrifices of those who pathed the way. On February 16, 2009, in the last great promo of his career, an emotional and sombre Piper schooled Jericho:

> *"Mickey Rourke is my friend, and I watched his movie, The Wrestler. And yes, I cried. The movie is not about a bunch of old timers that want another run. The movie is about the honour and respect we have for everyone. The movie is about the pain physically and emotionally and most importantly, why we do what we do: for the thrill of performing.*

> *"I have people that come up to me and they say, 'Hey Roddy,' we remember when you slapped Mr T. And I have people that come up to me and say, 'When my grandad was alive, we watched you shave Adrian Adonis' head.' And Chris, you want to bury these moments. No, these moments are to be celebrated."*

Piper went a step further a couple of years later, describing alleged encounters with the ghost of Adrian Adonis at his family home, in a pair of shows on the Biography Channel. In June 2012's *Celebrity Ghost Stories*, Piper recounted their friendship, before explaining that he and his children experienced strange noises and shadows in the house, which Piper interpreted as his late friend "looking out for him."

The following month, on the anniversary of Adonis' death, Piper made a pilgrimage to Newfoundland while touring to visit the spot where the van crashed and pay his respects once again. Eighteen months later, the topic was revisited for *The Haunting of Roddy Piper*, prompting plenty of derision from a disbelieving wrestling community. Regardless of the authenticity of the claims, Piper clearly believed what he felt and saw, even if this was just the manifestation of his own subconscious.

Despite a lack of effort by WWE over more than three decades, the legacy of Adrian Adonis exists and endures in different ways. Some are more uplifting than others. When other accidents have befallen wrestlers and wrestling personalities on the same day of the year as the Newfoundland crash, Adonis' name became associated with a perceived '4th of July curse' within the industry.

In 1989, Jason the Terrible (Karl Moffat), Davey Boy Smith and Chris Benoit were involved in a head-on collision while travelling in Jasper, Alberta, ending Moffat's career. In 1990, Brutus Beefcake suffered catastrophic facial injuries during a parasailing accident. And four years later, WWF referee Joey Marella perished in yet another wrestling-related car crash.

The 'curse' seems to have halted there, although fatal wrestling road accidents persisted. Many others, including Vivian Vachon, Jerry Blackwell, Junkyard Dog, and Randy Savage met a similar fate.

A more positive legacy for Adonis lives on today; online, in music, and in sly references snuck into wrestling shows by savvy commentators. Whereas Vince McMahon's mention of the "late Adrian Adonis" upon Dick Murdoch's entry at the 1995 *Royal Rumble* was an anomaly at the time, mentions creep in more often than they once did.

Some are less than complementary, such as when Matt Striker rebuked Vickie Guerrero on a December 22, 2010, episode of WWE*'s SmackDown* for possessing the *"face of Adrienne Barbeau and the body of Adrian Adonis."* His counterpart, JBL, was more flattering, namedropping Adonis often during the 2010s, usually in relation to a sleeper hold.

Wrestlers have taken the 'Adonis' name in later years, in part as a tribute to Keith Franke. Former WWE wrestlers Sam Adonis and Chris Adonis have both found success on the independent circuit with new identities that reference the late Buffalo native. Ex-ECW world champion Tommy Dreamer has made no secret of his love for Adonis and revealed in 2020 that he once pitched to return to WWE with an 'Adorable' persona of his own.

At WWE's Hall of Fame ceremony in 2019 both Bret Hart and Brutus Beefcake mentioned Adonis in their acceptance speeches, each recipient thanking their former colleague for his involvement at pivotal points in their careers. And whenever someone gets their head shaved due to a match stipulation, be it Kurt Angle, Serena Deeb, Molly Holly, or Vince McMahon himself, thoughts turn to the same fate which befell Adonis years earlier.

The cultural impact of Adrian Adonis stretches far beyond wrestling. Scratch the surface and there are plenty of references to Adonis scattered around pop culture.

Australian sports commentator Michael Schiavello adopted 'Good night, Irene!" as one of his knockout signature catch-cries, such a fan growing up was he of the 'Adorable One.' He even borrowed the line for the title of his 2020 autobiography, having become so strongly associated with the phrase.

In a similar vein, tennis wild-child Nick Kyrgios was once compared to Adonis by sports-caster Chris Fowler for his ability to play 'bad guy wrestler' during a Miami Open match with Roger Federer in April 2017. In MMA, welterweight fighter Adrian Adonis Barnes predictably gained the nickname "Adorable" during his brief career.

The 'Adrian Adonis' name has been adopted by a Toronto-based hip-hop producer, and the same city was home to glam rockers Nova Rex, which employed model and singer Vincent "Adrian" Adonis as its vocalist a few years ago.

Critically acclaimed hip-hop collective Jedi Mind Tricks name-checked Adonis in their 2000 track 'Muerte' *("Death is upon us, we slam like Adrian Adonis")*, as did rapper Milo on 2013's "Prop Joe's Clock Repair Shop" (*"Put flowers in my hair like Adrian Adonis / I don't really care my dude I'm pompous"*). Less celebratory is the third track on metal group Beg's eponymous 2017 EP (*"Keith Franke Decapitation Fascination,"*) touching as it does on the confusion and conjecture some have maintained over how he died.

Time has passed quickly, and 2023 marks 35 years since the death of Keith 'Adrian Adonis' Franke. That number is particularly stark when you consider Franke has now been dead longer than he was alive.

For so many years there has been no spotlight, but that may soon change. A scheduled episode of '*Dark Side of the Ring*' will give fans old and new a chance to get to know another side of Adrian Adonis. For family, it will be a gentle reminder of the man they still miss.

What matters most is family. Franke's oldest daughter is a nurse practitioner with several years in emergency/trauma nursing. His youngest daughter is an elementary school teacher and has her master's degree in school counselling. Franke has seven grandchildren, six girls, and one boy.

What of his legacy within wrestling? There are plenty of examples across social media and podcast interviews in which the great and the good of professional wrestling have highlighted Adonis' influence on their own careers.

From Stone Cold Steve Austin (*"Adrian Adonis was one of my favorite workers. He was such a great heel"*) to Sheamus (*"Roddy Piper vs Adrian Adonis was one of my favs as a kid"*) to Tony Khan (*"Watch your back in the afterlife, Hot Rod. Adrian Adonis has been up there for 27 years plotting to shave your head"*) sometimes it seems like everyone loves Adrian Adonis.

Maybe not so forgotten after all.

Chapter 21: Legacy

"It's kind of ironic, I believe it was 1981 that Adrian and I first sold out the Civic Center in St Paul.

"And you're still cheering me, only in '81 it was 'Jesse sucks!'

"The main thing was you were cheering then, you're cheering now."

- *Jesse Ventura's gubernatorial election victory speech, November 3, 1998*

Keith Franke lived fast and died young. That is the story as most know it. More than one person interviewed in the process of writing this book expressed the sentiment that, while the manner of his death was tragic, they were not surprised that he died. There was a sense that the real surprise lay in the fact that he died in the way he did rather than, say, an accidental drug overdose, or maybe a heart attack. Then, maybe, he would fit more comfortably on the list in our minds of all the other young dead wrestlers from the 1980s and 90s.

As a young boy, Franke loved pro wrestling. No different to lots of young children who have found themselves captivated by hulking superheroes playing out weekly struggles between good and evil. Fascinated by Sammartino, Blassie, the Graham Brothers and more, he would watch them on television before growing up to share a dressing room with many of the men he idolised as a youngster. The consensus from those who knew him is that Keith Franke took wrestling incredibly seriously. At least, he did when he started.

Overwhelming evidence points to bad habits which crept in after developing a fondness for the extracurricular activities which presented themselves to pro wrestlers on the road. Drug abuse and partying took over early enough that even his AWA tag team partner, future Governor of Minnesota Jesse Ventura, tired of having to babysit him. Nevertheless, his career grew. A divisive character among his fellow wrestlers, those close to him recall a roguish character full of pranks and laughs. Those who weren't remember a bully, especially to newer or younger grapplers.

In all the testimony about Franke, if one thing competes with wrestling in his life-long affections, it is family. His love for Bea is clear, meeting one night in Bakersfield, choosing to take her around the country with him before settling back in her hometown to raise their two daughters. Despite being an orphan, he enjoyed a supportive family unit and knew a balanced home was the key to a happy life. He told Roddy Piper to make sure he had the same, and his friend took the advice to heart.

Franke never lived to enjoy more than a fraction of the sedate domestic existence he hoped would bring him peace. That bliss is reflected in eldest daughter Angela's memories of growing up in a household of love and laughter:

> *"You know, he was a fun one because he'd come home and [there would be] no rules, it was just fun time and my mom was the one because she was with us every day. So that's what I remember."*

His younger daughter Gena reflected on the nature of her parent's relationship, and the affection her mother still holds for her late father. She said:

> *"No relationship's perfect but they never fought. He was smitten madly in love with her, they loved each other, called four or five times a day [from the road]. That's when it really hit her that he was gone – when the calls stopped. They had a great relationship; she still loves him and misses him."*

Keith Franke was a man who loved nothing more than to confuse and perplex people. He was not a people-pleaser – unless you count the way an effective heel plays his part in entertaining a paying audience. As Adonis, in all of its transitions, Franke was a malcontent who revelled in making people uncomfortable. A superlative worker at his 1980-82 peak, and, initially, a great talker, both faded when he stopped taking care of his talents but neither totally left him.

Adrian Adonis the character was a hard person to love. That is especially true for those who did not know him well or follow him closely. The exploitative and manipulative manner of the gay cross-dresser gimmick set wrestling back years – although he alone is not to blame for this. He did plenty to give people the impression that he did not care: the offensive gimmick, the drugs, the weight gain, the bizarre behaviour.

His career as a high-level worker was brief in hindsight, which might explain some of the possible apathy. But Franke wanted to scale the mountain. In many ways, he did just that.

The influence he had on other wrestlers cannot be denied, both with those he worked with and in the modern era. He shared the ring with opponents that stretched across generations – from Flair, Race, and Brisco, to Vader, Owen Hart and Shawn Michaels; he was a proponent of the big-bumping style perfected by Ray Stevens and today closely associated with Michaels.

Adonis, along with Gorgeous George, Goldust, and many others, became a necessary touchstone for exploitative wrestling characters within the industry, and no exploration of sexuality or homophobic sentiment in wrestling can capably be constructed without mention of these personalities. Adonis' presence in this set has thrown a shadow over the remainder of his body of work which he was unable to move himself out of. Worse still, his massive weight gain left an indelible mark on the minds of many.

Franke must bear some responsibility for both flaws. What if the 'Adorable' gimmick was foisted on him by Vince McMahon, playing a game for his own enjoyment? Some theorise that McMahon resented Adonis' weight gain and devised a character so humiliating as to break his spirit and force him to willingly leave the WWF. That is conjecture. The only evidence is that which the audience witnessed, as "Adorable" Adrian injected WWF programming with the type of adolescent humour that McMahon always valued.

All wrestling fans enjoy the notion of McMahon as 'Mr Burns'-esque bully, but it does not explain why Adonis was not simply fired before the storyline began if his weight was such an issue. Some claim the gimmick was just as much Adonis' idea, or that he at least enjoyed the stature and payday it brought. Others claim he hated every minute of it. Perhaps his opinion of it changed with the wind.

What is clear is that Adonis did not have to do the gimmick if he did not want to. It was profitable, and the best paid employment he could hope to find in his field in order to support his family, but not his only option. Likewise, with his fluctuating weight. Eventually, on both points, he realised the damage both had done to his reputation and resolved to change everyone's opinion. He simply ran out of time to do so.

The story of his matches became that of his career, as he played the heel to be vanquished in order for others to look good. To ultimately be looked beyond. Despite his status somewhere in between forgotten man and laughing-stock, Adonis has attained an improbably high level of acclaim among 'true' pro wrestling fans. Performers and experts rank him among their favourites, often citing him as inspiration for getting into the business.

The historical significance of the *WrestleMania III* match with Piper alone cannot be overstated. Alongside the epic Hogan-Andre showdown, Adonis and Piper's frantic brawl created the template for what makes a 'WrestleMania moment.' The match revitalised Piper as a babyface, launched the solo career of Brutus Beefcake, and is the only element of Adonis' career revisited by modern-day WWE with any regularity.

The match was an equally seminal milestone in Piper's career. *WrestleMania III* was replayed on FS1 in the States in May 2020 as part of the channel's television deal with WWE. The resultant airing of Adonis and Piper's antics in the Silverdome prompted, briefly and improbably, the name of 'Adrian Adonis' to trend worldwide on Twitter for possibly the first time ever, as fans old and new shared their thoughts on the vintage show.

The feud formed the basis of a collection of Piper clips on the WWE Network in recent years (aptly named '*Revenge is Adorable'*); and Adonis remains one of only three people to have their head shaved at a *WrestleMania*. He was followed by Molly Holly in 2004, and the chairman himself, at the hands of Donald Trump, nearly 20 years to the day that Adonis was shaved bald.

Beyond Piper and *WrestleMania*, you have to squint to make out Adonis' fingerprints across the pro wrestling landscape but they remain. Adonis was responsible, with Ventura, in following the Freebirds' example and establishing the trend for cool heel tag-teams in the early 1980s, with their shades, fedoras, and feather boas.

The pair had an outlandish sense of style, both verbal and visually, that borrowed from all areas. That sense of expression has been embodied by plenty of teams since, from the Hollywood Blondes to the New Age Outlaws, to the New Day. Adonis is also part of a select group with the likes of Ray Stevens, Terry Gordy, and a few others, to be associated with not one but two great tag teams. His reputation is further secured through the impact he made during significant runs in the WWF and the AWA, plus notable stays in Texas, Portland, Japan, and California.

So, to that final great question regarding Adrian Adonis; does he deserve to be in a wrestling Hall of Fame? Such discussions are mildly distracting but ultimately futile affairs. There are multiple versions for one thing, the most famous being the WWE Hall of Fame; *the Wrestling Observer* Hall of Fame; the Professional Wrestling Hall of Fame (PWHF) and Museum in Texas; the George Tragos/Lou Thesz version, or the Cauliflower Alley Club. Adonis is not a member of any.

The WWE Hall of Fame was created on a whim in 1993 simply to honour the passing of Andre the Giant and is not a hall of fame in the recognised tradition. With no nominations or voting, entrants to the WWE Hall of Fame were for many years determined by one man – Vince McMahon.

His family are keen to see it happen, but it remains unlikely. The archaic and offensive "Adorable" gimmick would subject WWE to needless criticism for the sins of more than three decades ago. The company has made great strides to operate as a thoughtful and inclusive employer. Why diminish that work by celebrating a character who did just the opposite?

The WWE could always 'spin' the Adonis character and laud his coming out on *Tuesday Night Titans* as a sign of its forward-thinking nature all along, when in fact it was quite the opposite. Stranger things have happened, especially in the brazen WWE. Muraco considered the question and did not see an obvious answer for Adonis' omission. He said:

> *"I don't know why he's been overlooked. Maybe because he was only in the limelight for a short, short time, those years, a year or two in Minneapolis, a year or so in WWE that he was there. I don't know if it's the gay gimmick, a lot of guys like Adrian Street and some of those other guys did that type of [gimmick]. I don't know. In my opinion he certainly deserves to be in all those, whatever Hall of Fame there is, he was that talented, he was that good.*

In the main, it does not matter. What matters are the memories he still holds of his late friend. Muraco added:

> *"I think of fun and good times. We were together in Florida, I was single, he was single, Florida was a good place, we lived close to each other."*

Tom Touchstone's thoughts nowadays are touching. He reflected:

> *"I would tell people the persona in the ring was so far from who he was; very intelligent, loving, considerate."*

Likewise, Joey Gaynor is one of the many who will never forget Keith Franke. He said:

> *"Number one, I'm honoured and privileged to have known him and find out we're far relations, as far as we know. To learn a lot about the wrestling business from him. To know someone like that. He was a wrestling mentor, would call him on the phone and get advice, on building feuds. We just didn't get to work together is the only regret I have.*
>
> *"Otherwise knowing him was inspiring. He was great, he was funny, [wrestling] was all he talked about. Innovative. Someone who broke ground. You can't erase history. And he's part of it. Fantastic athlete and a real high IQ. He was a smart man. And he liked my mom's eggs and bacon!"*

Maybe one day we will all find space for Keith Franke. A star in the WWF and the AWA (back when being a star in the AWA still mattered), he spent over a year as one of the top heels in the Federation during one of the hottest periods of the company's existence, headlining a house show run against the mighty Hulk Hogan.

He remains one of the only WWF title holders from the boom period not in the WWE Hall of Fame, and one of the only people to appear at two of the first *WrestleMania* shows not in. He had an influence on the likes of Bret Hart, directly through their friendship on the road, and Shawn Michaels, indirectly, as another purveyor of the Stevens-Flair big-bumping (and over-selling) style.

There are the motifs he introduced, whether people realise it or not. The first man to use the DDT as a finisher, long before Jake Roberts; he used a sharpshooter before Hart; and a sleeper before DiBiase. He sprayed fragrance before Rick Martel was a "Model;" he was a member of the Hart Foundation and the Dangerous Alliance; he created the 'Barber'; owner of the leather jacket with which Piper inspired Rousey; the last man to share a ring with Bruno Sammartino at the Garden, and the last to do so anywhere with Jack Brisco. Handed the original NWA belt by Lou Thesz. One of the last to be hired by the late Vince McMahon Senior, and a WWF champion on the day he passed away. And creator of one of the most indelible moments in the WWE's history, alongside his closest friend.

Adonis' standing with the company has started to appear less frosty in the last few years. He was considered relevant enough to feature on Heyman's enormously popular DVD set in 2014. At the NXT *Takeover* event in April 2018, commentators alluded to Adonis by name when the androgynous Velveteen Dream made his way to the ring. In the most direct reference yet, newcomer Tehuti Miles debuted on WWE programming in September 2020 under the ring name Ashante Adonis.

Franke, and especially his loved ones, should not have their feelings forgotten because the chance at a comeback was lost. Adonis knew he had work to do to regain people's belief as a wrestler, and to replace the prancing image of him that had stuck in their minds. He knew it would stick forever unless he took his training seriously again and went back to work. So, he went back to work. In Japan, and then in Newfoundland. And he never came home.

So, did we all forget about Adrian Adonis? Maybe we never knew him in the first place. It seems many moved on from him the moment they put down that newspaper in July 1988.

Others, those who loved him, never forgot. Those who knew the real Keith Franke loved him. They think about him still. And that is more than nothing at all.

Goodnight, Adrian Adonis.

Goodnight, Keith Franke.

Goodnight, Irene.

Chapter 22: Must-see matches

Examining the career of a wrestler through the medium of his or her best matches is an inexact science. It is a subjective task, and if the study relates to a wrestler from many years ago, harder still. Footage dating back years is more easily available than at any time in the past, but it can often be difficult to fully grasp the impact or importance of a match watched in isolation.

Like listening to a single song without experiencing the full album which accompanied it, context is everything. Picking the 'best' or 'most important' matches for any pro wrestler will always have its pitfalls. The below list is nevertheless a worthwhile starting point.

In the interest of convenience, match selections have been restricted to those which remain in circulation, easily accessible to anyone via YouTube, Peacock, the WWE Network, or similar. If taped, dates reflect when the match aired.

Keith Franks & Roddy Piper vs Tank Patton

NWA Hollywood; June 22, 1977; Olympic Auditorium, Los Angeles, CA

Possibly the oldest footage of the man who would later become Adrian Adonis available to view online. Grainy footage from the Olympic Auditorium opens with babyface Patton cutting a promo for legendary announcer Jimmy Lennon. Patton comments on his plan to run "Franks, the little blonde punk" out of town before dealing with Piper.

The surviving footage of the match itself is brief, a little over three minutes, and consists of Patton steamrolling the villains, over enthusiastic Spanish commentary. Needless to say, both Piper and Franks are far skinnier than they would be years later. After losing to a torture rack, Franks clears out to allow Piper to make the sneak attack, complete with some mean looking chair shots to Patton's head.

Adrian Adonis, Ron Starr, George Wells & Hector Guerrero vs Buddy Rose, Roddy Piper, Tim Brooks & Ed Wiskowski

Pacific Northwest Wrestling; April 7, 1979; Portland Sports Arena, Portland, OR

A red-hot match from the glory days of the Pacific Northwest territory, as Rose's Army take on the area's top babyfaces, live from the Portland Arena. Rose, Piper,

Brooks and Wiskowski faced down the babyface tag champs of Adonis and Starr alongside Wells and Guerrero in a main event from Portland's weekly television show.

The elimination-style match (or "devil take the hindmost") predates the WWF's Survivor Series-style bouts by nearly a decade and makes for terrific action. Things look bad for the good guys after eliminations for Wells and Guerrero, leaving Adonis and Starr outnumbered. From there, the match does not go to plan for Rose's Army.

Adrian Adonis & Ron Starr vs The Sheepherders

Pacific Northwest Wrestling; July 14, 1979; Portland Sports Arena, Portland, OR

Younger fans tracking down this match will be just as amazed by the different representation of the Sheepherders – or Bushwhackers – as Adonis. The same gurning and gesturing are present, but Butch and Luke are a more vicious, violent interpretation of the family-friendly clowns who would enter the World Wrestling Federation a decade later.

The pair are perfect foils for the Portland fan favourites of Adonis and Starr, resulting in a short but hard-hitting battle. Adonis in particular is on great form as he works hard to put over the new arrivals to the area, throwing himself into a turnbuckle and rebounding into the air with maximum force after missing a standing leg-drop. The Sheepherders win this non-title two out of three falls bout to set up a rematch the following week with the belts on the line.

Adrian Adonis vs Buddy Rose

Pacific Northwest Wrestling; August 31, 1979; Portland Sports Arena, Portland, OR

After splitting from Starr once the tag titles had been relinquished, Adonis had one of his only singles babyface runs. With plans to move on to the AWA, he was quickly programmed with Portland's top heel Buddy Rose. A series of exhilarating matches followed, many built around gimmick stipulations.

In one encounter, Adonis and Rose each had an accomplice (Steve Pardee and Rip Rogers) handcuffed to ringside to avoid interference. This was followed by an intense 14-minute two out of three falls bout. Big bumps, convincing selling, believable facial contortions, this match had it all, and the Portland crowd ate it up.

The East West Connection vs The High Flyers

AWA; March 1, 1981; Minneapolis Auditorium, Minneapolis, MN

There are plenty of meetings between Ventura-Adonis and Brunzell-Gagne during their long-running AWA feud to choose from. One of the longer outings took place during the Connection's year-long reign as AWA tag champs. The 23-minute title defence ends in a dissatisfying no-contest but there is plenty of entertaining action before the conclusion is reached.

In front of a packed house at the company's home turf of the Minneapolis Auditorium, the match gets off to a slow start with plenty of mat-based rest holds, before slowly ramping up in the second half. Adonis is at the centre of things of course, flying over the ropes, getting stuck in the ropes, and generally giving plenty of spotlight to the babyfaces, as well as the power moves of Ventura.

Adrian Adonis vs Bob Backlund

WWF; January 18, 1982; Madison Square Garden, New York, NY

This match represents arguably the high point of Adonis' in-ring career: challenging for a major world title in the main event of a major televised card live from the number one arena in the world – and leaving victorious, no less. Adonis' win was by referee's decision which was a ploy to set up a rematch, and not enough to secure the title. Adonis repaid the faith shown in him by both Backlund and promoter Vince McMahon Senior in this epic encounter. For more than 30 minutes, Adonis and Backlund complement each other perfectly and give the fans their money's worth.

From his open-handed slap to the champion's face as the opening bell rings, Adonis exudes attitude and charisma, and sneers his way through perhaps the best match of his life. After the customary slow build, the combatants up the ante for the final third of the match, to maximum effect. The screams of terror from the crowd when Adonis' throws 'Goodnight Irene' on the prone champion show how over the move was and how readily they bought the idea of Adonis as a genuine threat to the title.

Adrian Adonis vs Bob Backlund

WWF; March 28, 1982; Capital Centre, Landover, MD

249

Backlund, Adonis and McMahon were delighted with the chemistry the pair had, which led to a second MSG match, as well as several more meetings in the spring of 1982. One of the most entertaining of these is this lumberjack match, which aired on the USA Network at the time, pre-dating the WWF's weekly national timeslot with the station nearly two years later.

Adonis and Backlund wear each other down quickly, with both leaving the ring to fend off the respective heel and face lumberjacks at different points. Meanwhile, Adonis has all of his reliably impressive highlight spots on display – the thwarted running bulldog into the corner post, and getting tied in the ropes, to name just two. Both men look suitably exhausted at the end of this gruelling 15-minute match-up.

Adrian Adonis vs Tatsumi Fujinami

New Japan; July 30, 1982; Dolphin's Arena, Nagoya, Japan

Fresh from his original nine-month stay in the WWF, Adonis journeyed to Japan to participate in the summer tournament in a mixture of singles, tags and six-man tags. Entering to the *'Superman'* movie theme and accompanied by his WWF manager Freddie Blassie, Adonis goes toe-to-toe with future all-time great Fujinami, a ten-year veteran but only in the early stages of his career as a heavyweight.

The ten-minute match ebbs and flows, with plenty of rest holds, but never gets boring, before reaching an exciting crescendo. Adonis pulls out all the stops, switching his offense to power moves, including his local finisher, the inverted Atomic Drop, and an impressive dropkick from the top rope. Blassie gets involved for an unsatisfying finish to what up to that point had been an entertaining bout.

Adrian Adonis vs Bob Orton Jr

Southwest Championship Wrestling; May 26, 1983; The Summit, Houston, TX

Whether you consider the Southwest Championship Wrestling heavyweight title a true wrestling world title (most do not) it was the closest Adrian Adonis ever came to winning one, save for his encounters at the Garden with Backlund. The company introduced the belt to accompany its short-lived and unlikely status as a national television entity on the USA Network, making a lot of noise about inviting other champions to compete for their new title.

In reality SWCW had to make do with those on the roster plus a few guest stars, and the tournament was a rather humble affair in the end. The final though, between two men who would work together extensively later in their careers, was a technical wrestling masterclass, with Adonis reversing a small package for the victory after 15 minutes.

Adrian Adonis vs Andre the Giant

New Japan; June 8, 1984; Aomori Civic Gymnasium, Aomori, Japan

Adonis' New Japan matches from the early 1980s are littered with plenty of gems. This is to be expected considering how much local crowds appreciated a wrestler who could combine multiple styles of wrestling and do so believably. In many ways, Adonis' early 80s output and the discerning Japanese fans were made for each other. Adonis and Andre fought multiple times in singles, tags and handicap matches throughout the early part of the decade in the AWA, WWF and overseas.

This match captures probably the last time in both men's' lives when they are still mobile in the ring, though still has all the shortcuts Andre would come to rely on – bearhugs, chops, and plenty of time outside of the ring. By no means a classic but worth tracking down for the novelty, and to see Adonis work hard to make Andre look like a monster.

Adrian Adonis & Dick Murdoch vs Sgt Slaughter & Terry Daniels

WWF; July 23, 1984; Madison Square Garden, New York, NY

The nine-month tag title reign of Adonis and Murdoch featured many great matches as the hard-hitting odd couple put away all comers in 1984. This was wrestling's pre-pay-per-view era, so their most high-profile match is up for debate. A strong contender would be their title defence against the combination of Sgt Slaughter and his young Cobra Corps recruit, Private Terry Daniels.

The 17-minute match was part of a packed Madison Square Garden card which also featured Wendi Richter and Cyndi Lauper famously triumphing over Captain Lou Albano and the Fabulous Moolah on MTV to kickstart a new boom period for the WWF. Though none of the other matches aired on network television, several were well worth a watch. A fun match, Adonis and Murdoch take turns letting the less experienced and diminutive Daniels get some punishment before Slaughter rides to the rescue. The faces briefly threaten to take the titles with a near fall from a Daniels cross-body but Adonis and Murdoch eventually prevail.

Adrian Adonis & Dick Murdoch vs Antonio Inoki & Tatsumi Fujinami

251

New Japan; December 7, 1984; Osaka Prefectural Gymnasium, Osaka, Japan

An underappreciated gem from the final match of New Japan's 1984 MSG Tag League, Adonis and Murdoch faced off against the legendary Japanese pairing of Inoki and Fujinami. Adonis is visibly larger by this point compared to his trips to Japan just two years earlier, and this may explain why Murdoch takes a lot of the match for his team.

He still plays his part, acting as the perfect foil for the two Japanese superstars to the delight of the crowd, with plenty of brawling and pratfalls. While Inoki and Fujinami were victorious on the night after a hard-fought 33 minutes, Adonis and Murdoch clocked up enough wins over the course of the round-robin tournament to win overall.

Adrian Adonis & Dick Murdoch vs Jack & Jerry Brisco

WWF; December 28, 1984; Madison Square Garden, New York, NY

Yet another excellent Madison Square Garden outing for Adonis; who would blame him for pulling out all the stops when wrestling in the most famous arena in the world? With only weeks left of their title reign and WWF tenure, Adonis and Murdoch delivered probably their most impressive in-ring work, thanks in large part to the identity of the opponents. NWA Champion Jack Brisco was one of the greatest grapplers of his generation, with brother Jerry certainly no slouch.

The match ended in a double count-out after 27 minutes, which would logically suggest that a rematch was planned, wherein fans would get a definitive finish. The match starts slow but gets going when Adonis and the younger Brisco are in. This is notable for being the first U.S. match of Adonis' career to receive a rating from Dave Meltzer's *Wrestling Observer* newsletter, attracting a respectable three stars.

Adrian Adonis & Dick Murdoch vs Barry Windham & Mike Rotundo

WWF; January 21, 1985; Hartford Civic Center, Hartford, CT

A full version of this match has never surfaced and is an important lost treasure of vintage WWF wrestling, on a par with the Bret Hart and Tom Magee match that had so many searching their old VHS tapes. Taking place at a house show, the final four minutes of the match were spliced into an episode of WWF television two weeks later, with commentary added in the studio by Vince McMahon.

The match is weirdly shot, appearing to have been filmed on a hand-held camera at ringside, enforcing the idea that the title change was a last-minute decision. Even so, the start of the match has never aired and may not have even been recorded. Not a fascinating match, but an important moment for Adonis nonetheless as a significant chapter in his career came to an end.

Adrian Adonis & Randy Savage vs Tito Santana & Bruno Sammartino

WWF; July 12, 1986; Madison Square Garden, New York, NY

The summer of 1986 was also notable for Adonis forming a short-lived alliance with Randy Savage and taking on the pairing of Sammartino and Santana. After an inconclusive meeting at the Garden a month earlier, the teams met to settle things in a cage, as was customary in the era.

A wild and woolly brawl, the match is significant as one of the final WWF cage matches to take place in the traditional wire cage as opposed to the more famous blue bars, as well as being the final ever appearance in the Garden of the legendary Sammartino. There could only be one winner of course, but all four men play their part, particularly Savage, in this intense tussle.

Adrian Adonis vs Hulk Hogan

WWF; July 26, 1986; Philadelphia Spectrum, Philadelphia, PA

Adonis and Hogan, friends and travelling buddies through their time in Japan and the AWA, fought many times during the early part of their career. Adonis would do his trademark selling job to make the man behind 'Hulkamania' look a million dollars. That was another lifetime. By the summer of 1986, Hogan was into his third year as WWF Champion, the company was on fire, and Adonis had undergone a radical transformation.

One thing had not changed, and that was Adonis's knack for making Hogan look strong. That was something Adonis knew how to do whatever shape he was in, and he was one of a handful of heels to get a main event house show run with Hogan at this point. Aired on the PRISM Network from the Philadelphia Spectrum, this is textbook 1980s Hogan, and Adonis did a sterling job as the vanquished heel.

Adrian Adonis, Harley Race & Randy Savage vs Roddy Piper, Junkyard Dog & Ricky Steamboat

WWF; February 23, 1987; Madison Square Garden, New York, NY

This six-man elimination tag match was so unusual by the WWF's standards at the time, announcer Howard Finkel had to spend nearly a minute explaining the rules to the crowd. The match was one of several practice runs that took place throughout 1987 as the company perfected the 'Survivor Series' style of match which proved popular on pay-per-view and is still used to this day.

Steamboat, Savage and Race specifically worked their socks off to deliver a tremendous encounter, with Adonis and JYD – the two least effective workers – sensibly offloaded early. Watching this match, it is easy to see why the formula, tweaked somewhat, encouraged the WWF. Four stars from the *Wrestling Observer*.

Adrian Adonis vs Roddy Piper

WWF; March 29, 1987; Pontiac Silverdome, Pontiac, MI

No list of this kind would be complete without this match. While most of the supposed 93,000 fans in the Pontiac Silverdome had no idea, this match had added significance for Piper and Adonis far beyond settling a months-long feud. Friends for more than a decade, it would not have escaped the minds of either man as they looked across the ring from each other that ten years earlier they plied their trade together in front of a much smaller crowds for much less acclaim. Now they were the centre of the wrestling universe.

The match is deliberately brief, and in the final great performance of his life, Adonis makes his best friend look like a superstar. The match is full of now legendary moments, from Piper being the only man on the card to forego the buggy and walk to the ring, to Adonis' priceless reaction to seeing himself in the mirror. An all-time classic.

Adrian Adonis & Bob Orton Jr vs The Midnight Rockers

AWA; February 28, 1988; Minot, ND

An interesting curiosity, as Adonis clashed with future Hall of Famer Shawn Michaels during their time together in the flailing AWA towards the end of his career. The Rockers were essentially killing time until they were welcomed back to the WWF but put in some excellent performances during this period. Adonis, announced for this TV match at an eye-watering '400 pounds,' is perhaps at his biggest and leaves a lot of the work to Orton.

Adonis' ring work is slow and plodding as you might expect but he still largely holds up his end of the affair, incredibly even pulling off his trademark corner turnbuckle flip. A double count-out after fifteen minutes sees Michaels and Jannetty retain the AWA tag belts.

Adrian Adonis & Dick Murdoch vs Big Van Vader & Masa Saito

New Japan; June 19, 1988; Korakuen Hall, Tokyo, Japan

Another novelty worth tracking down, and another brief encounter bridging the divide between two different wrestling generations, as Adonis shares the ring for the only time with Big Van Vader. Six months into his New Japan career, Leon White had been transformed into a monster heel. The job for Adonis, as it had been so many times, was to give his all to make the opponent look good.

Still very large during this return to Japan after a three-year absence, Adonis sells like crazy to help Vader shine, and takes excellent bumps in the process. By no means a classic, the match is certainly worth watching for the chance to view Adonis as he took his first steps to rebuilding his wrestling reputation. He died fifteen days later.

Bibliography

Books

Albano, Lou, and Philip Varriale. *Often Imitated, Never Duplicated: Captain Lou Albano*. GEAN Publishing, 2008.

Atlas, Tony, and Scott Teal. *Atlas: Too Much ... Too Soon*. Crowbar Press, 2014.

Backlund, Bob, and Rob Miller. *Backlund: From All-American Boy to Professional Wrestling's World Champion*. New York, Sports Publishing, 2015.

Beefcake, Brutus, and Kenny Casanova. *Brutus Beefcake: Struttin' & Cuttin'*. WOHW Publishing, 2019.

Blassie, Fred, and Keith Elliott Greenberg. *Listen, You Pencil Neck Geeks*. New York, Pocket Books, 2003.

Brisco, Jack, and William Murdock. *Brisco: The Life and Times of National Collegiate and World Heavyweight Wrestling Champion Jack Brisco (Second edition)*. Crowbar Press, 2013.

Brunzell, Jim. *MatLands: True Stories from the Wrestling Road*. Minnesota, 2015.

Devito, Basil, and Joe Layden. *WWF Wrestlemania: The Official Insider's Story*. New York, Harper Entertainment, 2001.

Duncan, Royal, and Gary Will. *Wrestling Title Histories (Fourth edition)*. Waterloo, ON, Archeus Communications, 2000.

Freedman, Jim. *Drawing Heat (Second edition)*. Crowbar Press, 2014.

Funk, Terry, and Scott E. Williams. *Terry Funk: More Than Just Hardcore*. New York, Sports Publishing, 2012.

Hart, Bret. *Hitman: My Real Life in the Cartoon World of Wrestling*. Toronto, Random House Canada, 2007.

Hart, Jimmy. *The Mouth of the South: Jimmy Hart Story*. Toronto, ECW Press, 2004.

Heenan, Bobby, and Steve Anderson. *Bobby the Brain: Wrestling's Bad Boy Tells All*. Chicago, Triumph Books, 2002.

Hogan, Hulk, and Michael Jan Friedman. *Hollywood Hulk Hogan*. New York, Pocket Books, 2002.

Hornbaker, Tim. *Death of the Territories*. Toronto, ECW Press, 2018.

Johnson, Rocky, and Scott Teal. *Soulman: The Rocky Johnson Story*. Toronto, ECW Press, 2019.

Kenyon, J Michael, and Scott Teal. *Wrestling in the Garden, volume 2: 1940-2019*. Crowbar Press, 2019.

Mooneyham, Mike. *Mid-Atlantic Wrestling Memories*. Crowbar Press, 2013.

Piper, Roddy, and Robert Picarello. *In the Pit with Piper*. New York, Berkley Boulevard Book, 2002.

Schire, George. *Minnesota's Golden Age of Wrestling*. Minnesota, Minnesota Historical Society Press, 2010.

Shields, Brian. *30 Years of Wrestlemania*. Indianapolis, DK Publishing, 2014.

Shields, Brian. *Main Event: WWE in the Raging 80s*. New York, Gallery Books, 2006.

Stamp, Dennis, and Chris Duke. The Stamp Collection: True Stories from the Ring. CreateSpace, 2014.

Starr, Ron, and Rock Rims. *Bad to the Bone: 25 Years of Riots and Wrestling*. California, Flying Body Press, 2016.

Steele, George, and Jim Evans. *Animal*. Chicago, Triumph Books, 2013.

Tapper, Jake. *Body Slam: The Jesse Ventura Story*. New York, St Martin's Press, 1999.

Toombs, Ariel, and Colt Tombs. *Rowdy: The Roddy Piper Story*. Canada, Random House, 2016.

Ventura, Jesse. *I Ain't Got Time to Bleed: Reworking the Body Politic from the Bottom Up*. New York, Signet Books, 2000.

Verrier, Steven. *Gene Kiniski: Canadian Wrestling Legend*. North Carolina, McFarland, 2018.

Verrier, Steven. *Professional Wrestling in the Pacific Northwest*. North Carolina, McFarland, 2017.

WWE Encyclopedia Updated & Expanded (second edition). Indianapolis, DK Publishing, 2012.

Websites

Armdrag: http://armdrag.com

Ancestry: www.ancestry.com

Cagematch: www.cagematch.net

Camel Clutch Blog: https://camelclutchblog.com

Cauliflower Alley Club: www.caulifloweralleyclub.org

Dory Funk: https://dory-funk.com

The History of WWE: https://thehistoryofwwe.com

IMDB: www.imdb.com

The Internet Wrestling Database: www.profightdb.com

Kenmore East Alumni Association: www.kealumni.org

Legacy: www.legacy.com

Maple Leaf Wrestling: https://mapleleafwrestling.blogspot.com

Mid-Atlantic Gateway: www.midatatlanticgateway.com

Newspapers: www.newspapers.com

Newspaper Archive: https://newspaperarchive.com

Nikkan-spa: https://nikkan-spa.jp

Not In Hall of Fame: www.notinhalloffame.com

Online World of Wrestling: www.onlineworldofwrestling.com

OSW Review: http://oswreview.com

Pro Wrestling History: www.prowrestlinghistory.com

Pro Wrestling Stories: https://prowrestlingstories.com

Pro Wrestling Wiki: https://prowrestling.fandom.com

Ring The Damn Bell: https://ringthedamnbell.wordpress.com

SLAM Wrestling: https://slamwrestling.net

Tokyo Sports: www.tokyo-sports.co.jp

United Press International: www.upi.com

World Wrestling Entertainment: www.wwe.com

Wrestling Classics: www.wrestlingclassics.com

Wrestling Data: www.wrestlingdata.com

Wrestling Observer/Figure Four Online: www.f4wonline.com

World Wrestling Insanity: www.worldwrestlinginsanity.com

Online articles

Bateman, Oliver (2018). *The Ironic Masculinity of Adrian Adonis.* https://www.splicetoday.com/pop-culture/the-ironic-masculinity-of-adrian-adonis

Hamar, Jacob (2015). *Incredibly Talented & Largely Forgotten: The Tale of Adrian Adonis.* http://camelclutchblog.com/incredibly-talented-largely-forgotten-the-tale-of-adrian-adonis/

Hamlyn, Kris (2016). *Adrian Adonis: the Lewisporte Tragedy That Killed an American Wrestling Star.* http://secreteast.ca/2016/07/adrianadonis/

Hunsperger, Kevin (2018). *Remembering Adrian Adonis 30 years later.* http://www.my123cents.com/2018/07/remembering-adrian-adonis-30-years-later.html

Ward, Marshall (2013). *Adrian Adonis: A Look Back on the Anniversary of His Death.* https://www.wrestlenewz.com/exclusive-articles/adrian-adonis-a-look-back-on-the-anniversary-of-his-death/

The Wrestling Professor (2017). *Backstage Fights: Dan Spivey vs Adrian Adonis.* http://www.armpit-wrestling.com/dan-spivey-vs-adrian-adonis/

Newspapers and Magazines

Canyon News

Castro Country News

Central Maine

Huffington Post

People Magazine

The Alberni Valley Times

The Amarillo Daily News

The Bakersfield Californian

The Buffalo News

The Charlotte News

The Farmington Daily Times

The Hereford Brand

The Metro-West Herald News

The Palm Beach Post

The Philadelphia Inquirer

The Rocky Mount Telegram

The Tampa Tribune

The Toronto Sun

The Vancouver Province

The Washington Herald

Wrestling Publications

Figure Four Newsletter

Inside Wrestling

Pro Wrestling Illustrated

Pro Wrestling Torch

Sports Review Wrestling

The Wrestler

Wrestling Observer Newsletter

WWF Magazine

WWF Raw Magazine

Audio, video and digital content

18th & Grand: The Olympic Auditorium Story. Directed by Stephen DeBro. 2021

Adrian Adonis: Tribute to the Golden Boy Facebook page

Between The Sheets podcast, Apple podcasts

Kayfabe Commentaries: www.kayfabecommentaries.com

Main Event Radio podcast, YouTube

Monte & The Pharaoh, YouTube

Portland Wrestlecast podcast, www.f4wonline.com

RF Video: https://rfvideo.com

Something To Wrestle With podcast, Apple podcasts

Talk Is Jericho, Apple podcasts

The Hannibal TV, YouTube

The Lapsed Fan podcast, Apple podcasts

The Steve Austin Show podcast, Apple podcasts

Title Match Wrestling podcast, YouTube

Wrestling Gold DVD. VCI Video. 2001

Wrestling Observer Radio, www.f4wonline.com

Wrestling Shoot Interviews, YouTube

WWE Network

X-Pac 1,2,360 podcast, YouTube

Acknowledgements

This book would not have been possible without the help, support, guidance, and contributions of numerous people. I want to thank everybody I spoke to or communicated with about Keith "Adrian Adonis" Franke in the development of this project, including those who are referenced in the book, and several more who are not.

I would especially like to thank Keith's widow, Bea Franke, and his daughters, Angela Perides and Gena Banta, for their blessing and support throughout. Immense thanks in no particular order to Gilbert Hernandez, Greg Oliver, Bill Apter, Karl Stern, Fumi Saito, Tom Hankins, Rip Rogers, Don Muraco, Jerry Jaffe Sr and Jr, Terry Daniels, the late Lanny Poffo, Tom Touchstone, Tully Blanchard, Jerry Brisco, Paul Neiss, Dave Meltzer, Joey Gaynor, Adrian Street, Joe Kolkowitz, Jim Valley, the late Bert Prentice, Tim Hornbaker, George Tahinos, George Napolitano, Scott Teal, Brian Blair, the people at Fantagraphics, Kevin McElvaney and the team at *Pro Wrestling Illustrated*, and all at *WrestleTalk*.

I would also like to give credit to the various written sources credited throughout the text, which have proved invaluable as historical reference tools. Chief among these were the *Wrestling Observer* and *Pro Wrestling Torch* newsletters.

A special thanks to all my friends and family for their support, in particular my mother, sister, children, and wife, who were a constant source of encouragement.

A note on the title

The title of this book draws from a number of ideas, each of which I want to take this opportunity to acknowledge.

The phrasing of the title evokes two specific inspirations. Firstly, *Flowers for Algernon*, the award-winning 1966 science fiction novel by Daniel Keyes which tells the story of a man who undergoes a troubling transformation.

Secondly, 'Flowers for Adrian Adonis,' a poem in the 2014 collection, *The Dead Wrestler Elegies* by W. Todd Kaneko, which mines the history of professional wrestling to examine complex relationships between fathers and sons.

Flowers, ribbons, scarves, and more, were the accoutrements thrust onto Adrian Adonis upon his transition to the "Adorable" persona, and there is no more appropriate prop to draw attention to than the 'feminine' trappings he made his own.

264

The expression 'to give someone their flowers' has grown in popularity in recent years, particularly online. The sentiment is a noble one; we should not wait until someone has passed away to give them their due credit. Instead, let them know they are appreciated while they are around to hear it.

Franke is long removed from hearing any praise and instead it is left to loved ones to visit his graveside and reminisce. When they do, they leave flowers for Adrian.

Made in the USA
Monee, IL
23 March 2023

30431392R00154